Working as a Professional Translator

What does it take to be a professional translator in the 21st century? What are the opportunities and challenges of a career in translation? How do you find that first job? How do you ensure that work remains sustainable over time? Combining industry insights, the latest research in the field of translation studies and a career coaching approach, this textbook takes aspiring translators on an explorative journey that helps them answer these questions for themselves so they can become the professional translators they aspire to be.

Each chapter of this hands-on guide opens with key questions that budding translators might typically ask themselves and encourages them to reflect on their relevance for their own situation through regular discussion points and 'Topics for discussion and assignments'. Targeted suggestions for further reading at the end of each chapter guide users in deepening their knowledge. Written primarily for students on translation courses, the accessible language, tone and design of this book will appeal to anyone who is thinking of embarking upon a career in translation. Additional resources are available on the Routledge Translation Studies Portal.

JC Penet is Senior Lecturer (Associate Professor) in Translation Studies at Newcastle University, UK, where he is currently the Director of the MA in Professional Translation. Since joining the School of Modern Languages in 2010, he has taught on a wide range of undergraduate and postgraduate courses in translation studies, including on translation theory; the language service industry; CAT tools and project management; institutional translation; and interpersonal relations, emotions and well-being in the translation profession. Through his 'Translation Networks' project (2014–2018), he established lasting networks with local language service providers and freelancers in North East England.

Routledge Introductions to Translation and Interpreting
Series Editor:
Sergey Tyulenev is Professor of Translation Studies and
Director of Postgraduate Research at the School of Modern
Languages and Cultures, Durham University, UK.

<u>Advisory Board</u>
Luise von Flotow, University of Ottawa, Canada
Ricardo Munoz Martin, University of Bologna, Italy
Kobus Marais, University of the Free State, South Africa
Nike K. Pokorn, University of Ljubljana, Slovenia
James St André, Chinese University of Hong Kong, China
Michaela Wolf, University of Graz, Austria

Routledge Introductions to Translation and Interpreting is a series of
textbooks, designed to meet the need for teaching materials for translator/
interpreter training. Accessible and aimed at beginning students but also
useful for instructors designing and teaching courses, the series covers a
broad range of topics, many of which are already core courses while others
cover new directions of translator/interpreter teaching.

The series reflects the standards of the translator/interpreter training
and professional practice set out by national and international competence
frameworks and codes of translation/language service provision and are
aimed at a global readership.

All topics combine both practical and theoretical aspects so as to ensure
a bridging of the gap between the academic and professional world and all
titles include a range of pedagogical support: activities, case studies etc.

Most recent titles in the series:

Translation Tools and Technologies
*Andrew Rothwell, Joss Moorkens, Maria Fernández Parra, Joanna Drugan
and Frank Austermuehl*

Writing a Translation Commentary
Penélope Johnson

Working as a Professional Translator
JC Penet

For more information on any of these and other titles, or to order, please go to https://www.
routledge.com/Routledge-Introductions-to-Translation-and-Interpreting/book-series/RITI

Additional resources for Translation and Interpreting Studies are available on the Routledge
Translation Studies Portal: http://routledgetranslationstudiesportal.com/

Working as a Professional Translator

JC Penet

LONDON AND NEW YORK

Designed cover image: © Getty Images | Peshkova

First published 2024
by Routledge
4 Park Square, Milton Park, Abingdon, Oxon OX14 4RN

and by Routledge
605 Third Avenue, New York, NY 10158

Routledge is an imprint of the Taylor & Francis Group, an informa business

© 2024 JC Penet

The right of JC Penet to be identified as author of this work has been asserted in accordance with sections 77 and 78 of the Copyright, Designs and Patents Act 1988.

All rights reserved. No part of this book may be reprinted or reproduced or utilised in any form or by any electronic, mechanical, or other means, now known or hereafter invented, including photocopying and recording, or in any information storage or retrieval system, without permission in writing from the publishers.

Trademark notice: Product or corporate names may be trademarks or registered trademarks, and are used only for identification and explanation without intent to infringe.

British Library Cataloguing-in-Publication Data
A catalogue record for this book is available from the British Library

ISBN: 9781032115566 (hbk)
ISBN: 9781032115573 (pbk)
ISBN: 9781003220442 (ebk)

DOI: 10.4324/9781003220442

Typeset in Sabon
by Newgen Publishing UK

Access the Support Material: http://routledgetranslationstudiesportal.com

Contents

About the author	*vii*
Series editor's foreword	*ix*
About this textbook	*xi*
Acknowledgements	*xvi*

PART I
Joining the profession   1

1   What skills and qualifications do I need?   3

2   Career paths: Freelance, in-house or portfolio career?   23

3   No translator is an island: Setting up your support
    networks   41

4   Finding that first job   58

PART II
On the job   75

5   Dealing with clients   77

6   Managing your translation projects   101

7   Managing translation quality   128

vi *Contents*

PART III
Continuing to grow as a professional translator 151

8 Understanding your market and marketing your business 153

9 Keeping it sustainable 174

Bibliography 203
Index 218

About the author

Dr JC Penet is Senior Lecturer (Associate Professor) in Translation Studies at Newcastle University (UK), where he is currently the Director of the MA in Professional Translation. Since joining the School of Modern Languages in 2010, he has taught on a wide range of undergraduate and postgraduate courses in translation studies, including on translation theory; the language service industry; CAT tools and project management; institutional translation; and interpersonal relations, emotions and well-being in the translation profession. Through his 'Translation Networks' project (2014–18), he established lasting networks with local language service providers and freelancers in North East England.

In 2016, he co-founded, with Dr Olga Castro (University of Warwick, UK), the Association of Programmes in Translation and Interpreting Studies, UK & Ireland (APTIS) with the aim of advancing research into translator education for the public good. Between 2017 and 2021, he served as the first President of APTIS. The association, which soon brought together around 25 HE institutions from all over the British Isles, has helped create mutually beneficial connections between academia and the language industry.

His research interests lie in the fields of translator studies/language industry studies and translator education. More specifically, his current research endeavour explores the impact of recent developments in the language industry (such as changing production and workflow models as a result of increased automation) on the financial, physical and psychological well-being of professional translators. To that end, he is currently a co-investigator with Dr Joseph Lambert (Cardiff University, UK) on the British Academy-funded project 'Chasing Status: The Sustainability of the Freelance Translation Profession in the United Kingdom', led by Dr Callum Walker (University of Leeds, UK).

Another, related question his research seeks to answer is the impact these developments have on the way we understand and deliver translator training. A recent research project co-led with Dr Fernandez-Parra (Swansea University, UK), for instance, investigated the way(s) in which Trait Emotional Intelligence theory – and what we know about the role of

viii   *About the author*

emotions in professional translating – can be applied to translator training to help students develop the adaptive expertise they will need to thrive in the language industry. Recognising as part of this research project that taking a coaching approach to emotion-management could be a particularly apt way to help students, he became a certified life coach after successfully completing a Postgraduate Certificate in Coaching with the University of Warwick in 2023.

Series editor's foreword

Working as a Professional Translator is a milestone of a sort – it is the fifth textbook in the Routledge Introductions to Translation and Interpreting series. Now the focus is on the practical aspects of starting and advancing one's career as a professional translator. The title uses the term 'translator' inclusively: interpreters will find here a great deal of useful advice as well.

First, a bit of background to explain the rationale for this textbook. Traditionally, translator/interpreter training programmes have emphasised teaching how to translate and/or interpret, where translating and interpreting have been limited to the linguistic skills necessary to produce a text in one language based on a text in another, and to the cultural expertise requisite for handling sociocultural elements of the source text in order to render them appreciable in the target language. But being a translator or interpreter is more than all that. It is also the ability to present oneself and act as a professional; it is also the knowledge of how to find one's niche in the industry, how to deal with a client, how to keep records of one's work, etc. etc.

So far, training programmes have paid little attention to the nitty-gritty of plying the trade of translator/interpreter. Such down-to-earth details are usually bypassed as unworthy of academic attention. Budding translators and interpreters should consider themselves lucky if they have been advised how to write a CV or offered guidance on pros and cons of working as a freelancer vs. as an in-house translator; internships, if they are an option within the programme's curriculum, may provide a glance into the professional world the would-be professional is to face after graduation. Yet such scraps of information, if provided, are but drops in the ocean of the practical wisdom that is vital when starting or developing one's career as a translator or interpreter.

The inclusion of this textbook in the series aims to fill this glaring gap.

Emphatically, like all publications in the series, this is a textbook. Every care has been taken and every effort has been made to ensure that the presentation style is accessible to the novice and would be suitable for use either by a trainee aided by a trainer or by an autodidact. Each chapter contains

x *Series editor's foreword*

various features which will foster active engagement with the topic explained and stimulate discussion in a group.

The textbook *Working as a Professional Translator* is written by Dr JC Penet, Senior Lecturer in Translation Studies at the University of Newcastle, UK. Professional aspects of translation are the focus of Dr Penet's research and teaching. He is an experienced and reliable guide to the world of professional work as a translator or interpreter.

Sergey Tyulenev
September 2023

About this textbook

What does it take to be a professional translator in the 21st century? How much should one know about the translation industry before starting work as a professional translator? What does the job involve and what are the different possible career paths for translators? What are the opportunities and challenges of a career in translation? How to find that first job as a professional translator? What does it take to be a successful professional translator? How to ensure that the job remains sustainable over time?

Combining industry insights and the latest research in the field of translation studies with a career coaching approach, the entry-level textbook *Working as a Professional Translator* takes aspiring translators on an explorative journey that helps them answer these questions for themselves so they can become the professional translators they aspire to be. Even though it was written primarily with students on a postgraduate translation programme in mind, its accessible language, tone and design will appeal to anyone who is thinking of embarking upon a career in translation.

Approach in this textbook

There is so much to say about professional translating in the present day. As we will see throughout this book, it is a vast and rapidly evolving field. So much so that '[i]t has [now] become something of a truism to say that the pace of developments in professional language mediation has been exceedingly fast' (Massey et al., 2023: 326). Because of this, writing an introductory-level textbook about work as a professional translator has sometimes felt like shooting at a moving target. Deciding what to include and what to leave out often involved difficult decisions. Nevertheless, choices had to be made. I therefore used my long-standing experience as a translator educator to identify some of the current key issues for budding professional translators in the 21st century. The result is a textbook that gives as extensive an overview of professional translating as possible while hopefully remaining relevant, useable and accessible throughout.

xii *About this textbook*

Working as a Professional Translator is thus primarily about helping students turn translation into a career. As pointed out by some translation studies scholars, however, 'translation is in motion' (Dam et al., 2019: 1). Indeed, some of the recent developments in the language industry have made the concept of translation increasingly blurry. Hence the need to clearly define what I mean by translation here. For the purposes of this textbook, translation shall be understood as the remunerated interlingual mediation of written texts. As well as the more traditional forms of commercial and literary translation, it thus encompasses relatively new forms of translation such as localisation, transcreation and AVT (audio-visual translation).

Work as a professional translator, however, is about much more than translation itself. The European Master's in Translation (EMT) Competence Framework, for instance, names four other core competences besides 'Translation Competence' that professional translators should acquire before they enter the job market: 'Language and culture competence', 'Technology competence', 'Personal and interpersonal competence' and 'Service provision competence' (EMT, 2022). *Working as a Professional Translator* shares this more holistic view of professional translating as a career that requires both 'hard' and 'soft' skills. It is therefore designed in a way that allows readers to reflect and work on all these skills and competences.

Similarly, this textbook also shares the EMT's view that translator education and training:

> should equip students not only with a deep understanding of the processes involved, but also with the ability to perform and provide a translation service in line with the highest professional and ethical standards. (ibid.: 4)

This is because professional translators are, first and foremost, service providers. *Working as a Professional Translator* will therefore introduce readers to the concept of quality in translation and some key industry standards (such as, for instance, ISO 17100:2015 Translation Services – Requirements for Translation Services), while helping them (further) develop their own professional and ethical maturity as translators through reflective activities.

This is, in fact, a key aspect of *Working as a Professional Translator*. When other books on the topic sometimes adopt a descriptive, context-specific approach based on their author's personal experiences, this textbook rests on the idea that each individual will experience professional translating in his or her own unique way depending on their circumstances. Factors such as employment status, geographical location, language pairs or area of specialisation all influence how one operates and feels as a professional translator.

Inspired by career coaching, *Working as a Professional Translator* therefore chooses to put aspiring translators at the centre of the entire process by encouraging them to use the latest, most relevant research or industry information to reflect on what this might mean for them in their own context.

About this textbook xiii

As part of this reflective approach, it also encourages them to explore their own values, strengths and interests alongside key aspects of professional translating so they can start building their own ideal – and, importantly, sustainable – career path in the translation industry. This is because, as a personal coach, I fundamentally believe in the ability of each individual to 'create ideas, decide for themselves and move their situation forward' (Starr, 2021: 8) through questions and reflection in a way that is both meaningful and transformative.

Content of this textbook

Working as a Professional Translator contains three main parts broken down into nine chapters. The three main parts aim to follow the natural progression of an early career as a professional translator.

Part I ('Joining the profession') encourages readers to reflect on the skills and qualifications they will need to join the profession (Chapter 1) and the career path(s) they may want to follow as translators (Chapter 2). It also draws their attention to the importance of developing relevant professional support networks (Chapter 3) and of researching the translation industry (Chapter 4) before joining the ranks of professional translators.

Part II ('On the job') invites readers to discover key aspects of working as a professional translator in the 21st century, namely dealing with clients as intercultural experts (Chapter 5), managing sometimes complex translation projects (Chapter 6) as well as defining and ensuring translation quality for said projects (Chapter 7).

Finally, Part III ('Continuing to grow as a professional translator') encourages readers to adopt a longer-term view of their work by exploring market opportunities (Chapter 8) and by engaging with the concept of self-care (Chapter 9) in order to ensure the job remains sustainable over time.

Using this textbook

Instructors

Working as a Professional Translator is primarily aimed at instructors with students on Translation Studies programmes that are new to translation as a profession. The design of the textbook should make it easy to use on a typical one-semester module introducing students to this important topic. All the chapters are based around key questions to explore with students during the taught sessions. They all contain opportunities for guided reflection and suggested topics for discussions and assignments, as well as recommended further reading.

Despite counting nine chapters only, *Working as a Professional Translator* contains enough teaching materials and activities for eleven two-hour sessions. This is based on the typical pattern of delivery for a one-semester module in xiv *About this textbook*

the UK, which usually consists of a one-hour weekly lecture followed by a one-hour weekly seminar over eleven weeks. Given their central importance, the two longer chapters on translation project management (Chapter 6) and on quality management (Chapter 7) are intended to be taught over two weeks. My recommendation for Chapter 6 would be to focus on assessing and quoting in the first week and on launching and monitoring the project in the following week. Similarly, for Chapter 7, I would recommend focusing on defining translation quality in the first week and on quality management (including through the use of translation tools and technology) in the next week. All the remaining chapters can be taught as self-contained lecture + seminar sessions. For each chapter, my advice would be to use the lecture session to unpack, discuss and illustrate the content with students. The seminar could then be used as a student-led session using the suggested 'Topics for discussion and assignments' as a starting point.

Of course, not all programmes are in a position to dedicate so much teaching time to this topic. For instructors with more limited time, I would recommend focusing on the more process-oriented Chapters 4–8 in your sessions and treating the remaining chapters (Chapters 1–3 and Chapter 9) as of secondary priority. This is because, despite their overall importance, Chapters 1–3 and Chapter 9 can be seen as slightly less central to the process of working as a professional translator. As all chapters have been written with independent study in mind, my suggestion would be to set these chapters either as pre-reading or as further reading to the taught sessions on Chapters 4–8.

Every chapter also features regular discussion points. Instructors are encouraged to use these questions as a way to start whole-group discussions and/or smaller group conversations. Similarly, the regular 'Topics for discussion and assignments' contain a range of activities that encourage students to work through the content of this book both on their own and with fellow course mates. While some of these activities can be carried out in class, instructors may prefer to set others as preparation work for the session or as follow-up activities set, for example, on the Virtual Learning Environment. Finally, instructors are advised that additional suggested topics for discussion and assignments as well as other relevant teaching resources can be found on the TS Portal.

Students

Students are the primary target audience of *Working as a Professional Translator*, as this textbook has been designed to be used on specialised undergraduate or postgraduate programmes in translation studies. However, it was also written with independent study in mind. Indeed, its accessible content and style mean that anyone thinking of a career in translation will find it a valuable resource.

About this textbook xv

Students using this book are encouraged to question the latest research and industry information presented to them in and for their own context so they can start using it to forge their *own* path into the translation industry. This is because there is no secret recipe to becoming a successful professional translator. Neither is there, for that matter, a universal agreement on what 'successful' means ...! Each student will have his or her own vision of what a successful career as a professional translator looks like based on their own values and aspirations. The objective of this textbook is, therefore, to give students a *map* (knowledge about the translation industry and what professional translating is about) and a *compass* (professional and ethical maturity) to navigate the brave new world of the translation industry, some of which remains uncharted territory ...

To that aim, each chapter opens with key questions that budding translators might typically ask themselves, such as, for example: 'What skills do I need to work as a professional translator?', 'How can I start building my own, tailor-made support network?', 'What is my professional responsibility to clients as a translation service provider?', 'Which marketing mix should I adopt?' and so on. It then defines some key concepts and introduces students to the latest and most relevant research and industry information on the issue, and encourages them to reflect on its relevance for their own situation through regular discussion points and 'Topics for discussion and assignments'.

Students are strongly encouraged to take the time to pause and reflect for each of the discussion points indicated by a bullet point in the form of a question mark (?), especially if they use this book for independent study. My suggestion would be that they make a few quick notes of their answers so they can revisit them six months to a year later to see how their thinking on some of the issues presented has evolved. Similarly, students will find that the mix of activities contained in the 'Topics for discussion and assignments', which are designed to help them grow both their professional and their ethical maturity, can be used as building blocks to start concretely planning their emerging careers as professional translators.

Acknowledgements

If, as the proverb goes, it takes a village to raise a child, then it takes another whole village to write a textbook! So many people have contributed to the writing of this book, both directly and indirectly. I realise, of course, that it will not be possible to name them all here; I can only apologise to anyone I have unintentionally overlooked in the following remarks. I will therefore start by thanking the whole village from the bottom of my heart.

More specifically, I would first like to thank the series editor Professor Sergey Tyulenev (Durham University) for offering me the unique opportunity to write this textbook as part of his fantastic new series. I am eternally grateful for all the trust, support and guidance he has so generously provided me with throughout all the stages of this book.

There are many other translation studies colleagues and friends I would like to thank for their support. Despite some of the challenges of working as an academic in translation studies in the 21st century, I feel incredibly lucky to belong to such a brilliant and generous community of practice. First of all, a massive thank-you to Dr Joseph Lambert (Cardiff University) and Dr Callum Walker (University of Leeds) for their generous comments and insightful suggestions on all the draft chapters, and for the many thought-provoking chats that ensued. A massive thank-you, too, to Dr Olga Castro (University of Warwick) and Dr Maria Fernandez-Parra (Swansea University) for their help, feedback and encouragement with this book. I would also like to thank Dr Jennifer Arnold (Newcastle University) and Professor Dorothy Kenny (Dublin City University) for helping me believe in my ability to write it. Finally, I would like to thank all the brilliant fellow academics I have quoted in this book; I can only hope you find I have put your work to good use here.

I also owe a debt of gratitude to all the professional translators who have contributed to this book. Among them, I must name a few of my former students who now work as professional translators: Rachel Cross, Michelle Deeter and Lucy Makepeace. Thanks so much for so generously making the time to share your rich and varied experiences with me. Thank you, too, to Jessica Rainey for your insightful feedback on the draft version of Chapter 2.

Acknowledgements xvii

A great many other professional translators have contributed to this book through all the conversations we have had on professional translating. I owe them a massive thank-you, too.

I must also thank my past and present translation studies students at Newcastle University. You have been the first to discover – and work with – the draft chapters of this book. Your willingness to engage with the content, and to share your own perspectives and ideas, has been instrumental in helping me make sure that the final version of this book meets your learning needs as my primary target audience.

A great many thanks to the editorial team at Routledge for your support, guidance, patience and understanding throughout the entire process. A big thank-you, too, to Frances Tye for her careful copyediting.

Last, but certainly not least, my biggest thanks must go to my family as the people who have had no choice but to put up with me during that stressful time that writing a book can be. A huge thank-you to my wife, Helen, for her unwavering love and support throughout ... and for indulging my numerous rambling conversations about professional translating over the last couple of years. Helen, as a fellow academic working in a completely different field, I appreciate that this may not always have been your preferred topic of conversation. I am also incredibly grateful to you for all the concrete (making sure I had the time to work on the book; proofreading everything etc.) and emotional (believing in me; encouraging me every step of the way etc.) support you have given me since I took this on. Thanks, too, to my two wonderful children, Alannah and Cian, for helping me retain an acute sense of perspective by keeping me rooted and grounded in your love throughout.

Despite all the wonderful help and support I have received with this book, any omissions, inaccuracies or other errors are definitely my own.

Part I

Joining the profession

1 What skills and qualifications do I need?

Key questions we will explore in this chapter:

- What skills do I need to work as a professional translator?
- What are translator competence models? Why are there different models and how can they help me develop the right skills as a professional translator?
- How do I make sure I have the right qualifications to become a professional translator?

1.1 Not all linguists are translators ...

Some long-held myths about translation as a profession can prove difficult to bust. One of them is that proficiency in a foreign language is all it takes to set up stall as a translator. To some, translation is an obvious profession to get into for anyone who speaks at least two languages. Find yourself a good – online – dictionary and you will be okay!

On the other end of the spectrum, others argue that there is no future for the translation profession now that computers can already do as well – if not better – than most translators can. Why would you even want to become a translator when everyone can instantly access free translation apps on their smartphones?

Both myths, in fact, result from the same core misconception about translation: that translation is, essentially, *just* about languages. There are good reasons why many still hold this view. One of them is the enduring legacy of **pedagogical translation,** that is to say the way translation has been – and largely continues to be – taught in foreign-language classes. Indeed, it remains common practice to set languages students 'translation tasks' that require them to translate either random sentences or excerpts from journalistic and/ or literary texts in a completely decontextualised way. Often, they must do so without the help of dictionaries or any other resources. The objective, here, is purely linguistic, as the aim of these tasks is either to help students improve

DOI: 10.4324/9781003220442-2

4 *Joining the profession*

their command of the foreign language or test it. Unfortunately, what they also do is reinforce the belief that translation is just about your command of the two languages. What they do not do, however, is help develop **real translation competence** or, indeed, test it.

This is not to say that translation has nothing to do with languages: far from it! Being proficient in at least one language other than your language of habitual use remains an essential prerequisite to becoming a translator. To be a successful translator, you need an excellent command of both your first language and your other languages. Language-learning classes must therefore precede and accompany translation classes. And later, throughout your career as a translator, you will continue working on your languages – not least your first language! – by increasing your knowledge of the terminology in the areas in which you work and by watching how it evolves over time (see Chapter 9). This notwithstanding, **language competence** on its own is not enough to work as a professional translator.

As we will see not just in this chapter, but throughout the rest of this book too, professional translating is vastly different from pedagogical translation. If most linguists can translate (albeit with varying degrees of success), not all linguists are translators. As well as language competence, professional translators must fully grasp the context of the translation work they are carrying out, know where and how to look for the right information (by selecting and using the right resources), have second-to-none interpersonal and intercultural skills, be digitally literate and have the business acumen necessary to survive in this fast-changing, cut-throat industry. Or, to put it in other words, today's professional translators must be '*experts in multilingual multimedia communication engineering*' (Gouadec, 2007: 17, my emphasis).

How do we know this? A quick Internet search with the words 'translator + vacancy' will take you to a multitude of job advertisements for translation positions, such as the following anonymised ad I came across in early 2021 (see Box 1.1):

Box 1.1 English into Hungarian Translator

United Kingdom
£22,000–£25,000 a year - Full-time, Permanent
[Paragraph introducing the translation company]

Main Tasks:

- Translate a variety of text types and subject matters
- Transcreate
- Review, post-edit machine-produced translations
- Terminology research

What skills and qualifications do I need? 5

- Create and maintain translation memories
- Create and maintain style guides
- Occasional meetings with client contacts
- Occasional visits to clients for product demos, briefings ...

Key requirements:

- Translators must master the target language at mother-tongue level
- Cultural awareness
- Translation qualification and min. 2 years of experience
- Willingness to learn new things and to go the extra mile
- Ability to review work of others, edit and provide feedback
- Ability to work under pressure without impacting quality
- Good time management, versatility
- Professional approach and commitment to quality
- Able to work autonomously as well as within a team
- Good eye for detail and ability to pay attention to multiple references
- Client-orientation

Optional, but welcome skills:

- Familiar with MemoQ and Trados, Smartling
- Ability to translate/transcreate marketing-type messages
- Experience translating for the e-commerce and finance sector
- Optional: Ability to translate from another source language

Language:

- Professional level of English (Required)
- Target language at mother-tongue level (Required)

How to apply:
Send CV and letter of motivation.

Source: https://uk.indeed.com/jobs?q=Translator%20Vacancy&vjk=3dcd8b2
b46c97dea&advn=6968501819191432

Unsurprisingly, there are only a couple of references to languages in the ad; prospective candidates must master the source language, English, at 'professional level' and the target language, Hungarian, at 'mother-tongue level'. Judging by this ad, it seems that a candidate's command of languages is mostly a prerequisite. This may well be because the 'main tasks' the hired English-to-Hungarian translator will have to perform seem to correspond perfectly to

6 Joining the profession

Gouadec's definition of translators as 'experts in multilingual multimedia communication engineering' (Gouadec, 2007: 17). If you are new to the world of translation, it is very likely that you will not be familiar with some of these (e.g. 'post-edit machine-produced translations', 'terminology research', 'create and maintain translation memories', 'create and maintain style guides'). Similarly, you may well be puzzled by some of the required skills, especially what the ad calls 'Optional, but welcome skills' (e.g. 'familiar with MemoQ and Trados, Smartling' or 'ability to translate/transcreate marketing-type messages'). This ad is yet another reminder *that there is much more to translation than meets the eye*, and that trainee translators therefore need to develop a whole range of skills (other than just linguistic) in order to be job-ready.

1.2 What does it take to be a translator, then?

It was this very question that encouraged some translation scholars to look into the concept of 'translator competence' more empirically. Their objective was to give a holistic definition of translator competence that could be adopted by translator training programmes wanting to make sure their graduates had the necessary skills to enter the job market.

1.2.1 The strategic translator: PACTE's Translation Competence Model

In the late 1990s, a group of researchers at the Autonomous University of Barcelona (Spain) felt that translation studies as a discipline needed to come up with a generally accepted definition of translation competence (Orozco and Hurtado Albir, 2002: 375). Similarly, they believed that previous models of translation competence were more the result of – sometimes valid – hunches about what it takes to be a professional translator rather than proper empirical research. As a result, they decided to set up the **PACTE** research group. In Catalan, PACTE stands for 'Procés d'Adquisició de la Competència Traductora i Avaluació'. This name makes the research group's objective of researching the way translation competence can be acquired and assessed rather explicit. In the first instance, the group came up with an initial understanding of translation competence, which they defined as 'the underlying system of knowledge and skills needed to be able to translate' (PACTE, 2000: 99). They also started developing a **holistic translation competence model** they could use to carry out an exploratory study of translation competence with five professional translators (PACTE, 2000). Following this initial study, the research group reviewed their definition of translation competence to include a translator's attitude towards the translation task at hand. Translation competence was now defined as the '**underlying system of knowledge, abilities and attitudes required to be able to translate**' and their proposed translation competence model was revised to accord with what they called the 'Strategic sub-competence' at the heart of the model (PACTE, 2003). Figure 1.1 shows you PACTE's revised translation competence model.

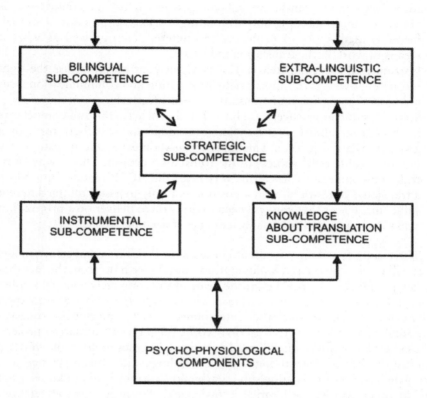

Figure 1.1 PACTE's revised Translation Competence Model (from PACTE, 2003: 60)

What does this model, which integrates the results of empirical-experimental research, tell us about translation competence or, to put it plainly, what it takes to be a professional translator? According to PACTE's model, translation competence is made up of five '**sub-competences**' (often called 'competences' in other models) one needs to acquire to become a competent translator, namely:

- **Bilingual sub-competence:** This is the obvious one! Bilingual sub-competence means having an excellent command of two languages. You should note, though, that this sub-competence in PACTE's model also includes 'influence control', that is, the ability to code-switch without interference from one language to the next;
- **Extra-linguistic sub-competence:** This is about your general knowledge, and more specifically about how much you know about (1) the culture(s) and sub-cultures of your language pair(s) and (2) subject-specific fields (that you may have to translate in);

8 *Joining the profession*

- **Knowledge-about-translation sub-competence:** This sub-competence is about you understanding how translating works (e.g. processes required, methods used, types of problems encountered, etc.) as well as what it means to work in the translation industry;
- **Instrumental sub-competence:** This is about your ability to use the right resources as well as the appropriate information and communication technologies to carry out your translation work effectively;
- **Strategic sub-competence:** Last, but certainly not least, this sub-competence is about your ability as a translator to adopt an overall strategy for a given translation project. This means you should be able to plan, carry out and evaluate the success of the translation project. This is why 'strategic sub-competence' lies at the very heart of PACTE's model. Indeed, as a translator you should be in a position not only to assess all the different sub-competences that you will need to draw on to deliver on a project, but also to compensate for any shortcomings if need be.

There are a few things we should note about PACTE's competence model that will matter to you as a budding translator. As we have seen, the fact that 'Strategic sub-competence' lies at the heart of the competence model implies that you, as a professional translator, will be expected to act as an expert who can draw on all your other, interconnected sub-competences to design and implement a macro-strategy that works for a given translation project. The **expert knowledge** you will need to activate in order to do so, however, is not just theoretical. Even though both 'Extra-linguistic sub-competence' and 'Knowledge-about-translation sub-competence' are mostly about **know-what** (or, in other words, 'declarative knowledge'), 'Strategic sub-competence', 'Bilingual sub-competence' and 'Instrumental sub-competence' are all about **know-how** (i.e. 'procedural knowledge'). What this means is that practice and experience matter.

We should also note that, in PACTE's model (Figure 1.1), only the last sub-competences – 'Knowledge about translation', 'Instrumental' and 'Strategic' – are specific to translation work. Indeed, the first two sub-competences can be required for other, non-translation-related jobs in the language industry. The last three sub-competences are therefore the ones that will allow you to develop **expertise** as a professional translator. This is, in any case, what PACTE's 2004 pilot test seems to confirm. The aim of the test, which involved professionals working with foreign languages, was to clearly identify the distinguishing features of translation competence and, as a result, validate PACTE's revised model. For this test, three professional translators and three foreign-language tutors were asked to (1) carry out translation tasks with their screens being recorded, (2) fill in questionnaires asking them to reflect on the translation problems they encountered and (3) take part in retrospective interviews while viewing their screen recordings (PACTE, 2005). The objective, here, was to test each group's 'Instrumental', 'Knowledge about translation' and 'Strategic' sub-competences, as both groups already

What skills and qualifications do I need? 9

shared the 'Bilingual' and 'Extra-linguistic' sub-competences. The results of this pilot test confirmed that 'the degree of expertise influences the translation process and product' (PACTE, 2005: 618). In other words, these are the three sub-competences you as a linguist must develop to become a successful professional translator.

Take a few minutes to reflect on the implications of PACTE's model for your own development as a budding professional translator:

- Do you agree that the three sub-competences 'Instrumental', 'Knowledge about translation' and 'Strategic' are key to developing professional expertise as a translator? How have you been developing them on your current translation programme?

1.2.2 *The productive translator: Göpferich's Translation Competence Model*

Because it was rooted in empirical research, PACTE's holistic translation competence model was one of the first – and one of the most influential – models of its kind. It was also the first one that tried to show how all competences relate to each other. This does not mean, however, that it was the only one. My objective, here, is not to take you through the whole history of translation competence models ... this could prove somewhat tedious! Nevertheless, research in the acquisition of translation competence has become a prominent field of inquiry in translation studies over the last two decades, and I would therefore like to introduce you to two other key models that have influenced our thinking on translation competence.

The first such model is the one developed by German translator and academic Susanne Göpferich as part of her 2007 research study 'TransComp'. What made Göpferich's different from preceding studies was its longitudinal character. Over a three-year period, 'TransComp' looked at the development of the translation competence of twelve undergraduate students of translation, and compared it to that of ten professional translators. Integrating previous research on translation competence, not least PACTE's, Göpferich developed her own model, which she used as the framework of reference for her own study (see Figure 1.2).

Just like in PACTE's model, 'Strategic competence'–that is, the translator's expertise defined as his or her ability to draw on all the other sub-competences to implement an overall strategy – lies at the heart of this model. Similarly, 'Communicative competence', 'Domain competence' and 'Tools and research competence' in the model can be seen to broadly correspond to PACTE's 'Bilingual sub-competence', 'Extra-linguistic sub-competence' and 'Instrumental sub-competence'. It is worth noting, though, that Göpferich mentions the use of **computer-assisted translation (CAT)** tools and **machine translation (MT)** explicitly under 'Tools and research competence'

10 Joining the profession

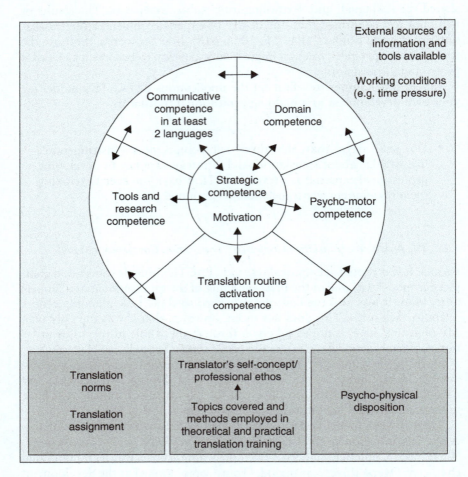

Figure 1.2 Göpferich's Translation Competence Model (from 2009: 21)

(Göpferich, 2019: 92). This is most likely because hers is a more recent model that acknowledges the impact of advances in translation technology on translation competence.

What makes her model different from PACTE's, however, are the 'Translation routine activation' and 'Psychomotor' competences. The **'Translation routine activation' competence** requires you to quickly recall and apply standard transfer operations that often lead to acceptable translations in the target language (Göpferich, 2009: 22). Obviously, this competence is one you primarily acquire through experience. Indeed, the longer you have practised as a translator working in a specific language combination and specialising in a specific domain, the quicker you will find translation

What skills and qualifications do I need? 11

solutions that are acceptable for the context in which you are operating. This, in turn, will increase your productivity and make your future as a professional translator more financially sustainable.

Similarly, the **'Psychomotor' competence** in Göpferich's model deals with the 'psychomotor abilities required for reading and writing (with electronic tools)' (ibid.: 22). This has to do with the translator's 'cognitive load', that is, the amount of information their working memory must process at any given time. This makes perfect sense! Imagine that you, as a professional translator, are not very good at typing. The extra cognitive effort it takes for you to type your translation will impact on your capacity to solve translation problems. In other words, the more brain energy you spend on typing, the less brain energy you have left to deal with arguably more important, translation-specific issues. As a professional translator, you should therefore strive to improve your psychomotor skills in order to free up some brain space for problem-solving.

- Concretely, what could you do to (further) develop your 'Translation routine activation' and 'Psychomotor' competences as a budding professional translator?

As you can see, the 'Translation routine activation' and 'Psychomotor' competences encompass some elements of PACTE's 'Knowledge-about-translation' sub-competence, while bringing new dimensions to the model. Through these two competences, Göpferich, who worked as a technical writer before becoming an academic, acknowledges the importance of productivity for professional translators more explicitly. This is because translation is, after all, a business.

1.2.3 The market- and technology-savvy translator: The European Master's in Translation's Competence Framework

A recognition that translation is a business and that a professional translator's competences should meet the needs of the **translation service industry** was also at the heart of the European Union's attempt to develop its own comprehensive model of translation competence.

Due to its policy of multilingualism, which means that it currently has 24 official languages, the European Union (EU) is one the biggest employers in the translation industry – both in Europe and worldwide. From the mid-2000s, however, the EU began to find it increasingly difficult to recruit translators with both the language competence and the other professional competences required of a professional translator in the 21st century. One of the reasons behind this, it believed, was that the content of some of the translation programmes from which students graduated was,

12 Joining the profession

at times, 'potentially incompatible with the requirements of the profession' (Chodkiewicz, 2012: 38). To address this, the European Commission's translation service, also known as the 'Directorate-General for Translation' (DGT), worked in partnership with academics and professional translators to develop a framework of reference of the competences translation students needed to acquire in order to 'meet agreed professional standards and market demands' (EMT, 2020). Since then, the European Commission's DGT has used the Competence Framework to award its quality label **European Master's in Translation (EMT)** to European postgraduate translation programmes that can prove that the content of their teaching helps students acquire these competences.

Known as the **Wheel of Competences**, the first iteration of the Framework launched in 2009 (see Figure 1.3). It aimed to define 'the basic competences that translators need to work successfully in today's market' (EMT, 2020). Placed at the heart of the 'Wheel', the 'Translation service provision' competence is clearly the one that stands out in this model. It replaces the 'Strategic' (sub-)competence of PACTE's and Göpferich's models. Although it integrates elements of the 'Strategic' (sub-)competence such as planning, management and self-evaluation, there is greater emphasis, here, on the **business and marketing skills** needed to offer translation services in a professional context (e.g., approaching new clients, negotiating rates with clients, budgeting your translation project).

The EMT's Competence Framework has since been updated twice (in 2017 and 2022) to reflect the impact technological change has since had on 'the way translation services are performed' as well as the evolution of market needs in the translation industry (EMT, 2017: 2). The reworked versions therefore sought to address the way **artificial intelligence and social**

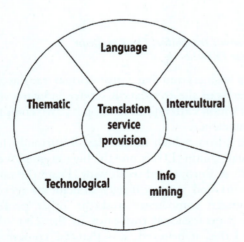

Figure 1.3 EMT 'Wheel of Competences' (from EMT, 2009: 4)

What skills and qualifications do I need?   13

media had 'considerably changed people's relation to communication in general, and to translation in particular' (ibid.) by putting renewed emphasis on the importance of developing the **digital literacy** of future professional translators.[1]

In the reworked versions of the Framework, the number of competences has been reduced to five, namely:

- **Language and culture competence:** This is very much like the bilingual/communicative competence of other models, as it 'encompasses all the general or language-specific linguistic, sociolinguistic, cultural and transcultural knowledge and skills that constitute the basis for advanced translation competence' (EMT, 2022: 6). Because this competence is not specific to professional translating, it serves as a prerequisite to all the other competences of the Framework;
- **Translation competence:** In the EMT Framework, this competence is akin to PACTE's 'Knowledge-about-translation' sub-competence, to which it adds a strategic (e.g., quality control procedures) as well as a thematic dimension (that is, the ability to work on domain-specific, media-specific and situation-specific types of translations). Rather topically, with this competence the EMT Framework also recognises that 'machine translation (MT) represents a growing part of the translation workflows, and that MT literacy and awareness of MT's possibilities and limitations is an integral part of professional translation competence' (EMT, 2022: 7);
- **Technology competence:** Added in 2017 in recognition of the fact that technological change in the translation industry is fast-paced and unrelenting, this competence stresses the importance for translators of developing 'the knowledge and skills used to implement present and future translation technologies within the translation process' (EMT, 2017: 9). The 2022 version goes even further by saying that professional translators should have the knowledge and skills not just to implement, but also to 'advise' clients on the use of, translation technologies in the translation process (EMT, 2022: 9).This means they should develop a good understanding of how machine translation works and its potential impact on translation quality (see Chapter 7);
- **Personal and interpersonal competence:** This competence is about the so-called 'soft skills' students are expected to develop to enhance their employability. This includes managing your work and your stress, keeping to deadlines, being able to work in teams (including in 'virtual, multicultural and multilingual environments, using current communication technologies'), understanding the organisational and physical ergonomics of your working environment and being able to self-evaluate and to engage with continuing professional development. In line with the Framework's emphasis on digital literacy, this competence also mentions the ability to 'us[e] social media responsibly for professional purposes' (EMT, 2022: 10);

14 *Joining the profession*

- **Service provision competence:** In the reworked versions of the Framework, this competence still contains many of the dimensions of the 'Translation service provision' competence from the 2009 Wheel of Competences. Indeed, this competence implies the ability to monitor new market requirements, to find and hold on to new clients by understanding their needs, to negotiate rates and deadlines and to manage the whole translation project (including quality insurance), and so on. The 2022 Framework, however, also insists on the importance of ethical practice for the profession. It therefore stresses the importance of learning to 'critically assess and work within the ethical principles (such as confidentiality, fair competition, impartiality) defined in codes of ethics' and to 'network with other translators and language service providers [...] so as to improve individual and collective professional visibility' (EMT, 2022: 11).

Interestingly, in both the reworked versions of the EMT Framework, 'Translation service provision' no longer lies at the heart of the model. In fact, there is no one competence at its heart, as all are considered to be of equal importance. What is more, the personal and interpersonal dimensions that used to be part of 'Translation service provision' now form a new competence of their own in the latest versions of the Framework: 'Personal and interpersonal'. This means that while the reworked Frameworks give increased recognition to the technological competence a translator should possess in this day and age, they also put renewed emphasis on all the **'human', 'soft' skills** a translator should acquire, too. Made exclusively of **'transferable skills'**, that is, the skills that are valued in most jobs, the 'Personal and interpersonal' competence has thus become key for anyone wanting a career in the translation service industry. As a result of this, training as an expert in 'multilingual multimedia communication engineering' (Gouadec, 2007: 17) should equip you not only with all the competences you need to become a successful translator, but also with a whole range of transferable skills that will stand you in good stead should you choose to pursue a different career.

TOPICS FOR DISCUSSION AND ASSIGNMENTS 1.1

Empirical research into translation competence acquisition (e.g. PACTE, TransComp) and collaboration between academia and the translation industry (EMT) has resulted in the development of influential translation competence models such as the ones we have just discussed. These three models share quite a lot in common, but they also emphasise different skills and competences that trainee translators should develop to become professional translators. Have another look at each model. With a course mate, discuss the following questions:

What skills and qualifications do I need? 15

- What are, according to you, the key differences between the three translation competence models?
- If you had to choose one model, which one do you think would work best in and for your own context? Why is that?
- Do you feel there are other important translation skills ('competences') that are missing from the three models we discussed? What competence(s) would that be?

1.3 Make sure you develop the right skills

From its beginnings, the ultimate objective of research into the acquisition of translation competence has been to ensure that you as a trainee translator develop the right skills on your chosen translation programme.

This was the case, for instance, for the PACTE research group. One of their main objectives was to help develop 'new pedagogical models that advocate competence-based training' based on their own competence model validated through experimental research (Hurtado Albir, 2015: 257). In the same vein, the pan-European EMT Framework was developed with the specific aim of ensuring that the students who study on an EMT-accredited postgraduate translation programme develop the necessary professional skills to meet market demand. In both cases, the objective is noble; it is part of a wider movement sometimes known as the **'professionalisation turn'**[2] in translation studies (Krajcso, 2018: 682).

It may well be that your chosen translation programme does not use a competence model as a yardstick, and that is fine. There is no magic formula, and the skills and competences you will want to develop for your future career in translation will also be partly based on your own personal objectives and the context in which you think you will operate as a translator. In any case, though, you should always take the time to reflect on the skills and competences your translation programme is helping you develop so you can identify existing strengths and any potential gaps you may still have.

According to Zita Krajcso in her article 'Translator's competence profiles versus market demand' (2018: 704), at the very least you should aim to develop skills and competences in the following three key fields before entering the job market:

- Translation field
- Technological field
- Operational field

Based on a review of recent industry and graduate surveys, Krajcso believes that the translation field is generally well covered on most translation programmes (ibid.). The **technological field**, however, can be more problematic, as not all programmes put as much emphasis on developing the technological skills you will need to 'respond to ever changing technological

16 *Joining the profession*

challenges' (ibid.: 705). And yet, as a trainee translator you should seek every opportunity not just to train in the use of specific translation tools, but also to develop your **knowledge and understanding** of some of the key principles behind **language technology** as this will help you confidently adapt to future new tools when and if the need arises.

What is more, you should also make sure you develop the skills that will allow you to deal with **operational issues** such as project management, quality management, marketing, risk management and so on. Indeed, this is an area where a '**real gap**' (ibid.; my emphasis) can be found between many translation graduates and industry, as most starting translators need these skills as soon as they graduate to launch their careers as self-employed or freelance translators. The skills that will allow you to do that are more general personal attributes that potential recruiters value, as attested by the anonymised job ad in Box 1.1: curiosity ('willingness to learn new things'), stress management ('ability to work under pressure'), time management ('good time management'), flexibility ('versatility'), professionalism ('professional approach'), individual and teamwork ('able to work autonomously as well as within a team'), 'client-orientation' and so on. These are also known as 'soft skills', as opposed to the 'hard' translation skills I mentioned earlier.

From all this we could conclude that, as a trainee translator entering the market in an age of ever-increasing use of technology in the language industry in general, and of the automation of the translation process in particular, you should see developing your skills and competences in the 'operational' and 'technical' fields as being perhaps as important as developing those in the 'translation field'. One could argue, after all, that **neural machine translation (NMT)** is 'destined to turn most translators into posteditors one day, perhaps soon' (Pym, 2013: 488). When and if this happens, a translator's role may no longer be to identify the best possible solutions to a given translation problem but to select between solutions suggested by machine translation. This represents, according to translation scholar Anthony Pym, 'a very simple and quite profound shift' as it significantly changes the nature of the translator's role (ibid.: 493). This shift justifies, according to him, adopting a simplified skill set for translation training programmes whereby you as a budding translator should, first and foremost (ibid.: 494–496):

- **Learn to learn** (e.g. learn to use new technical tools quickly and evaluate critically them for a given task);
- **Learn to trust and mistrust data** (e.g. learn to check machine-translation output based on provenance and client specifications);
- **Learn to revise translations as texts** (e.g. ability to conduct stylistic revising).

We can therefore see two particular soft skills, **curiosity** and **flexibility,** as vital for us translators in the age of automation. Yet, they are not enough: in order to revise the output of machine translation, we also need to hone

What skills and qualifications do I need? 17

'traditional and unique human skills such as first language proficiency and mastery of language skills that involve creativity' (Rodríguez de Céspedes, 2019: 113).

If what you need to be a successful professional translator is second-to-none language skills and soft skills such as curiosity and **creativity**, then why is a traditional languages degree not enough? Have we not gone back full circle? No, we haven't, because now we are all aware that while these skills are crucial, they should be developed alongside other important skills. This was also the conclusion of the EMT Competence Taskforce in their introduction to the latest version of the EMT Framework, published in 2022:

> This updated framework reflects the need for [...] human skills by reiterating the importance of linguistic, sociolinguistic, cultural, and transcultural skills. This does not mean a narrower focus, but rather *an awareness of human skills as a differentiator in a technologized employment market*, where linguistic, critical, and ethical competences can combine to produce a transversal skill set to equip graduates for the future. (EMT, 2022: 2, my emphasis)

Before we move on, take a few minutes to have a look at the programme specifications for the translation programme you are currently on to answer the following questions:

- How does my programme allow me to develop the skills I need to become an independent, critical user of language technology (i.e. 'learning to learn' and 'learning to trust and mistrust data')?
- How does my programme help me to enhance the human skills I need to succeed in the language industry (e.g. curiosity, flexibility, professionalism)?

TOPICS FOR DISCUSSION AND ASSIGNMENTS 1.2

National translator associations and/or initiatives often offer advice to budding translators with regard to the skills they will need to join the profession. For instance, the UK's National Network for Translation (2007–16), a government-funded programme that aimed to encourage young people to join the translation profession, listed the following skills on its website:

1. Professionalism
2. Networking skills
3. Attention to detail
4. Flexibility/adaptability

18   *Joining the profession*

5. Organisational skills
6. Writing skills
7. General knowledge
8. Analytical skills
9. Research skills
10. Subject knowledge
11. Curiosity
12. Excellent knowledge of the foreign language
13. IT skills
14. Picking up new ideas quickly
15. Good cultural awareness
16. Love of reading

Source: http://www.nationalnetworkfortranslation.ac.uk/resources/what-are-skills-required

Activity 1.1 Which of these skills do you think are so-called 'soft skills' (i.e. general attributes you may already possess) and which of them are 'hard skills' (i.e. skills specific to the translation industry that you may still need to develop)?

Activity 1.2 How does this list compare with the competence models discussed previously in this chapter? Are there any important skills missing from this list?

Activity 1.3 Now, spend some time searching the Internet to see if you can find a similar list of skills translators should have for the country where you'd like to work as a translator and/or the countries of your other language(s)? These are often published by national professional associations of translators and/or online careers advice websites. Is the list similar to the one above or does it put greater emphasis on a specific kind of skills (e.g. more on 'soft skills' or more on 'hard skills' etc.)? What do you think this may mean about the way that country sees translation as a profession?

Activity 1.4 Take some time to research advertised translator jobs online in your selected country. Have a look at 5 to 10 of them and write down the advertised skills they seek in a candidate, both explicitly and implicitly. If you found a list of skills for the previous activity, how does it compare with the list of skills taken from the advertised translator jobs? What about you? Do you feel you have the required skills?

Activity 1.5 Finally, have another look at the programme specifications of the programme you are currently on. How can it help you (further) develop the kind of soft and hard skills typically required of professional translators? Among the soft skills it can help you develop, which ones are 'transferable',

What skills and qualifications do I need? 19

meaning that they can easily be transferred to another job should you wish to explore different career paths (e.g. time management, problem-solving etc.)?

1.4 Which qualifications do I need to work as a professional translator?

As most translator trainers will tell you, this is one of the questions we get asked the most ... and with reason! Maybe you are a final-year modern languages student who wonders whether you need to study on a specialised translation programme to be able to work as a professional translator. Or an undergraduate student currently on a specialised translation programme who wonders whether you should complete a specialised postgraduate programme in translation to be employable as a translator. Or a postgraduate translation student who wonders whether you will need to have a specific professional accreditation to get work as a translator.

Unfortunately, there are no straightforward answers to any of these questions. This is because of the status of translation as a profession. Despite the fact that translation is far from being a 'new' profession, unlike others (e.g. medicine, law, architecture etc.) it has not yet achieved full professional autonomy. It remains, at best, **an emerging profession** (Pym et al., 2012: 81–82). Indeed, full professional autonomy for translators would involve protected status for their profession, put into effect through regulatory scrutiny by professional associations and/or governments. In most countries, translation is **not a regulated profession**. This means that there is no specific legal requirement in terms of the educational qualifications one should have in order to call oneself a 'translator' or to be hired as one (ibid.: 20). There are, of course, notable exceptions to this. Some countries, for instance, have measures in place to protect the status of the translators of legal documents, such as sworn translators or certified translators. However, these measures vary from one country to the next, and do not fully protect the title of translator (ibid.). In the absence of such regulatory scrutiny, any attempts to regulate who can work as a professional translator remain largely self-imposed through the relevant **professional associations** (see Chapter 3).

Concretely, this means that professional translators are not obliged to comply with specific rules regulating access to the profession. To put it simply, in most countries there is no specific qualification one has to attain to work as a professional translator. This does not mean, however, that it is right to work as a professional translator without having the required competences and/or qualifications. This is an **ethical issue,** after all. Many professional translator associations recognise that issue. They therefore have some guidelines around this in the codes of ethics or codes of conduct that their members must sign up to. Members of the Australian Institute of Interpreters and Translators, for instance, may only 'undertake work they are competent to perform in the languages for which they are professionally qualified through training and credentials' (AUSIT, 2012: 5).

20 Joining the profession

Another way for professional associations to ensure a minimal level of qualification can be to give full membership only to professionals who have achieved **certification** (also called 'accreditation' in some countries) (see Hlavac, 2013). Certification is the recognition of members based on their degrees or exams. In the UK, for instance, professional translators who want to become members of the Chartered Institute of Linguists (CIOL) must have an undergraduate degree in languages and three years' professional experience as a translator, or a postgraduate degree in languages and two years' professional experience. Failing that, prospective members can choose to take one of CIOL's own certification exams (see https://www.ciol.org.uk/member). These attempts, however, can be limited in their scope and in their reach. In China, for instance, certification schemes by professional associations remain 'limited and experimental' (Setton and Guo Liangliang, 2011: 91). By contrast, certifications appear to be highly valued in Iran, where they are seen as an important way to enhance the status of the profession by guaranteeing that members have the required level of competence (see Kafi et al., 2018 and McDonough Dolmaya, 2022). In many countries, professional associations can leverage this kind of power on the profession as gaining membership of such associations often gives professional translators more visibility and greater access to clients (see Chapter 3).

Besides professional associations, **industry standards** are another source of self-imposed regulation through certification in the translation industry. First published in 2015, the international standard **ISO 17100: 2015 'Translation Services – Requirements for Translation Services'** is a good example of this. This standard details what is required to deliver quality translation services. For translation service providers (TSP), being ISO 17100-certified is a way to demonstrate that you meet widely recognised, high-quality professional standards. The original standard dealt with the expected professional competences under the heading '3.1.3: Professional competences of translators'. Just like many professional associations, however, it failed to establish a clear link between the expected competences and a minimal level of qualifications (International Organization for Standardization, 2015: 6). Interestingly, though, the amendment '3.1.4: Translator qualifications' was added to the standard in 2017 (International Organization for Standardization, 2017a: 6). You will find the amendment in Box 1.2.

Box 1.2 ISO 17100: 2015+A1:2017

3.1.4 Translator qualifications

The TSP shall determine the translator's qualifications to provide a service confirming to this International Standard by obtaining documented evidence that the translator fulfils at least one of the following criteria:

What skills and qualifications do I need? 21

a) has obtained a degree in translation, linguistic or language studies or an equivalent degree that includes significant translation training, from a recognised institution of higher education;
b) has obtained a degree in any other field from a recognised institution of higher education and has the equivalent of two years of full-time professional experience in translating;
c) has the equivalent of five years of full-time professional experience in translating.
(International Organization for Standardization, 2017a: 6)

This amendment on translator qualifications can be seen as a positive step towards greater recognition of translation as a profession. However, the last criterion still allows for translators to work with no formal qualifications. In most countries, one could hardly imagine a similar list for nurses, where the last criterion would allow for a nurse with no formal training to be recognised as qualified provided they had the equivalent of five years' full-time professional experience! One should add, too, that there is absolutely no obligation for translation service providers to adhere to ISO 17100:2015.

The **absence of minimal educational requirements** to become a professional translator means that we can expect a huge range of disparity in what professional translators know about translation. This disparity, I would argue, can be detrimental to the credibility of translators and translation practice, especially in an age of increased competition from low-cost online translation platforms and free access to MT. As mentioned earlier, despite or maybe because of the absence of regulatory scrutiny that protects the status of professional translators, '[i]t is professional identity, and not measurable parameters, which provides the structuring principle [...] of the translation profession' (Sela-Sheffy, 2022: 173). For this **professional identity** to be realised, professional translators must behave professionally, and therefore ethically, beyond the prescriptive guidelines of codes of conduct. It is, for instance, our ethical duty as professional translators to constantly seek to enhance our knowledge about translation by engaging with the latest developments in the field. Doing so on an individual level will help enhance the collective status of translation as a profession. Whether we have achieved a formal qualification in translation or not, we as professional translators should therefore engage in continuous professional development throughout our entire careers (see Chapter 9).

TOPICS FOR DISCUSSION AND ASSIGNMENTS 1.3

Take some time to research advertised translator jobs online in your selected country. Have a look at five to ten of them.

22 Joining the profession

- What are the required qualifications (if any) for the job ads you selected? Are these specific to translation? If not, is membership of a professional association required?
- Whether or not specific qualifications in translation are required, in what ways do you think your having a qualification in translation could contribute to the collective visibility and the good reputation of translation as a profession in your chosen country?

Notes

1 Digital literacy, here, is defined as having acquired 'generic digital competencies.' These include

> information and data literacy, i.e. knowledge and skills related to information and data processing, storage and management. Moreover, they also include the ability to critically evaluate digital information, online interactions and online tools. Further competencies include the ability to find and communicate information, to share digital contents and to use digital communication and collaboration practices as well as social media. Finally, data security and risk management play an important role. (Nitzke et al., 2019: 294)

2 Professionalisation in this context is defined as

> the process to give a student the qualities, competences and skills worthy of and appropriate to a person engaged in the paid occupation of translation by means of a prolonged training and a formal qualification, so as to gain initial employment in translation, to maintain employment, and to be able to move around within the translation labour market. (Thelen, 2016: 123; Krajcso, 2018: 682)

Further reading

Krajcso (2018) provides an interesting contrasting analysis between existing translator competence frameworks and industry surveys to ascertain whether skills profiles match the needs of the current European translation market.

Rodríguez de Céspedes (2019) offers a thought-provoking article on the challenges of the automation of the translation workflow for translator training.

2 Career paths

Freelance, in-house or portfolio career?

> **Key questions we will explore in this chapter:**
>
> - What are the different possible career pathways for me as a budding professional translator?
> - What can I expect the role of a freelance and of an in-house translator to be?
> - How should I go about deciding between the roles of in-house and freelance translator? What if I can't decide?

2.1 The translation profession: Complex, fragmented but happy?

Chapter 1 aimed to help you reflect on the skills and qualifications required to become a translator both in general and in the country of your choice. In this chapter, we will have a closer look at all the potential career options for you as a translator. Before we do, though, it may be a good idea to remind ourselves of the reasons why the translation profession remains an attractive proposition, while mentioning some realistic concerns.

First of all, the global language services industry was valued at $60.5 bn in 2021 and it is projected to grow to nearly $85bn by 2026 (Nimdzi, 2022). Not just that; there is also some evidence that a career as a professional translator can be fulfilling. This is, in any case, the finding of a 2016 study by Helle V. Dam and Karen Korning Zethsen in an article entitled: ' "I think it is a wonderful job": On the solidity of the translation profession.' Having researched the occupational status of translators in Denmark for over a decade, Dam and Zethsen were all too aware that translation as a profession is often perceived as being associated with both **low pay and low status.** In this study, the two professors asked 15 professional translators to write about what they felt it is like to be a translator. The translators were selected on the basis that they had been working as professional translators for a while; all of them had at least eight years' experience as staff translators

DOI: 10.4324/9781003220442-3

24 *Joining the profession*

in the field of commercial translation. Even though their answers confirmed the low-pay, low-status issue often associated with translation as a profession, they also demonstrated 'a rather widespread enthusiasm about being a translator' (2016: 179). Indeed, their answers overwhelmingly showed professional translating to be 'an intellectual and creative challenge' that is '*exciting and satisfying*', and is 'varied, stimulating and never boring' as well as being 'important and therefore *meaningful*' (ibid.: 180, my emphases). Every job is different. Every text will give you a reading experience that you may never have had otherwise.

It is not just Danish translators who think that way! A similar study of the role, status and professional identity of translators and interpreters in China found that a majority of Chinese translators were also satisfied with their job and had no desire to change profession (Setton and Guo Liangliang, 2011). More recently, a survey of translators in Ireland and the United Kingdom showed that respondents showed high levels of **job satisfaction** (Courtney and Phelan, 2019). Even though such studies remain limited in their scope, they are a very welcome reminder that being a professional translator can remain attractive despite some of the **challenges** the profession has been facing of late, such as those around issues such as rates of pay, status and working conditions (see Lambert and Walker, 2022). Of course, these challenges are very real, as we will see in Chapter 9, and every budding translator should be fully aware of them. However, the fact that many professional translators continue to find the job fulfilling regardless may well comfort you in your decision to join their ranks!

Another reason why professional translating is 'never boring' may also be that what is meant by the word 'translator', and what is expected of the role, is constantly **evolving**. As we saw in Chapter 1, one needs to develop a whole range of both 'soft' and 'hard' skills to start performing at the level of a professional translator. This is something the professional translators involved in Dam and Zethsen's study were well aware of. Indeed, there is no denying that translating is an increasingly complex profession. This can be seen in the proliferation of **new job titles** that reflect the market expectation that translators will offer other services, 'add-ons', beyond translating, such as, for instance, post-editing of machine translation. Besides, technological advancements also mean that today's translators can be expected to deal with 'multilingual and multimodal digital genres' such as web content, videogames and smartphone apps (Schäffner, 2020: 80). This trend can be found the world over; it was also observed, for instance, in Sakwe Mbotake's survey of professional translators in Cameroon (2015). Because of the profound changes in the nature of the role of translator, one could be tempted to argue that it may be time to update the job title itself. Would 'interlingual communication engineer', for instance, not be a better reflection of what today's translators do? The jury is still out on that one ... as such a change may well further confuse the issue!

> - Which aspects of translation as a profession do you find most appealing? Conversely, which aspects of the profession do you worry about the most?

As well as being complex, the translation profession is also quite **fragmented**. Professional translators operate in a wide variety of settings which impact their working conditions. In most countries, the main work providers for translators are translation agencies and translation companies. Even though both are commonly called 'agencies' or **LSPs** ('Language Service Providers'), it is still possible to make a distinction between the two. Typically, **translation companies** employ their own dedicated teams of staff translators ('in-house translators') as well as using the services of self-employed translators ('freelance translators'). **Translation agencies**, however, act primarily as brokers between their clients and freelance translators. There are, of course, work opportunities for translators beyond translation agencies and companies. Some freelance translators, for instance, work directly with translation requesters. Similarly, some in-house translators are employed directly by companies or organisations that do not specialise in translation but need a translator on their books (as can be the case, for instance, for multinational financial service providers).

In any case, the most significant difference in **employment status** is to be found between in-house and freelance translators. Most surveys looking at the employment status of translators tend to agree that freelance translating is the most common form of translation employment across the globe. In many countries, around 70–80% of translators work on a freelance basis (see Pym et al., 2012). However, employment practices vary greatly from one country to the next as attested by the fact that this average is much lower in China – around 40–50% (ibid.). In the rest of this chapter, we will have a closer look at what it means to be an in-house and a freelance translator. We will start with freelance translators in recognition of the fact that this is the most common form of employment for most translators worldwide.

TOPICS FOR DISCUSSION AND ASSIGNMENTS 2.1

Activity 2.1 Recent research into the socio-economic status of translators shows that in quite a few countries translators perceive themselves as low-paid and low-status yet happy professionals (see Katan, 2011; Setton and Guo Liangliang, 2011 and Dam and Zethsen, 2016). Does this hold true for professional translators in the country where you would like to work as a translator and/or the countries of your other language(s)?

26 *Joining the profession*

Investigate for yourself by browsing online translator blogs as well as online translator forums for the country of your choice. Try to answer the following questions:

- What do translators say about their profession? Can you see a tendency emerging?
- Do translators there seem generally happy with their status as translator, or not? Why is that?

Activity 2.2 We know that the trend worldwide is for translators to be self-employed (see Pym et al., 2012). Search the Internet to try and find out what the figures are for the country where you'd like to work as a translator and/or the countries of your other language(s). In some countries, national associations of translators publish official figures, whereas in others you may have to rely on less reliable sources. Once you have found some figures, ask yourself the following questions:

- Are the figures you found for your chosen country in line with the global trend or is the employment pattern of translators different there?
- What does this mean for your prospects of working as a freelance translator and/or an in-house translator?

2.2 Going freelance

As we have just seen, many professional translators work on a 'freelance' basis. This means that they sell their translation services to clients. Undoubtedly, working as a freelance translator means that you have **more control** over your working conditions, as you are your own boss. You can decide, for instance, when and where you want to work and who for, and you can set your own conditions. However, being a freelance translator also means accepting a lower level of job security than you would enjoy as a staff translator. As a freelancer, you won't benefit from the security of a guaranteed, steady income and the profit you'll generate will likely fluctuate from one month to the next. You won't benefit from sick leave or paid annual leave either. For most people, working freelance therefore means enjoying greater work freedom but a bit **less security**.

As a freelance translator, the first thing you will need to do is not translate ... but **find clients!** (see Chapters 4, 5 and 8). The first step, therefore, is for you to clearly identify your potential clients: Who are they? Where are they? What is their core business? What are they trying to get done? Once you

Career paths: Freelance, in-house or portfolio career? 27

have answered these questions, you should ask yourself another couple of questions: Why should they want to employ your services (and not somebody else's)? How can they find you?

Because finding direct clients can be tricky for freelance translators new to the job market, you may decide to **work for translation agencies** as a way to get a foot in the door. The agencies are, in this instance, your clients. There are some significant advantages to having a translation agency as your client. You will be able to spend more time on what you really enjoy doing (translating!) instead of looking for clients and dealing with administrative tasks. The agency, for instance, will deal with managing the project and invoicing the end client (i.e. the translation requester). More often than not, your main contact at the translation agency will be a **'project manager'**. Employed as staff, the project manager's role is to manage the translation project for the end client on behalf of the agency. Sometimes, this can involve dealing with complex, multilingual projects.

Imagine, for instance, that Apple wants its new iPhone marketing materials translated into 50 languages. The project manager will be tasked with giving Apple a quote for the requested translation project, identifying suitable translators for the task among the agency's pool of freelance translators, organising the project's workflow, liaising with both the freelance translators and the designated contact, ensuring quality control, invoicing Apple at the end of the project and arranging payment for the freelance translators. A good project manager will know which questions to ask the end client to make sure the translation project meets their expectations. Because they have the necessary human resources to deal with **complex, multilingual projects** (i.e., project managers and a big pool of freelance translators), big multinational companies tend to work with such agencies. This, in turn, often means a steadier flow of work for the freelancers the agencies employ.

Despite all this, translation agencies sometimes have a bad press among translators because of the **rates** they set and the deadlines they impose on freelancers. It is true that the rate you will get from an agency can be half what you would get if you worked with direct clients. A recent survey of freelance translators in the United Kingdom, for instance, showed that translation agencies are 2.5 times more likely to ask translators to lower their rates than direct clients (see Inbox Translation, 2021). However, many agencies will give you access to the required translation **software** (which can be quite expensive to access otherwise) and they will also give you some **feedback** on your translation work. Working with an agency therefore provides you with some training on the job, which is very valuable for a budding translator.

All in all, if you accept agency assignments you will have to trade in some of your freedom as freelancer for some more security. This can involve, for instance, accepting a lower pay rate (which is often presented as fixed, although you can always negotiate), agreeing to take on a new translation project on a Friday afternoon that is due the following Monday or even agreeing to sign a non-disclosure agreement.

28 *Joining the profession*

Like any other business, you will find the good, the bad and the ugly when looking for a translation agency. Some translation agencies will set you unrealistic deadlines. As a budding translator, you have to be realistic as to how many words you can translate in a working day (also known as your '**daily throughput**'). Of course, this will vary according to your language combination and the degree of specialisation that is required. Still, around **2,000 words a day** seems to be a realistic guideline for starting translators. Agencies therefore tend to expect around 10,000 in five working days, but some agencies may send you a 20,000-word translation commission on a Monday morning that they want you to complete by close of play on the Friday. In such a case, you must ask yourself if you can realistically deliver without compromising your reputation as a professional translator. There is no easy answer, though, as you may well desperately need the work in order to keep afloat financially.

It is important to add, here, that this kind of dilemma applies to all freelance translators, whether they work with agencies or for direct clients. A big difference, however, is that it may feel easier to charge direct clients **a premium** for tight deadlines. Of course, you can also do this for agency assignments. If they want you and they don't have anybody else, they will likely pay you the premium. However, you have to be willing to walk away if they won't. In general, finding your own clients is more rewarding financially than taking on agency assignments, as you negotiate with them on your own terms. This is why many freelance translators who start off with agencies as clients try to gradually build their own **direct client base** on the side (see Chapter 5). You should never approach existing clients you may already work for via a translation agency to offer them your services directly, though. Not only would it expressly contravene most of the 'non-solicitation' or 'non-compete' clauses that form part of many agencies' sign-up contracts, it is also clearly **unethical** and could cause you long-term reputational damage. You will need to find clients yourself by marketing your services to them, often with the help of social media (see Chapter 9).

Having to find new clients is one of the reasons why you should not think that being a freelance translator means translating 24/7. The more you work with direct clients, the more you have to dedicate some time during your working week to two other important jobs: **marketing** and **admin**. The latter will typically involve following up on invoices and doing some accounting. All freelance translators should also dedicate some of their time to **Continuing Professional Development (CPD)**. CPD activities for freelance translators are very wide-ranging and can include taking courses on the latest translation technology, terminology courses in their field of specialisation, or marketing courses, and so on. What matters is that you keep learning on the job to make sure you keep on top of your game (see Chapter 9).

As a freelance translator, you should therefore not expect to be translating all the time. In his *Practical Guide for Translators*, Geoffrey Samuelsson-Brown

Career paths: Freelance, in-house or portfolio career? 29

shows that experienced freelance translators such as himself can spend up to a quarter of their working time on admin, marketing, networking and CPD (2010: 3). Even on the days when you are actually translating, you will find it difficult to sustain long, uninterrupted stretches on task. You will certainly need to take some **breaks** during the day to keep it sustainable (see Chapter 9). Depending on the difficulty of the translation task in hand, the cognitive demands of the job may also mean that there are days where you manage to translate for six full hours 'only'. This is something you will need to take into consideration when setting your rates with clients.

Consequently, some of the essential attributes you will have to draw on as a freelance translator are **self-discipline** and **resilience**: self-discipline, because you will need to find and set your own work and to self-motivate; resilience, because finding work can be very challenging at first. You may well have to apply to hundreds of translation agencies before one of them replies to you. Those who do reply will likely ask you to complete test translations before they offer you any work. Similarly, it will take time to build your own base of direct clients. You may well lose a few clients along the way, too. There will be quite a few bumps in the road ... and this is why it is very important for freelance translators to build their own support networks (see Chapters 3 and 4).

If life as a freelance translator appeals to you and you feel that you have what it takes to make a success of it, then you need to start thinking about the practical implications of setting yourself up as a freelancer. Obviously, these will differ depending on the country where you want to work, but the key principles remain the same. First of all, in most countries aspiring freelancers can choose between different legal statuses that have implications regarding their tax liability and access to welfare. In the UK, for instance, you can choose between setting yourself up as a 'sole trader' (i.e. as self-employed) or setting up a 'limited company'. If you are a **sole trader**, you and your translation business are just one legal entity. This means that you can keep all the profits from your work, but also that you are personally responsible for all the losses the business may incur. Technically, it also means that you can use your personal bank account for your business if you so wish. Yet, for accountancy reasons it is highly recommended you open a separate bank account for your business as it makes it easier to track all the business-related income and expenditure you will have to report in your annual tax return. When you set up a **limited company**, however, you create a business that hires you as a **limited company director**. What this means is that the profits you generate belong to the business, not you; the bank account for the business is kept separate from yours. It also means that, unlike a sole trader, you have limited liability for the losses the business may incur as you are, technically, an employee of the limited company you created. Despite this, many freelance translators choose to register as sole traders when they first set up their business as the process can appear more straightforward – and therefore less daunting – than setting up a limited company.

30 *Joining the profession*

This may seem rather complicated, but it is important that you understand the available legal options in your chosen context. This is because the **legal status** you opt for as a freelancer will almost certainly have implications for the amount of tax you must pay and your liability if the business goes bankrupt, as well as for your welfare and pension entitlements. One way to find out more about your options is to carry out an initial Internet search with the words 'legal status' + 'freelancer' + 'options' + [name of the country] for your chosen context. This should lead you to websites explaining the differences between the different statuses you can choose from as a freelancer.

- What are the different legal statuses under which you could set yourself up as a freelance translator in the country/-ies where you would like to work? Which one do you feel would be best suited to your own situation and needs?

Another thing to consider is how much **money** you will need before you even start operating as a freelance translator. As a freelancer, you will most likely work from home so you won't need to rent some office space. You will, however, need to equip yourself with a personal computer and reliable Internet access at the very least. Depending on where you work, you may also be expected to have a licence for specific CAT (computer-assisted technology) software in order to get some work ... and this can be quite pricy. You may also want to spend some money advertising your services by creating a sleek website or printing out business cards. Another expense you should really consider is some kind of insurance policy that protects you as a professional in case something goes wrong (see Chapter 5). This is not something most of us want to think about but, sadly, things do go wrong every now and then. As a freelance translator, for instance, a client may decide to sue you if they are not happy with your work or if they believe you have breached confidentiality. Such a policy – typically referred to as **professional indemnity insurance** (**PII**)–will protect you by covering the legal fees involved in defending the case as well as the compensation due if you lose it (see also Chapter 5). As a benefit to their members, some professional translator associations, such as the UK's Chartered Institute of Linguists, offer access to recommended PII providers with whom they have negotiated preferential rates.

All these upfront costs soon add up! Remember that the chances are you won't start earning money straightaway, as it will take time to find your first clients. You should therefore calculate how much money you will need for your own **daily expenses** (e.g. paying rent, grocery shopping, etc.) in the first few months of your business, on top of the money you will need to set the business up. Depending on your situation, this may mean that setting yourself up as a freelance translator is not financially possible in the first instance.

Career paths: Freelance, in-house or portfolio career? 31

If that's the case, why not consider other options such as working as an in-house translator for a few years before you go freelance?

- Based on what you have just read, what are *for you* the greatest advantages of working as a freelance translator? Conversely, what are the greatest drawbacks of freelancing?

2.3 Working in-house

The main advantages of working as an in-house translator are obvious. Inevitably, some of the 'perks' will vary depending on the legislation of the country where you work and the policies of the company that employs you. In most countries, though, salaried translators are entitled to paid annual leave, sick leave and parental leave. They often have access to a pension scheme and, sometimes, to private health insurance. All this, of course, on top of a **guaranteed income**.

There are other advantages to starting your career in-house. Unlike freelance translators, you won't have to incur all the upfront costs required to equip yourself. Your employer will provide you with the necessary IT equipment and resources and, in most cases, they will also give you access to the necessary training to use them efficiently. It is very likely that you will also receive **regular, valuable feedback** on your translation work although, once again, this will depend on where you work. Globally, though, one of the main advantages of starting in-house is that you can gather some experience and further develop all the necessary skills and competences we discussed in Chapter 1 while you earn. Another advantage is that, in some respects, an in-house career may make it easier to achieve a good **work–life balance**. Indeed, unlike freelance translators you should not be expected to work weekends in order to meet a deadline. In most cases, your work contract will specify the days/times you can be expected to work as well as the overall number of hours your employer expects you to put in.

As I said before, all this will vary depending not only on the legislation of the country where you work, but also on the policies of the company that employs you. This is why you should not assume that **working conditions** are the same everywhere. Some in-house jobs will give you greater access to training and/or career development while others may give you shorter working weeks or more annual leave. Others still will provide a workload you find more interesting or they will simply pay more. To some extent, it is up to you to decide what is important to you at this stage of your career.

In any case, you would do well to always keep an eye out for opportunities. And there are many opportunities for in-house translators! This is because staff translators work in a great variety of contexts ... so much so that it would be nearly impossible to list them all. In what follows, I will

32   Joining the profession

focus on the main contexts in which in-house translators work: translation companies, translation agencies, commercial companies and governmental or international organisations.

2.3.1 Translation companies

Let's start with **translation companies.** Translation companies have translation and translation-related services at the core of their business. They employ their own staff translators even though they sometimes use the services of freelancers, too. They tend to specialise in certain language combinations and fields of expertise, although what they translate is largely dictated by the needs of their clients. Many translation companies pride themselves on offering a reliable, high-quality service to their clients that respects their exact requirements and preferences. This explains why they often hire budding translators as **'Translation Checkers'** before letting them translate for clients. In this role, you can expect to spend a lot of your time checking completed translations for potential errors, paying particular attention to key elements such as proper names, numbers and the like. On a typical day, checkers check around 2,000 words per hour. Once the company is satisfied with your work as a checker, they will gradually start giving you some translation work on the side. In most cases, the company's translators will go through your translation work with a fine-tooth comb and will give you detailed feedback so you can improve.

The feedback you get on your translation work will determine how quickly you are promoted to a translating role. Being a checker can sometimes feel like a thankless task as it takes time to move on to an actual translating role (usually one to two years). This is because translation companies want to make sure that you fully understand each of their clients' specific requirements as well as the company's own quality-control procedures. Nevertheless, starting as a checker is highly formative, as you get feedback from colleagues who are expert translators and you are likely to work with a wide variety of texts (depending on your company's clients, of course). Once you have made it to **Translator,** you can expect to translate between 2,000 and 2,500 words a day. There is room for further career progression in translation companies, as you can then be promoted to **Senior Translator,** with increased responsibilities. To sum it up, most translation companies will provide you with training and opportunities to progress but they will also expect you to 'be productive, guarantee 100% quality and uphold the company's values and ethical code at all times' (Gouadec, 2007: 97).

2.3.2 Translation agencies

The demands and training opportunities you are presented with will be similar to those of translators working for a translation company if you choose to work in-house at a **translation agency,** but your role will be different. As we saw earlier, translation agencies act primarily as brokers between their clients and freelance translators. Because of their business model, translation agencies hire more **project managers** than they do in-house translators. When they do hire staff translators, their job is to manage the work of the freelance translators employed by the agency and to check the quality of their translations. You will be doing some translating, but less than you would at a translation company. Your role as in-house translator at an agency is therefore very close to that of a project manager in that you are the one responsible for the full translation project and for liaising between the agency's team of freelancers and the clients. Because of this, you will be expected to have strong **organisational and interpersonal skills** as well as having an **eye for detail**. Translation agencies tend to offer fewer opportunities for career progression for translators who want to keep translating; if you want to move up, you may well have to move into a more managerial role.

2.3.3 Commercial companies

Translation companies and agencies are where you most expect to find in-house translators. However, many staff translators find work at **commercial companies** whose core business is not translation but where there is a strategic need to employ translators full-time. These are often – though not always – big multinational companies 'with full-blown translation departments [which] include Ericsson, Michelin, Spar, Carrefour, Sears, Eurocontrol, UBS, Air France, MacDonald's, Snecma, EADS, Boeing, PCW, all international banks, etc.' (Gouadec, 2007: 94). In smaller commercial companies, where there may not be a specific translation department, in-house translators tend to be based in the company's **documentation department** or its **marketing department**.

If you work as translator for a commercial company, you can therefore expect to regularly translate internal documents such as policies, procedures or training materials as well as reports for external stakeholders and client-facing documentation. Staff who translate marketing materials are sometimes called **'localisers'**. This name reflects the fact that a company's product and its marketing materials may need to be adapted to meet the cultural needs and expectations of foreign markets. Localisers is also what you call translators working in one of the fastest-growing industries in the last decade, the **gaming industry**. Video games often go global, which explains the need for localisers. Due to the high level of secrecy that surrounds the development of new video games, some companies such as Ubisoft have become major recruiters of in-house translators of late.

Whether you translate in-house for a video-game developer or a global food producer, a significant advantage of working for a commercial company is that you can really **specialise** in a given field. Indeed, most of your translation work will be related to the core business of the company; you will spend a fair share of your time '[raising] awareness of the importance of a clearly

34 Joining the profession

set-out in-house language policy covering issues such as terminology, phrase-ology, parts lists and bills of materials, concept definitions, technical writing and technical documentation' (ibid.: 95). So, if you are passionate about cars, then working as in-house translator for a multinational car manufacturer will be just the ticket! Some of you, however, will see this as a drawback as you may prefer to translate a more varied range of documents, especially at the beginning of your career. Still, another advantage of working for a com-mercial company is that the ones with big translation departments can offer you good **career progression** as a translator, with roles akin to that of Senior Translator.

2.3.4 Governmental and intergovernmental organisations

Translating in-house for **governmental or intergovernmental organisations** is, in many ways, similar to translating for commercial companies, but in this case you are doing so for the public service. One of the best-known governmental organisations is Canada's Translation Bureau, which supports Canada's official policy of multilingualism. Similarly, the best-known inter-governmental organisation is probably the UN (United Nations). Other, more regional intergovernmental organisations include NATO (the North Atlantic Treaty Organization), the EU (European Union) and the AfDB (African Development Bank). Unlike commercial companies, these organisations' translation needs arise from a **political commitment to multilingualism** that has become a legal requirement. This means that they recruit in-house translators mostly – although not exclusively – for the languages the organ-isation recognises as 'official' or 'working' languages. AfDB, for instance, has two working languages (French and English), whereas the UN counts six official languages (Arabic, Chinese, English, French, Russian and Spanish).

You should note that many of these organisations employ their in-house translators as **civil servants**. Where this is the case, only candidates who meet specific citizenship requirements may apply. The EU, for instance, only offers permanent in-house translation positions to applicants who can prove they have citizenship of one of its 27 member states. Once you are in the job, the nature of the work carried out by the organisation will dictate what you trans-late. Again, just like staff translators working for a commercial company, you can expect to translate **internal documentation** (e.g. policies, procedures, training materials, etc.) as well as **official documents** for external stakeholders (e.g. reports) and **public-facing documents** (e.g. information leaflets for the general public, press releases etc.). One of the main differences, though, arises from the fact that the translation departments of such organisations have a greater tendency to invest huge resources in **terminology management** and **quality-control** measures. This is because they routinely deal with legally binding documents where, potentially, translation errors such as not using a preferred term could have disastrous political consequences. As a result of these measures, the work of translators at such organisations may appear

Career paths: Freelance, in-house or portfolio career? 35

quite controlled and constricted. This, in turn, can lead to a sense of disempowerment and reduced agency among some translators (see Kang, 2019). However, work at such organisations usually offers second-to-none working conditions and excellent career progression.

- Based on what you have just read, what are *for you* the greatest advantages of working as an in-house translator? Conversely, what are the greatest drawbacks of working in-house?
- Were you to work as an in-house translator, which professional context (e.g. translation company, translation agency, commercial company or (inter)governmental agency) do you feel would work best for you?

2.4 Freelance or in-house: What shall I do?

Just like freelance translators, in-house translators need to be able to demonstrate that they can be efficient (meet deadlines on time), accurate (dot the i's and cross the t's), flexible (adapt to different fields, document styles and formats, client expectations and, sometimes, technologies) and resilient. Resilient because, as we've just discussed, there are times when staff translators might feel like cogs in the machine.

The latter point may help to explain why some studies have found that professional translators tend to 'find more **control** and **autonomy** as freelancers than as in-house translators' (Pym et al., 2012: 79, my emphases). Admittedly, as a freelance translator you will be in a position to choose the field(s) of expertise you want to specialise in (see Chapters 8 and 9). Yet, freelance translating will also offer you more limited career progression as, more often than not, your clients will pay more attention to the price you charge than to your 'experience, evidence of specialist knowledge, continuous personal development since qualifying or tangible evidence of quality management' (Samuelsson-Brown, 2010: 17). Then again, however, a survey of freelance translators in the United Kingdom found that:

> The more successful [freelance translators] are able to use their market position to exert substantial control over areas like pay and deadlines. In addition, the lack of traditional career structure means that many translators have actively chosen freelance work and that even those who were originally forced into it would not now take an in-house job. (Fraser and Gold, 2001: 682)

Given all this, you may find it difficult to decide which career path would be best suited to you. Another factor to influence your decision could be the **socio-economic status** of a freelance versus an in-house translator. Rather

36   Joining the profession

conveniently, in the last decade or so, translation studies scholars have started carrying out empirical research work into this. While some studies focus on the status of the profession at large, others look into translators' status-perception and job satisfaction based on the context in which they work. If you are still undecided, such studies could help you have a clearer idea of what might work best for you.

In Denmark, for instance, a 2011 study tried to understand the differences in the perceived professional status of translators based on whether they worked freelance, for a translation company or for a commercial company. The researchers asked 244 Danish translators some questions around their salary/income, the recognition of their education/expertise, their visibility and their power/influence; these four parameters are believed to be indicators of status in Denmark (Dam and Zethsen 2011: 979). They also asked them how they perceived their status as translators in society. Overall, the staff translators working at commercial companies rated their **occupational status** higher than those working for a translation company or freelance did, and the scores for agency and freelance translators were quite similar (ibid.: 984). These results were confirmed by the question around translators' perceived **visibility** at work and by clients; the translators working for commercial companies rated their visibility as high whereas freelancers rated it low (ibid.: 991). However, freelance translators reported the highest levels of **income,** while translators working for commercial companies reported the lowest ones (ibid: 986). Similarly, freelance and translation company translators shared a stronger sense of **professional identity** and a greater tendency to see themselves as **highly skilled professionals** than those working for commercial companies. Finally, in-house translators working for commercial companies reported significantly higher levels of perceived levels of **influence at work** than translation company or freelance translators (ibid.: 993). Unlike what Dam and Zethsen had initially expected, the results for in-house translators working at a translation company were more closely aligned to those of freelance translators than those of staff translators working for a commercial company. This led them to conclude that: 'Being a staff translator, on a permanent contract with stability in employment and income [...] may after all not be that important in a status context, but it remains to be investigated which factors are decisive' (ibid.: 994).

Of course, this study was specific to the Danish context, but its finding that the difference in **employment status** (freelance versus in-house) may not be the strongest indicator of perceived professional status does provide some food for thought. A recent Finnish survey subsequently tried to find out whether a professional translator's **domain of specialisation** had an impact on their perceived status and job satisfaction. They partly replicated Dam and Zethsen's study but made a distinction between literary translators, non-literary translators and audio-visual translators (aka 'subtitlers'). What they found was that, even though literary translators are generally believed be the ones with the highest status, there was, in fact, no real link between a

Career paths: Freelance, in-house or portfolio career? 37

translator's domain of specialisation and how they perceived their status as a translator (Ruokonen and Mäkisalo, 2018). With no ready-made answers available, your best option is to further explore the working conditions for all these different career paths for yourself so as to find the best fit for you. The following activities will help you do just that!

TOPICS FOR DISCUSSION AND ASSIGNMENTS 2.2

To help you decide the kind of translator you want to be, it may be helpful for you to understand not just what the various professional contexts involve, but also what motivates you both personally and professionally. The following activities will therefore help you do that.

Activity 2.3 Spend some time browsing the Internet to try and find out more about the most common working conditions for both freelance and in-house translators in the country of your choice. Bear in mind that, with the explosion of remote work, the country where you're based may be different from the country where you are officially employed and/or where your clients are based. This could have implications for some of your answers to the questions below (e.g. access to health cover, pension etc.). Still, here are a few questions you should aim to answer when trying to decide whether freelance or in-house would work best for you:

- What kind of tasks will have I to carry out on a day-to-day basis? Can I feel excited about them?
- How many hours a day and how many days a week should I expect to work? Will this work with my other life goals and commitments?
- How much can I expect to earn at the beginning of my career? Will that be enough for me?
- Will I have access to health cover, annual leave, sick leave, parental leave? Will I be contributing towards a pension?
- Will I feel challenged enough in the role? Will there be room for me to grow over time?

Activity 2.4 Now, let's see how what you have found out for Activity 2.3 could match with what you know about yourself by using a **values exercise** that will help you reflect on your own professional and personal values.

Have a look at the list of core values in Table 2.1. As values are also culturally determined, you may feel the list in Table 2.1 does not accurately reflect what you would see as core values in the culture you are from. If this is the case for you, then please carry out an Internet search with the words 'list of core values' in the language of your chosen culture in order to find a more appropriate list of values you can use for this exercise. When you are done, take some time to choose five values (no more, no less!) from the list that you

38 *Joining the profession*

Table 2.1 List of core values commonly used by leadership institutes and programmes

Authenticity	Creativity	Justice	Recognition
Achievement	Determination	Leadership	Responsibility
Adventure	Fairness	Learning	Security
Authority	Faith	Love	Self-Respect
Autonomy	Fame	Loyalty	Service
Balance	Friendships	Meaningful Work	Spirituality
Beauty	Fun	Openness	Stability
Boldness	Growth	Optimism	Success
Compassion	Happiness	Peace	Status
Challenge	Honesty	Pleasure	Trustworthiness
Citizenship	Humour	Poise	Wealth
Community	Influence	Popularity	Wisdom
Competency	Inner Harmony	Religion	
Contribution	Kindness	Reputation	
Curiosity	Knowledge	Respect	

Source: Adapted from: James Clear, 'Core Values List' (n.d.), https://jamesclear.com/core-values

feel best represent what matters for you in your personal life. Then take some time to choose five values from the same list that you feel best represent what matters for you in your professional life. These can be the same values as the ones you chose for your personal life, but they can be different, too.

Activity 2.5 Now that you have found out more about the working conditions for both freelance and in-house translators (Activity 2.3) and you have selected five key values that best reflect what matters to you in both your personal and your professional life (Activity 2.4), please discuss the following with a course mate:

- In which professional context (freelance vs. in-house) do I feel I am most likely to realise my core professional values? What about my core personal values?
- On balance, based on what I know about my own values and about the working conditions for in-house and freelance translators in the country where I'd like to work, which professional context do I feel will most likely suit me as an individual? Why is that?

2.5 Life is what happens while you're busy making other plans ...

Or so the saying goes! Now that you've spent some time trying to figure out whether you'd be best suited for a career as a freelance or as a staff translator, allow me to throw a metaphorical spanner in the works: **chance**. Ask any professional and they will likely tell you that chance has played a big role in the way their career has developed. There is, in fact, a whole career guidance

Career paths: Freelance, in-house or portfolio career? 39

theory dedicated to this: planned **happenstance theory**. Originally developed by American scholar John D. Krumboltz, happenstance theory recognises the simple fact that, as we've just mentioned, 'Chance plays an important role in everyone's career. No one can predict the future with any accuracy' (Mitchell et al., 1999: 116).

Concretely, this means you can't really plan your career once and for all as a student, because life is a constant flow of unplanned and unpredictable events. Or, in other words, it's ok if you don't know whether you want to be a freelance or an in-house translator just yet. You should remain **flexible** enough to constantly reassess your options in order to 'create a satisfying life in a constantly changing work environment' (ibid.: 117). Planned happenstance does not mean that you should just wait with your fingers crossed in the hope that everything will magically fall into place. What it means, though, is that you need to learn to 'recognize, and incorporate chance events into [your] career development' by learning 'to take action to generate and find opportunities' (ibid.: 117).

With happenstance theory, unplanned events are therefore desirable and it is ok for you to be indecisive about your next career move as this means you remain **open-minded**. This is an important mindset to have if you are to make the most of the opportunities life throws at you. Similarly, you should strive to develop a set of other key qualities: **curiosity** (to explore new opportunities), **persistence** (to deal with potential obstacles), **flexibility** (to address changing circumstances), **optimism** (that the new opportunities are attainable) and **risk-taking** (in the face of unknown outcomes) (ibid.: 118).

Planned happenstance theory is highly relevant to us, as a significant number of professional translators end up having as many careers as a cat has lives as a result of **chance events** (or, one could say, 'seized opportunities'). In fact, a lot of us develop what is known as 'portfolio careers'. A **portfolio career** is a career in which 'individuals develop a portfolio of skills that they sell to a range a clients' (Templer and Cawsey, 1999: 71). For translators, this often means selling our services as an occasional interpreter, a translator trainer, a language tutor, a content writer or even a project manager, for example. What else we do besides translating will be largely guided by the opportunities that arise around us as well as those we seek to create. Despite the rather traditional view that a 'successful' translator should be able to live off translating only, having a portfolio career is extremely common in the profession.

This was confirmed by David Katan's survey of 1,000 translators and translation professionals worldwide, which found that portfolio careers were mainstream among them: 'Over two-thirds (69%) of respondents "also" had a second role, while over half (54%) had a third role "at times". This is apart from the 75 (8%) who vaunted a fourth role, which mainly centered around teaching' (Katan, 2011: 68). We should not see portfolio careers as a translator's failure to live off translation only. On the contrary, we should see it as a true testament to the wide range of **transferable skills** a translator possesses and their ability to make the most of life's vicissitudes. Of

40 *Joining the profession*

course, freelance translators are more likely to develop a portfolio career than in-house translators. However, we know that there are, on balance, more freelance translators than in-house translators. What's more, it is not uncommon for in-house translators to end up working freelance due to a change of circumstances. Developing a portfolio career is, therefore, a very real prospect for many aspiring professional translators.

Similarly, planned happenstance theory should also make us acknowledge that not everyone who studies translation will work as a professional translator all their lives, if at all. This is why I can only encourage you to reflect on all the transferable skills you are developing as a trainee translator that you could apply to non-translation jobs throughout your working life. If you haven't completed them already, the section 'Topics for discussion and assignments 1.2' in Chapter 1 can help you with that.

Further reading

Dam and Zethsen (2016) uses Bourdieu's concepts of habitus and capital(s) to explore professional translators' relatively high levels of satisfaction with their work despite the perception that the profession sometimes offers sub-standard working conditions.

Mitchell et al. (1999) offers an excellent explanation of the role of planned happenstance and its corollary, open-mindedness, in career planning.

3 No translator is an island
Setting up your support networks

Key questions we will explore in this chapter:

- Why do networks matter to me as a budding professional translator?
- What kind of professional support networks can I join as a professional translator? How do I decide which will work best for me?
- How can I start building my own, tailor-made support network?

3.1 Translators in the age of networks

The first two chapters aimed to give you a clearer idea of the skill set needed to become a translator and, just as importantly, of what the job involves for both in-house and freelance translators. After reading these two chapters, it should become clear to you that translators do not work in complete isolation, despite regularly spending long, solitary hours working on a given translation job. As 17th-century English poet John Donne famously wrote in his 'Meditation 17':

> No man is an island, entire of itself; every man is a piece of the continent, a part of the main.

Donne's main point in his meditation is that we, as human beings, are all connected to each other. We are all part of society and we need that connection to others. It is vital to our own well-being.

Times have changed since Donne wrote this, but it still holds true. And translators are no exception; they cannot be true hermits. Not just because it would be bad for their own well-being (which it would ...), but also because it would impact negatively on their ability to do the job properly. Have another look at the job advertisement for an English-to-Hungarian translator in Chapter 1 (see Box 1.1). You will see that one of the key requirements for applicants is for them to be '[a]ble to work autonomously

DOI: 10.4324/9781003220442-4

42 *Joining the profession*

as well as within a team', closely followed by 'client-orientation'. One could be tempted to read the latter to mean producing translations that meet client requirements only. Yet, the emphasis in the European Master's in Translation's (EMT's) revised versions of the Competence Framework on the need for translators to have 'Personal and interpersonal' as well as 'Service provision' competences suggests that the ability to connect not only with the client as a key stakeholder, but also with other important stakeholders in the translation process, matters as well (see EMT, 2022: 10– 11). Translators need to have the soft skills to liaise and negotiate with them when the need arises. Seen that way, translation is fundamentally an **interpersonal activity**.

This idea of translation as an interpersonal or, one could say, social activity had a big influence on what is known as the **'functionalist' approach** to translation. As I have already explained, the object of this book is not theoretical. Nevertheless, I must say a few words about this approach, as it may help you situate your work as translator. Until the functionalist approach emerged in Germany in the late 1970s and early 1980s, translation studies in the Western world mostly discussed translation in terms of equivalence to the source text. According to translation scholar Anthony Pym, the functionalist approach broke away from that tradition in two ways. First, it 'propose[d] that a translation is designed to achieve a purpose' (Pym, 2014a: 43). Second, and perhaps more importantly, it also accepted that the purpose of the target text, which is 'the dominant factor in the translation project' (ibid.: 43), may be different from the purpose of the source text. Concretely, this means that the same source text can be translated in many different ways depending on its **intended purpose** (see Reiss and Vermeer, 1991). Translators consequently need to understand the intended purpose of the target text they will produce from the translation situation. This, in turn, may imply having to clarify the target text's purpose with their client(s) and various other stakeholders also involved in the translation process. Therefore, as Pym aptly puts it: 'the linguistic frame of the equivalence paradigm becomes much wider, bringing in a series of professional relationships' (2014a: 43).

Who are, then, these other stakeholders you will likely have to develop professional relationships with? Finnish scholar Justa Holz-Mänttäri, who also viewed translation as a purpose-driven activity, identified **six key players** in what she called the 'translatorial action' (see Figure 3.1).

As you can see from Figure 3.1, the **ST producer**, that is, the author of the source text, can sometimes be involved in the translation process. Other key stakeholders who, unlike the ST producer, are always involved in the process, are the **Initiator**, that is, 'the company or individual who needs the translation', and the **Commissioner** (Munday et al., 2022: 108). The latter is the individual or agency who contacts the target text (TT) producer (ibid.). Sometimes, but not always, the Initiator and the Commissioner are one and the same. Once the translation has been commissioned, the **TT producer** gets involved. The TT producer can consist of just one translator, or of a whole

No translator is an island: Setting up your support networks

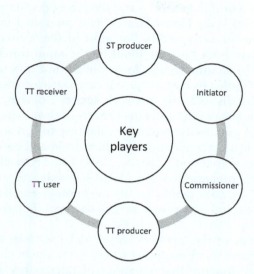

Figure 3.1 Holz-Mänttäri: Key players involved in translatorial action (based on Munday et al., 2022: 108)

team of translators, for more complex, collaborative projects. It may also consist of other colleagues at the translation agency/company, whose role it is to assist with delivering the translation project (e.g. terminologists, revisers or project managers). Finally, once the TT has been produced, it is used by both a **TT user** and a **TT receiver**.

Let's take the translation of a leaflet advertising the latest model of a washing machine, to illustrate the difference between TT user and TT receiver. The TT *user* will be the salesperson using the translated leaflet on the shop floor as part of their sales strategy. The shoppers reading the leaflet the salesperson handed out to them, however, are the TT *receivers*. Their needs and expectations regarding the purpose of the leaflet, and what it should contain, may differ. Whereas the salesperson may want the TT to insist on the modern, fancy design of the washing machine and how silent it is, a shopper may feel it should highlight other information such as the machine's energy consumption, its load capacity or its maximum spin speed. In other words, the salesperson needs the translation to prioritise the advertising function of the leaflet so it can assist them in their job. Shoppers, on the other hand, might expect it to prioritise what they view as key information about the model they are considering buying. From the ST producer to the TT receiver, all key stakeholders are likely to have **different needs and expectations** of a given translation project. It is the translator's role as expert to take these into consideration by communicating effectively and, if necessary, negotiating with their client(s).

44 *Joining the profession*

There is no denying that the world in general – and the job of translator in particular – has changed a lot since Holz-Mänttäri first published her model of translatorial action in the early 1980s. For most of the Western world, many of the changes have been brought about by the rapid transition from an industrial society to an **information society** in the last quarter of the 20th century. The latter has led to the concurrent emergence of what Spanish sociologist Manuel Castells calls the 'network society', that is, a new form of social organisation born of the combined effects of the crisis of industrialism, the emergence of grassroots movements fighting for greater social justice and, last but not least, a 'revolution in information and communication technologies' during that period (Castells, 2004: 19). The backdrop to this new form of social organisation is a globalised restructuring of the world's economies and societies thanks to 'the technology-enabled circulation of goods, services, capital and people across borders' (Folaron and Buzelin, 2007: 626).

Castells borrowed the concept of the 'network' from social sciences to describe the seismic change in social relations and practices in the age of globalisation. A **network** is an 'open structure' that is made up of 'interconnected nodes'; it evolves by adding or removing nodes according to needs (Castells and Cardoso, 2006: 7). This new organisational model, which was made possible by the technological advances of the time (including, from the 1990s, the Internet), is therefore characterised by 'large-scale organizational flexibility, scalability and coordination' (Stalder, 2006: 183). If this new 'network' model is **more flexible** than the former industrial model of social organisation and economic production it replaces, it can also appear **more complex**. It is worth noting, here, that despite being originally presented as a Western ('Euro-American') phenomenon, the network society has now become 'the major organisational form of our globalised information age' (Tang and Gentzler, 2009: 170). Its consequences can increasingly be felt by professional translators the world over.

Castell's network society matters to us professional translators in two ways. First of all, it has led to the emergence of '**production networks**' that are characterised by 'the **outsourcing** of activities that were previously done in-house' (Abdallah and Koskinen, 2007: 675; my emphases). In the translation industry, this has meant the gradual disappearance of many in-house translator jobs at commercial companies whose core business is not translation. Many of these now choose to outsource translation projects to translation agencies on a need basis, for the greater flexibility this offers them. Translation agencies, in turn, also prefer to sub-contract the work to freelance translators for the flexibility it gives *them* to complete a wider range of projects, including more complex, multilingual ones. As illustrated by Figure 3.2, one of the consequences of these changes in the translation industry is that: 'the horizontal and personal relationship between the client and translator who are familiar with one another, or are perhaps within the

No translator is an island: Setting up your support networks

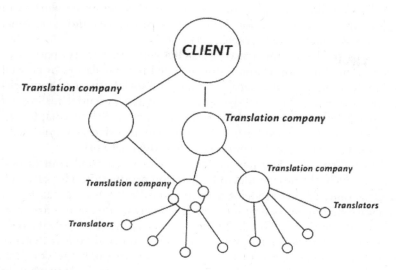

Figure 3.2 Translation production network (from Abdallah and Koskinen, 2007: 677)

same organization, is giving way to **a vertical network** where the end client may be several links away from the actual translator, with no contact or interaction between them' (ibid.: 676; my emphasis).

This new, more complex production structure, which involves **more partners and intermediaries** – sometimes located in different part of the world – challenges previous models such as Holz-Mänttäri's. To go back to our example of the translation of a leaflet advertising the latest model of a washing machine, in the new model of translation production, the 'Client' could be a global brand wanting the leaflet translated into 50 languages by a certain deadline. The client is therefore very likely to employ the services of one or several translation agencies (called 'translation companies' in Figure 3.2) that have the resources to deliver such a complex, multilingual project by said deadline. In turn, the chosen translation agencies may decide to outsource part of the project to a fellow agency if, for instance, they lack the required language expertise to deliver. Finally, each translation agency's project manager will likely outsource the work to an army of individual translators who are on their database of trusted freelancers (based on language expertise and availability). Individual translators working on this project are therefore unlikely to be in a position to clarify and/or negotiate with the client whether they should prioritise the needs of the target users (i.e. the leaflet's advertising function) or of the target recipients (i.e. its informative function). Indeed, we can no longer assume that translators can communicate and negotiate directly with their clients, and in fact this is increasingly rare in the **agency-mediated procurement model** which is now so prevalent

46 Joining the profession

in the translation industry. As a result, these new production networks can lead to a growing sense of isolation for freelance translators and, over time, diminished job satisfaction (Moorkens, 2017: 467).

This leads us to the second reason Castell's network society matters to us. It tells us something important about the need for translators to be well connected by forming part of a network. First, the **social aspect** of networks can help them improve their well-being and fight the potential feelings of isolation caused by a more complex production network (see Chapter 9). However, there are other, more prosaic reasons why translators should dedicate some time to creating and maintaining their own networks.

Marie-Luise Groß is a German academic who researched translators' support networks in the new model of translation production. Her research makes it clear that, in this model where increased outsourcing has led to more translators being sub-contracted as freelancers, translators are 'creative knowledge workers' (Groß, 2010: 98). As such, they 'rely heavily on their personal professional knowledge'. They must therefore 'ensure their competitive advantage on the labour market through the constant improvement of their unique selling propositions' (ibid.). With that in mind, a translator's social and professional networks are therefore essential to both **exchange knowledge with and learn from other translators**: 'When facing a cognitive deficit, having the possibility to ask someone for support or additional information can be of great help to a knowledge worker' (ibid.: 100).

Developing these networks makes a lot of business sense for professional translators in a network economy characterised by 'interaction and mutual dependency': '[N]odes must be connected in order to survive; in a network, no one node can exist or act alone' (Abdallah and Koskinen, 2007: 6). Or, to quote Donne's Meditation 17 again: 'No man is an island, entire of itself ...'. Budding translators should therefore aim to become **'networked lone fighters'** (Groß, 2010: 9), as opposed to just 'lone fighters'. This will help them thrive in the translation industry. To help you with this, the rest of this chapter will explore the various different networks – both online and offline – you can join as a professional translator and how these can support you and your work.

3.2 Traditional support networks: Professional associations

Whether you work freelance or in-house, there are quite a few different types of support networks you can access as a translator; it is really important for both your personal and your professional development that you be aware of them from the get-go.

The more traditional translation networks tend to be **'profession-oriented networks'** (McDonough, 2007: 796). National and international associations of professional translators are a good example of such networks that focus primarily on translation as a profession. The main aim of these networks

No translator is an island: Setting up your support networks 47

is to 'defen[d] the rights of language professionals, promot[e] profession-alism, enhanc[e] the status of language professionals and improve[e] working conditions' (ibid.). Research has shown that, as a budding translator, you are 'particularly prone to economic exploitation and moral hazard' (Groß, 2014: 4) due to the inevitable gap you need to bridge between your studies and the sometimes cut-throat reality of the translation industry.[1] Profession-oriented networks can help you navigate all this.

There are many **professional associations of translators** across the globe and many of the major, national ones are represented by FIT (Fédération Internationale des Traducteurs/International Federation of Translators, n.d.). Established in 1953, FIT now counts over 130 professional asso-ciations as its members, representing more than 85,000 translators in 55 countries. As stated on its website, FIT's objective is to 'bring together asso-ciations of translators and to promote interaction and cooperation between such associations' (FIT, 2022). FIT's ultimate aim is to advance the status of translation as a profession by 'promoting the harmonisation of professional standards and, generally, uphold[ing] the moral and material interests of translators throughout the world' (ibid.). As an association of associations, FIT may not seem directly relevant to you. However, as I have just mentioned, FIT counts among its ranks most of the major national associations of translators, such as ABRATES (Brazilian Association of Translators and Interpreters), APTIC Cameroun (Association of Professional Translators and Interpreters in Cameroon), ATA (American Translators Association), ITI (Institute of Translation and Interpreting, UK), TAC (Translator's Association of China) and UTR (Union of Translators of Russia), among many others.

FIT is therefore an excellent starting point for you to find out more about the relevant national association(s) you may like to join. To do so, just visit its website on 'www.fit-ift.org' and browse its 'Member Directory', which lists member associations by country. Bear in mind, though, that there exist many other professional associations for translators that are not listed by FIT. Some, more niche associations specialise in specific fields such as literary translation, audio-visual translation or game localisation. If they don't fall under the FIT umbrella, you won't find them listed on its directory and you will have to research them yourself. Depending on your own specialisation, you should try to find an association that is a **good match** for your own spe-cific profile. 'Topics for discussion and assignments 3.2' below will help you do that.

The exact **benefits** you will get from belonging to a professional associ-ation will vary depending on the association itself. Most of them, though, will allow you to keep abreast of the latest relevant developments in the pro-fession by sending regular updates via a mailing list, by organising annual meetings or by publishing their own journals. Many will also give you access to **forums** on their websites where you can ask other members for advice on specific translation(-related) issues. Last but certainly not least, some also

48 Joining the profession

act as a **marketplace** by allowing prospective clients to find a translator on their directory, which means that being a member may bring you some work. A good example of this is the 'Find-a-Linguist' directory on the website of the Chartered Institute of Linguists (UK), which allows potential customers to search for translators and interpreters in specific language pairs, and with specific specialist domains.

Arguably, though, the main appeal of professional associations for you as a budding translator is the access to the **ethical and legal support** most of them offer, which will help you navigate the 'economic exploitation and moral hazard' we discussed earlier (Groß, 2014: 4). Many professional associations of translators, for instance, have a **code of conduct and/or a code of ethics** – the two terms are often used interchangeably – that members must adhere to in order to become a member. This is the case for the UK-based professional association of translators ITI (Institute of Translation and Interpreting). Upon joining, the association's new members must agree to uphold its Code of Professional Conduct as approved by existing members. The ITI Code of Professional Conduct gives specific advice to members on what they should and should not do when **advertising their services** (Article 1.1), when they are faced with a **conflict of interest** (Article 1.2) or when they find themselves in a situation that is 'inconsistent with their **professional obligations**' (Article 1.3). The Code also makes it clear that ITI members should 'refuse work that they know to be beyond their **competence** either linguistically or because of lack of specialised knowledge' (Article 2.2), unless this work is sub-contracted to a translator with the required competence. Finally, it also gives guidance on managing **contractual arrangements** with clients (Article 2.5), engaging in **competition** with other translators (Article 2.7), respecting **confidentiality** (Article 3.1) and **being loyal** to fellow ITI members (Article 4.1).

There are obvious advantages to adhering to a code of professional conduct such as ITI's. First of all, by accepting to adhere to it you are signalling to both your clients and fellow translators that you intend to uphold the highest standards as a professional translator. As pointed out by Joseph Lambert, '[t]he codes act as a shared set of guiding principles and are a key element in the **professionalisation** of a practice, providing certain standards to uphold' (2023: 117; my emphasis). In a word, adhering to a professional code will increase your **trustworthiness** among colleagues and clients. What's more, a code of professional conduct can act as a first port of call when you are faced with **ethical and legal dilemmas** and/or ambiguous professional situations you have never encountered before. Still, according to Lambert, 'codes of ethics undoubtedly represent most working translators' primary point of contact (if not their only point of contact) with thought on ethics [...] and are a key tool in defining ethical translation and **informing ethical decision-making**' (ibid.; my emphasis). Imagine, for instance, the following situations, which illustrate some of the everyday dilemmas you may face as a professional translator.

No translator is an island: Setting up your support networks 49

- **Situation 1:** You have just started as a translator and you have been asked to translate a 6,000-word scientific article on the role of gastro-intestinal microbiomes in bats' viral hosting capacity. You have 48 hours to complete the translation. Should you accept this job?
- **Situation 2:** An agency has asked you to translate marketing materials for an international meat-production company. However, as a committed vegan and animal welfare activist, you have been campaigning against this company, which does not respect animal welfare. You have only recently started as a professional translator and you really need the money. You are also worried that turning down the job will not go down well with the agency and that they may even stop considering you for future jobs. Should you accept this job?
- **Situation 3:** A direct client sends you a document to translate that is very similar to a document you have already translated for an agency. You have saved the translation, so it is just a matter of locating the file on your PC and updating a few details. Should you accept the new commission and charge the client in full, or should you tell them and charge them a reduced rate? What about your contract with the agency? Could you be at risk of breaching confidentiality?
- **Situation 4:** Two weeks after you delivered a translation job to a client, they call you to say that they believe you have breached the agreement of confidentiality you had with them. They ask you to pay a hefty sum in compensation. You did not breach confidentiality, but you don't know how to go about proving you're innocent. You wonder whether it may not be easier to pay the compensation, but you also worry about what this would do to your reputation as a professional translator. What should you do?

Of course, no code of professional conduct will give you all the clear-cut answers you may feel you need in situations like these, but they can guide you through them. Take the ITI Code of Conduct, for instance. Article 2.2 on 'Competence' can help you with Situation 1, while articles 1.2 and 1.3 on 'Conflicts of interest' and 'Integrity' will guide your thinking on Situation 2. There are times, however, where you may need more specific guidance to come to a decision. This is arguably the case with Situations 3 and 4. In such a case, belonging to a professional association will give you the access you need to a support network of more **experienced professional translators** who can guide you through thorny situations. As a member of ITI, for instance, you have access to a discussion forum where you can ask your peers for some guidance and advice on ethical and other issues. In fact, professional associations such as ITI actively encourage their members to build support networks with fellow members by organising networks based on geographical

50 Joining the profession

location, language combinations, subject (e.g. food and drink, information technology, law and finance, medical and pharmaceutical, terminology etc.) as well as social support networks such as neurodiversity networks and parent networks. Many of them also offer access to (free) **legal advice**. ITI, for instance, gives its members access to a free legal helpline that could prove really helpful should you find yourself in situations such as the ones described in Situations 3 and 4.

Joining a professional association will therefore allow you to become a member of a community of practice based on shared values, where you can build both knowledge and social support networks with fellow translators. Often, though, there are **perceived barriers** to joining for translators new to the profession. One of these is membership requirements. Professional associations normally have strict **membership requirements** that are justified by the need for all members to meet agreed standards. In effect, this can mean that you must have specific qualifications and/or a couple of years' experience as a professional translator before you can join. Combined with the sometimes relatively high **cost of membership**, this can act as a deterrent for translators who have just set out their stalls. However, most professional associations also offer cheaper, dedicated membership levels (e.g. 'affiliate' or 'associate') to less-experienced translators who don't meet all the criteria for full membership yet. Even though they may not give you access to the whole range of services, such membership levels usually allow you to benefit from ethical and legal support by giving you full access to the association's networks. If you factor in the fact that it may also help you increase your trustworthiness among your peers and prospective clients, an 'associate membership' is therefore well worth considering.

Another common barrier that could stop you joining a professional association is ... **confidence!** As a new, less-experienced member, you may well worry that you don't have all the credentials to become part of such a community of practice and that you will come across as somewhat ignorant to your peers. If this is true in your case, then please rest assured that you won't be the only one with those fears and that longer-standing members of the association likely had the same doubts when they first joined. What is important, though, is that you find a professional association where you feel members trust and respect each other, so you are comfortable enough to start building the support networks you need for the rest of your career as translator.

TOPICS FOR DISCUSSION AND ASSIGNMENTS 3.1

Activity 3.1 Make a list of the professional associations (if there is more than one!) relevant to you as a translator in the country where you are based and/or where you would like to work as a professional translator (e.g. if you are originally from Japan but you are based in South Africa, you may like to look up existing translator associations in both countries). If you are from a

No translator is an island: Setting up your support networks   51

relatively large country, check whether there are professional associations for translators in the region where you live. At this stage, list all of them.

Activity 3.2 Based on your findings for Activity 3.1, determine which professional association(s) will be the best fit for you by asking yourself the following questions for each association:

- Where is it based? If it is based quite far from me, does it have a strong online presence?
- Does it specialise in specific language combination(s) and/or translation field(s) (e.g. literary translation, audio-visual translation, medical translation)? If it does, does this match my own requirements?
- Does it have a Code of Professional Conduct? If so, do I feel I can adhere to it?
- Does it have specific entry requirements for new members? If I don't meet them yet, does it offer specific membership levels (e.g. 'associate') to new entrants into the profession?
- What kind of benefits will membership to the professional association give me access to? (e.g. professional certification? Continuing Professional Development seminars/webinars? Regular updates with professional news via mailing list or journal? Legal helpline? Access to negotiated Professional Indemnity Insurance? Knowledge and/or support networks? Local social and/or professional events? Job opportunities? Discounts with IT software? etc.)
- Will joining increase my visibility and/or trustworthiness among both clients and colleagues?
- Will joining give me access to clients (both direct clients and agencies)?
- Will joining give me access to peer support networks that could help me navigate potential ethical and legal issues?
- Will joining offer me other forms of support that I find important as a budding translator?

3.3 Global support networks: Virtual communities of practice

Belonging to a professional association will help you build profession-oriented support networks. For some of you, a professional association's online presence may well be a decisive factor in your decision to join, especially if you're working from a geographically distant location that does not allow you to meet physically with other members on a regular basis. You may even prefer to belong to a community of practice that operates fully online, as you feel it works best for you. If this is the case for you, you may be reassured to hear that research into **online translator communities** has shown that the connections members make can be just as strong as for traditional, offline communities (see McDonough, 2007 and Groß, 2014). Whether it is 'offline' or online, what matters is that you do engage with a community of fellow professionals, as this will allow you to ward off the

52   *Joining the profession*

feelings of isolation translators sometimes experience in the new production model. In the process, you will also learn from and with your peers, which is very important for translators as knowledge workers. Last but not least, belonging to a community of practice will help you shape your sense of **professional and social identity** as translator.

Since the early 2000s, the development of the social web (or what is commonly called 'Web 2.0') has greatly contributed to the success of **virtual communities of practice** for translators. Their objective is to bring together professionals who want to discuss the act of translating itself, as well as related aspects of professional translating such as terminology management, the use of computer-assisted translation tools or marketing strategies for translators. As such, they are primarily 'practice-oriented' translation networks (see McDonough Dolmaya, 2022). These networks often act as a marketplace between professional translators and prospective clients, too. Of course, some national and international professional associations also provide the space for these discussions and may already act as a marketplace for translators as well, both online and offline. They remain, however, primarily profession-oriented networks.

On the other hand, Web 2.0. has opened up the possibility for online-practice-oriented professional translator networks to reach a much wider audience. Some of them have met **global success**. The site ProZ.com, for instance, which launched in 1999 as a 'membership-based website targeting freelance translators', counted an impressive worldwide membership of over 1 million users in 2022. On its website, ProZ boasts to be serving 'the world's largest community of translators' by 'providing access to state-of-the-art tools, educating and inspiring, fostering collaboration among positive, like-minded professionals' (www.proz.com). Similarly TranslatorsCafé, a site launched in 2002 to provide a 'very convenient way [for translators] to connect with others in the international community', counted over 410,000 registered members and 87,000 registered agencies in 2022. The site's main objective is to function as a **marketplace for professional translators** by giving them the opportunity to offer their services to the translation agencies registered on the site (www.translatorscafe.com). As well as this, members have access to varied resources such as 'Tutorials for translators', information on translation rates and, rather importantly, discussion forums. These are quite varied, and forums listed include the following: 'Jobs, outsourcers and payments', 'Translators and agencies', 'Working as a freelancer', 'On translation (theory and history of translation)', 'Literary translation', 'Beginners: Ask here!', 'Techniques', 'Resources', 'Legal and financial translation', 'Medical translation', 'Ethics and professionalism', 'Localization', 'Subtitling', 'Come together (to meet in the real world)', 'All about garbage (includes security issues)', 'Machine translation', and 'Computer work and your health', as well as language-specific forums and a forum where you can just 'chit-chat' with other members. Becoming a member of online communities such as ProZ.com and TranslatorsCafé is free, and there are no specific criteria to meet.

No translator is an island: Setting up your support networks 53

A past study into the strength of relationships among members as well as members' engagement with the discussion forums on TranslatorsCafé has shown that ties tend to be weak among members of online communities, as only a few members post regularly on the discussion forums (McDonough, 2007: 809). This may be partly explained by the fact that membership is free and that there are no prerequisites for joining. Indeed, this inevitably results in a more diverse membership, 'with varying levels of knowledge, experience and education' (ibid.: 801), which in turn can lead to **trust issues**. How do I trust that the other participants on the forum are giving me good advice if I don't know anything about their credentials? Another issue may be that some translators join in order to use the site as a marketplace but do not really want to network with other translators on the discussion forums. Nevertheless, the same study also shows that 'stronger ties exist among the subgroups of users who actively interact with others by posting and reading messages in the discussion and terminology forum' (ibid.: 809). What's more, quite a few members interact passively by regularly reading the posts in the discussion forums. The study concluded that despite the weak-tie relationships among members on such online communities, engaging with them is **globally beneficial** for professional translators as it gives them access to a global-practice-based network with a wide range of experience, language pairs and fields of expertise (ibid.).

These findings were confirmed by a later study into the benefits of belonging to a virtual community such as ProZ.com for professional translators. ProZ.com also acts as a marketplace for translators and gives them access to many resources and forums where they can ask other translators for help on specific issues. The survey found that the main reasons professional translators joined ProZ.com were finding work (56%), sense of community (54%), learning/benchmarking (42%) or networking/collaboration (30%) (Risku and Dickinson, 2009: 62). Based on members' responses, the study concluded that belonging to a virtual translation community offers many benefits to translators, such as 'exchanging information and knowledge with colleagues worldwide and access to rapid, qualified help' and 'giving and receiving advice and support [...] round the clock' as well as 'commercial benefits' (ibid.: 65). Several members also stressed the **social benefits** of belonging to a virtual network of fellow professional translators, saying it had increased their level of fun at work and that it had allowed them to build lasting social and professional relationships.

TOPICS FOR DISCUSSION AND ASSIGNMENTS 3.2

Let's find out more about online translator communities. Visit the website of TranslatorsCafé (www.translatorscafe.com), ProZ.com (www.proz.com) or another, similar virtual community you are familiar with. Browse the site's webpages and try to answer the following questions:

54 *Joining the profession*

- What do I need to do to register and to have access to potential clients?
- What kinds of resources will I have access to as a member that could prove useful to me as a budding translator?
- Which discussion forums do I think would be useful to me at the start of my career? Are there any posts I find helpful already?
- Will becoming a member increase my visibility and/or trustworthiness among both clients and colleagues?
- Will becoming a member give me access to clients (both direct clients and agencies)?

3.4 Building your own support networks

We have seen the potential benefits of joining both professional-oriented and practice-oriented translation networks for you as a budding professional translator. In parallel to this, though, you should also aim to build your own, **tailor-made support network**. This is something you can start doing straight away.

If you are on an undergraduate or a postgraduate programme in translation studies, you should consider having some of **your peers** on the course as part of your own network. Once you start as a freelance translator, you may need to seek their help as informal source- or target-language informers or even, depending on circumstances, as experts in a given domain. Imagine that one of your friends at university ends up working as a solicitor specialising in intellectual property after deciding to complete a law conversion course. Having them in your professional network could prove useful, not just if you needed help with a specific concept from intellectual property law for one of your translation jobs, but also if you had questions around intellectual property rights relating to your own work as a translator. Similarly, **your tutors** and other **professionals from the translation industry** you met on the course may be able to help you by providing recommendations, giving you continued guidance and support or introducing you to key contacts in the industry. All you need to do is keep in touch with them! Of course, how you go about keeping in touch with your former course mates and tutors will largely depend on the cultural conventions of the country in which you study. Increasingly, though, a great way to do so is on **social media** in general, and on social networking websites that specialise in professional networking such as LinkedIn in particular (MaiMai or InJobs in China, Skillsnet in Russia). LinkedIn, for instance, allows you to start developing your online profile as a student.

Social media is rapidly becoming the most popular way for budding translators to create and manage their own networks. Admittedly, though, its use is not – as yet – quite as widespread in Africa and Russia as it is in America and Europe. This notwithstanding, the greatest advantage of **social networking sites** is that, unlike sites such as ProZ.com or TranslatorsCafé, this time you're in control of your support network as you're the one who

No translator is an island: Setting up your support networks 55

decides who can join it. This means you should be able to trust the advice and support you receive from the members of this support network.

The most commonly used sites in Africa, America, Australia and Europe are LinkedIn, Facebook (often used for family and friends) and X (formerly Twitter). VKontakte is a very popular social networking site in Russia, whereas WeChat and Sina Weibo are the popular ones in China. Some sites, such as Facebook for instance, are used for both professional and personal networking. When this is the case, you should really consider creating a **professional profile** that is distinct from your personal one. This is rather important, as you would not want current or prospective clients stumbling upon potentially embarrassing pictures of you on your personal account on Facebook. In fact, you should also consider locking down your personal account to friends only so that non-friends cannot access it. This notwithstanding, having a **social media presence** will help you increase your visibility among fellow translators and potential direct clients. Most sites will allow you to post short comments and articles about what you do, the kind of training you have completed and so on, which will help you establish your digital presence (see Chapter 8). This could potentially mean more business coming your way. Recently, for instance, some freelance translators have started to be commissioned work from direct clients as a result of their posts about translation on their X (formerly Twitter) accounts. This remains marginal, but it is definitely something to consider in the age of social media.

Back in the physical world, another way for you to build your own support networks as a budding professional translator is to work in **co-working spaces** for at least part of the time. Co-working spaces are shared workspaces where people rent a desk space. The reason some people decide to work in a co-working space instead of working from home range from the facilities they offer (e.g. reliable Internet connection, desk space in a quiet and professional environment, access to meeting rooms etc.) to the possibility of networking and learning from other **professionals from different industries**. Imagine, for instance, that you are struggling to develop your online presence as a translator but that your desk is next to that of a self-employed web developer ... provided they need some help to make their services known in different languages, this could be a match made in heaven! The other advantage of working from a co-working space is **psychological**. For some freelance translators, it can be a way to overcome the greater sense of isolation that has come with the new production networks. You can feel like you belong to a community of other (mostly freelance) workers with whom you can share and exchange your experiences of the vicissitudes of setting up your own business. However, there are also some disadvantages of co-working spaces. First of all, they can be **expensive** at times ... especially when most freelance translators work from home anyway. Why, some would argue, pay for something you can do for free from the comfort of your own home? What's more, working from a shared office space can mean potentially **disruptive background noise** at times. It can also lead to **confidentiality issues** if you are

56 *Joining the profession*

working on sensitive documents. The solution to all this could be to work in a co-working space only occasionally, say one or two days a week. This would reduce the cost while still allowing you to make meaningful contacts with other freelancers, and learn from their own specific skills, in an arguably more inspiring professional environment than your own four walls.

Whichever way you decide to build your network, bear in mind that it will likely evolve over time. In her study of the support networks of freelance translators, Groß shows that budding freelancers tend to have a relatively large network, but that it is mostly made up of family, friends, former tutors/ employers and classmates/colleagues. After a while, you can expect this network to include fellow freelancers and industry professionals as well as actual and potential clients. In this second phase, your network will grow but the number of '**weaker ties**' you have to some of its members will grow, too. Later on in your professional life, however, as you become well established as a professional translator, you will likely have a strong support network of close colleagues and habitual clients. In this later phase of your network, the weaker ties will tend to disappear in favour of '**stronger ties**' that are based on 'emotional bonding and trust' (Groß, 2014: 181).

TOPICS FOR DISCUSSION AND ASSIGNMENTS 3.3

Different cultures and societies have different socialising – and, therefore, networking – styles. Similarly, each individual will have his or her preferred way to socialise. In pairs, briefly discuss the following questions:

- What would you say characterises the 'socialising style' of the culture(s) you identify with?
- What about you? What would you say is your own preferred socialising style?
- How might your answers to the first two questions influence how you go about developing your own tailor-made support network as a professional translator?

Note

1 A 'moral hazard' here can be understood as

> [A] situation in which a person or organization has no incentive to act honestly or with due prudence. The term is mainly used in the insurance world, where a typical example of a person exposed to moral hazard would be the owner of an insured car, who has little or no incentive to guard against theft. (Law, 2009)

No translator is an island: Setting up your support networks 57

As we saw in Chapter 1, professional translating remains largely unregulated in most countries. A perceived lack of repercussions may therefore make it tempting for some in the profession to act unethically and/or illegally in order to maximise profit.

Further reading

In their seminal article, Abdallah and Koskinen (2007) combine sociological studies of social capital and trust with Albert-László Barabási's real-world network model, as well as with interviews with professional translators, to review the roles of trust, loyalty and social capital in the contemporary network-based translation industry.

In his analytical review of over 200 professional associations, Pym (2014b) shows how a new, more interactive model is emerging for translator/interpreter associations as they become a place for social, pedagogical and political action that invent new ways of signalling translators' trustworthiness.

Risku et al. (2016) gives fascinating insights into the structures and complexity of three authentic translation networks (a freelancer's, a translation department's and an online amateur translation network's).

4 Finding that first job

> **Key questions we will explore in this chapter:**
>
> - What do I need to know before I start looking for a job in the translation industry?
> - How can I find out what employers are looking for?
> - How do I go about writing my CV and covering letter? Are there specific expectations for these? What about translation tests?

4.1 Research before job search!

Now that you have a clearer idea of what it takes to be a translator, and what the job involves, you may have decided that this is definitely the right career path for you! This is great, but how do you go about finding your first job? There is no denying that taking your first step into the translation industry can sometimes prove more daunting than one would like ... especially if you are aiming for an in-house position.

Inspired by **career guidance**, this chapter will help you adopt the right strategies on where and how to look for your first translation job. Even though Chapter 3 on the importance of support networks was relevant to all budding translators, its emphasis made it of particular interest to those of you choosing to work freelance. Similarly, this chapter will likely be of greater interest to those of you who want to start their career in-house, although many aspects of it (e.g. learning to understand global trends in the translation industry, writing up your CV etc.) will remain relevant to aspiring freelance translators.

Imagine that you have completed all the qualifications you need to work as a translator and that you are ready to look for your first role in the translation industry.

DOI: 10.4324/9781003220442-5

> • What do you think is the first thing you should do when looking for your first job as a translator?

Maybe you are tempted to go straight onto a job search website, type in the word 'translator' and answer all the job adverts that come your way. Well, this is certainly one way to do it (and sometimes it works!), although it may not always be the best. As a friend of mine with long-standing experience as a careers consultant always says: '**Research comes before job search!**' You need to be well informed about the job market for translators so you can make sure your expectations are realistically aligned with what is available out there. This means that you need to find out as much as you can about the current trends in the translation industry – both globally and locally – before you even start with your job search. In a nutshell, the more you know about the translation industry, the better prepared you are for your job search and the more successful you are likely to be.

A great way to find out about current trends in the translation industry is to consult recent reports that summarise the latest **industry intelligence**. There are quite a few of them concerning the language industry. One of the best-known global surveys is the one conducted by the Common Sense Advisory, which now goes by the name of **CSA Research**. CSA Research's aim is to deliver 'independent, objective, and comprehensive primary research focused exclusively on the global content and language services markets' (www.csa-research.com). It does so with its annual 'Language Services Market' report, which looks at overall trends in the language industry, including where current growth/opportunities can be found. Another leading language-industry intelligence company that regularly publishes global industry news and reports is **Slator.** As stated on its website, Slator's aim is to help clients 'make business sense of the translation and language technology markets through news and insights on demand drivers, funding, talent moves, technology and more' (www.slator.com). Finally, international market research and consulting company Nimdzi also deserves a mention here. **Nimdzi** also provides regular reports and market research on global trends in the translation industry with the aim of 'provid[ing] our clients with the insights they need to succeed on a global scale' (www.nimdzi.com).

Just like CSA Research, Slator publishes an **annual report** ('Language Industry Market Report') that provides 'a comprehensive view of the global language services and technology industry'. Its 2021 report, for instance, looked at the size, trends and growth areas in the language industry, while also exploring the future of the profession with chapters on 'expert-in-the-loop' machine-translation-enabled production models (as opposed to 'human-in-the-loop' models) and on 'frontier technology' (e.g. speech-to-speech translation). Aimed at LSPs (language-service providers), these reports are a great way for you to start your job search as they will give

60 Joining the profession

you very valuable insights into the direction the job market is taking globally. However, both CSA Research and Slator charge for access to their flagship annual reports. If you are still studying towards a degree, you may be able to access them via your institution's library portal. If not, you could contact your library to ask them to consider subscribing so you and your peers on the course have access to them. In any case, CSA Research, Slator and Nimdzi all publish freely accessible summary reports on their website which, for most of them, contain enough depth for you to develop a general understanding of the current direction of travel in the global language industry. What is more, Slator and Nimdzi both produce podcasts with industry news, which are freely available to everyone on their websites. Subscribing to such podcasts can be another great way to stay on top of language industry news.

While CSA Research, Slator and Nimdzi can help you keep up to date with the global trends in the language industry, you should also try to access **more 'local' (i.e. regional or national) reports** to have a better idea of the trends in the language industry for the job market you would like to enter. Such reports are often published by or in partnership with professional translator associations (see Chapter 3). In Europe, for instance, **EUATC** (European Federation of National Associations of Translation Companies) co-ordinates the annual publication of the 'ELIS – European Language Industry Survey' in partnership with ELIA (European Language Industry Association), FIT Europe, GALA (Globalization and Localization Association), the EMT University Network, LIND (the European Commission's Language Industry Platform) and WiL (Women in Localization). Based on a survey of European language-service companies, independent language professionals, representatives of training institutions, language departments, language-service buyers and language technology providers, this survey 'covers market trends, expectations & concerns, challenges and obstacles, as well as changes in business practices' in Europe (ELIS Research, 2022: 3). Unlike CSA Research's and Slator's reports, though, the ELIS report can be accessed free of charge provided you register on the survey's website: www.elis-sur vey.org.

In a similar way, **TAC** (Translators Association of China) regularly publishes reports on China's language industry. The latest one at the time of writing was its 2019 report, 'China Language Service Industry Development'. Based on a survey of 263 LSPs, this report showed that there had been continued growth for the sector in the preceding years and that the **main fields** from which LSPs received translation orders were 'information technology', 'education & training' and 'government international communication' (TAC, 2019). The most in-demand languages were English, French, Japanese, German, Russian and Spanish, but the report also highlighted a need for translators with less-common-but-sought-after languages such as Korean, Thai and Polish for instance (ibid.). By comparison, the Association of Translation Companies' 'Language Services Industry Survey and Report

Finding that first job 61

2021' highlighted that the three fields that were most in demand in the UK that year were 'creative services' (including marketing and advertising), 'technology' and 'life sciences' (including medical) (ATC UK, 2021: 14). The **services** most commonly provided by LSPs in the UK besides translation were 'subtitling', 'copywriting, transcreation, content creation', 'publishing', 'desktop publishing (DTP) & graphic design' and 'machine translation and post-editing' (ibid.: 13).

As you can see, beyond some of the **globally observed tendencies** in the language industry, more local reports will allow you to find out more about the **local trends** that are unique to a specific context. For you as a trainee or newly qualified translator, such reports may inform your thinking about which field(s) to specialise in, which language(s) to potentially add to your language portfolio, which other translation-related service(s) to offer, which technologies you should get more familiar with and where to look in order to optimise your chances of finding work.

TOPICS FOR DISCUSSION AND ASSIGNMENTS 4.1

Research comes before job search! The best way to start find out more about current trends in the translation industry is to scour the websites of global language industry-intelligence companies such as CSA Research, Slator or Nimdzi before looking at more local surveys and reports. Both global and local trends will inform your job search (if you are aiming for an in-house position) or the way you position yourself on the market (if you are thinking of a freelance career).

Activity 4.1 Fill in the column 'Global trend(s)' in Table 4.1. First, try to find out whether your library has access to either CSA Research's or Slator's annual reports. If not, use their online summary reports – as well as Nimdzi's – and go through your lecture notes to answer as many of the questions as possible. Pay particular attention to current areas of growth in the industry as well as predictions for the next few years.

Activity 4.2 Now, fill in the column 'Local trend(s)' in Table 4.1. First, you will need to find a recent language industry survey/report on the country or countries where you would like to work as a translator. Combine this with Internet searches to answer as many of the questions about current local trends in the language industry as you possibly can.

4.2 Research and ... more research!

If you look at the figures for the global language industry in the last few years, you will find that it is, by and large, a **thriving industry**. Your own research into the observed 'global trend(s)' for 'Topics for discussion and assignments

62 *Joining the profession*

Table 4.1 Researching trends in the translation industry

	Global trend(s)	Local trend(s)
What has been the observed trend in the language industry with regards to *growth* in the last few years?		
Geographically, where do we find the *biggest markets* in the language industry? Where are the *fastest-growing* ones? Are they one and the same?		
Which sectors of the global economy are currently the *greatest buyers* of translation services (e.g. tourism or science?)? Are there *new specialist domains* emerging as a result of growing demand?		
Which *language pair(s)* are currently the most in demand? Are there any other less common but highly sought-after language combination(s)?		
Apart from translating, which *services* do LSPs most commonly provide to their clients? Is it possible to spot any *new trends* emerging (i.e. relatively new services that are growing rapidly)?		
Which *technologies* do LSPs commonly incorporate into their workflow? Is it possible to spot any *new trends* emerging (i.e. relatively new technologies that are rapidly becoming more mainstream)?		

Finding that first job 63

4.1' will likely echo the findings of British scholar Joanna Drugan. In her review of market growth for the global translation industry, she noted that the hallmarks of globalisation – growing international trade and the age of the Internet – had led to 'insatiable demand for translation services that cannot be met with proprietary business models or the capacity of around 300,000 professional translators worldwide' (Drugan, 2013: 10).

Since the turn of the century, the global translation industry has indeed experienced continued strong growth with an increase in both the demand (volume) and reach (languages) of translation requests. This growth, which can partly be explained by the emergence of new content types (websites, software, apps, games and audio-visual material), was made possible by the adoption of new technologies (e.g. translation tools and machine translation). It has, however, also been accompanied by **new challenges** (e.g. tighter deadlines; dealing with 'streaming' multilingual content on websites and social medial; proliferation of new file formats; increasingly 'unstable' source content created by a team of contributors) (ibid.: 10–25). **Technological advances,** it would appear, have thus been a key factor behind the growth of the global language industry as well as being both a source of new challenges and a way to deal with them. In brief, they have allowed the language industry to grow big while making it increasingly more complex.

- What do you think these global trends mean for a budding translator like you trying to enter the job market today?

Before anything else, it is important to recognise that all the global trends you observe globally in the translation industry will not necessarily be mirrored in the local trends for the country or countries where you would like to find employment. You may have noticed this when completing 'Topics for discussion and assignments 4.1'. Even though the global trends give you the general direction of travel for the language industry, you need to continue drilling down to understand the **impact** of both the global and the local trends on what employers actually want when they advertise for a translation role. After research comes ... more research!

This is what Canadian academic Lynne Bowker did for Canada back in 2004 for an article called: 'What does it take to work in the translation profession in Canada in the 21st century?' Recognising the rapid changes in the translation industry, she decided to 'evaluate the state of the profession in Canada and to determine what employers are looking for' by 'analysing a database of [301] job advertisements for a variety of translation-related positions' (Bowker, 2004: 960). Admittedly, reporting the actual findings of this study here would serve little to no purpose. The study is now clearly

64 *Joining the profession*

dated and its results are relevant to a specific job market only. Despite all this, the **methodology** Lynne Bowker used in her study can help you prepare for your own job search.

First of all, Bowker searched job advertisements for all translation-related positions to build her database, not just ads advertising directly for 'translators'. In fact, she found that only just over half of the advertised translation-related positions in her database had the job title 'translator' (56%). The other advertised positions were for 'translator-revisers', 'localization specialists', 'revisers' and so on (ibid.: 962). This, per se, is quite significant as it reflects the fact that the profession has become more complex and fragmented (see Chapter 2) and that there are, therefore, **a variety of translation-related jobs** that can be advertised. Limiting your job search to the keyword 'translator' could therefore seriously hinder your chances of finding a position in the translation industry.

Bowker then looked into the language combination(s) that were most commonly requested in the job ads and where the jobs were geographically located. The latter allowed her to have a better idea of where translators were most in demand in Canada. We should note, though, that in some countries geographical location is becoming less relevant for translators with the rise of remote work, although it often continues to be a determining factor in access to in-house work opportunities. She subsequently looked at the domains that were most in demand in the ads, the level of education and type of qualifications sought by employers, whether applicants were expected to be certified by a recognised professional association and the number of years of experience that prospective employers wanted applicants to have. She also looked into the types of skills candidates were most commonly required to bring to the advertised positions. At the time of her study, the most sought-after skills in Canada were being 'computer literate' (60.5%), being a 'team player' (36.5%), being able to 'work under pressure' (36.5%) and having 'fluent written communication skills' (35.9%) (ibid.: 969). Finally, she checked the proportion of ads that required a knowledge of specialised translation technology. From all this she concluded that her database of job ads 'provides a means of gaining some insight into the current state of the translation profession in Canada, particularly as viewed from an employer's perspective' (ibid.: 971).

As we can see from Lynne Bowker's study, analysing job advertisements for translation-related jobs for a specific country can help you have a clearer idea of where the local translation industry is heading and, consequently, **what local employers expect** from the new generation of translators. Completing 'Topics for discussion and assignments 4.2' at the end of this section should help you get a clearer idea of not only what local employers want (language combinations, domains, degrees and/or other qualifications, professional accreditation, experience etc.), but also of the words they use to advertise these roles.

> - How do you think the methodology Lynne Bowker used in her 2004 study could help you with your own job search?

A first tendency you may observe first-hand when you start exploring the job market for translators is that prospective employers often look for a mix of translation-related 'hard' skills and more transferable 'soft' skills (see Chapter 1 for a more detailed discussion of these). Another interesting trend is that, of late, quite a few employers have become increasingly creative with the job titles they use to recruit people in translation(-related) positions. This is, in any case, something that Slator observed when they delved into the different job titles used on the LinkedIn profiles of people working in the language industry back in 2018. They counted no less than 600 different job titles (Bond, 2018)! While some of these were well-recognised job titles that have been around for a while (e.g. specialised translator, post-editor, reviser, checker, terminologist or localiser), 'others, such as transcreator, quality assurance engineer, Multilanguage UX designer and strategy consultant, [were] relatively new to the scene' (Angelone et al., 2020: 2). Such **diversification of job titles** in the language industry reflects the increasing diversity of services that are routinely offered in the field of multilingual communication.

Talking to the academic community about 'The Evolving Role of Language Service Provision', the Managing Director of translation company Sandberg, Anu Carnegie-Brown, confirmed this trend by reeling off an impressive list of roles open to translation graduates: translator, editor, translation checker, localisation expert, reviewer, language tester, language specialist, translation/localisation/transcreation project manager, project coordinator, project assistant, project executive, marketing manager, account manager, business development manager, vendor manager, resource coordinator, supply chain manager and talent manager (APTIS, 2021). Make sure, therefore, that you **keep an open mind** and **cast your net wide** enough when looking for your first graduate job as a translator/language industry professional …

Let's have a look at some of the roles that employ translation graduates but are not necessarily advertised as 'Translator'. Some of you may already be familiar with the terms 'localisation' and '**Localiser**'/'**Localisation specialist**'. A localiser's role is to 'give a product or service the look and feel of having been created specifically for a target market, no matter their language, cultural preferences, or location' (GALA, 2022). Translation is only one part of this process, which is often associated with the translation of apps and video games. Indeed, localisation also typically involves 'the expertise of […] language and tools specialists, programmers, engineers, project managers, desktop publishing specialists and marketing staff' (Folaron in Byrne, 2009). More recently, LSPs have also started hiring translation graduates as '**Transcreators**'. Just like localisation, transcreation involves adapting the product or service for the target market. However, transcreation, which can be seen as somewhere

66   *Joining the profession*

in-between translating and copywriting, is usually associated with the field of marketing (e.g. the creative translation of marketing campaigns). In a client-facing promotion video, the LSP RWS thus defines transcreation as 'the process of adapting your communications, both culturally and linguistically, to convey a specific experience. This creative service allows you to subtly flex text and images to suit each market's needs.' This process, they continue, is carried out by their 'bilingual copywriters', who 'possess deep cultural and linguistic expertise' (RWS Translation Services, 2022).

Both roles, 'localiser' and 'transcreator', have emerged as a result of the growing **variety of new media** for which translation happens, be it video games or digital marketing campaigns on social media. Both require you to be not just a good linguist, but also an (inter-)cultural expert with a good understanding of the media for which and on which you translate. The need to create **new professional profiles for translators** due to the changing nature of what the job involves is also felt in the translation services of some international institutions. The European Parliament's Directorate-General for Translation (DG TRAD), for instance, has stopped using the word 'translator' for its staff as they now have to work across a range of different media (text, audio and video). Instead, translators at DG TRAD are now known as 'intercultural and language professionals', tasked with 'translating, adapting, transcreating and revising all types of content in or into their mother tongue' (European Parliament Talent Selection Unit, 2021).

From all this we can conclude that the role of translator is **evolving constantly** and that some of these changes get reflected in the job titles used, and in the variety of roles open to translation graduates. It is paramount, therefore, that you take the time to familiarise yourself with the language industry in the country or countries where you want to work and with the terminology commonly used for advertised roles, so you are in a prime position to make the most of all potential opportunities.

TOPICS FOR DISCUSSION AND ASSIGNMENTS 4.2

In this activity, I would like you to carry out a small-scale 'repeat study' of Lynne Bowker's research by analysing the job ads for translation-related positions in the country or countries where you would like to work as a translator. As I said earlier, this activity may seem more relevant to you if you are aspiring to an in-house position. However, it will also be useful to those of you who are thinking of working freelance, as it will help you form a better understanding of the local translation market.

To carry out a small-scale repeat study of Bowker's, please proceed as follows:

1. Go onto job search websites for the country where you would like to work (e.g. 51job.com for China, bumeran.com.mx for Mexico, de.indeed.com for Germany or superjob.ru for Russia etc.);

Finding that first job 67

2. Enter the word 'translator', 'translation' or 'linguist' in the relevant language and look up four to five job ads (depending on where you are looking, you may need to go onto several job search websites);
3. For each job, take a few notes on the following:

Job title	
Languages required?	
Specific specialist domains required (if any)?	
Level of education and qualifications required (if any)?	
Is certification by a recognised professional association required?	
Years of professional experience required (if any)?	
Desirable/required skills (if any)?	
Is knowledge of a required translation technology required? If so, which one?	

4.3 Applying for that first job: CVs, covering letters and test translations

Once you have carried out all the necessary background research into the translation industry and identified suitable translation positions to apply for, you will need to start work on your job application.

4.3.1 CVs and covering letters

In most countries worldwide, a key document for any job application is your employment **CV** (short for **curriculum vitae**), or 'résumé' as it is called in North America. Both terms refer to a short, written document that applicants use to tell prospective employers about their relevant qualifications and work experience to date. To understand what CVs are all about, it can be helpful to approach them in the same way you would approach any other translation job. I say 'any other translation job' because, coming to think of it,

68 *Joining the profession*

writing up your CV is all about **translating your own educational and work experiences** into a document that can be easily understood by prospective employers. In fact, I suggest that you adopt the **functionalist approach** to translating for this task. At the beginning of Chapter 3 (Section 3.1), I quoted Anthony Pym to explain that, according to the functionalist approach, translation is designed to achieve a purpose and that a source text may therefore be translated in many different ways depending on the target text's intended purpose (Pym, 2014a). Similarly, all the education and work experience you have acquired to date could be translated into many different kinds of CV depending on your intended purpose. Indeed, the CVs you send to employers should be specifically tailored to each job you are applying for as well as adhering to the **cultural conventions** for this type of document in the country or countries where you are looking for work.

A good starting point, therefore, will be to understand the core nature of CVs as well as their **main communicative function** in the culture(s) where you are applying for translation jobs. According to Italian scholar Ira Torresi, CVs are 'highly formal and standardized texts' that are used by individuals '[who] want to promote themselves professionally' (2021: 43). It would be a mistake, therefore, to consider your CV as a text whose sole purpose it is to inform employers of all your educational and work achievements in an objective and detailed manner. As there is always an element of **self-promotion** at play, it may be more helpful to see it as a more subjective document, whose purpose it is to convince prospective employers to employ you by giving them carefully selected information about your past achievements.

However, it is important to note that some cultures consider that the core communicative function of a CV remains first and foremost that of **informing potential employers** about a candidate's past education and work experience in a matter-of-fact way, despite this element of self-promotion. These tend to favour the use of impersonal structures and nominal constructions in CVs. In other cultures, though, the self-promotion dimension of CVs is given far more importance. In such cultures, verbs that show agency, the pronoun 'I' and adjectives and superlatives are far more commonly used in CVs. In fact, these cultures sometimes see more informative CVs as too impersonal or not assertive enough. CVs, Torresi explains, are thus an example of '[a] promotional genre where conventions between the information-to-persuasion ratio varies between cultures' (ibid.: 54). This is why I will not give you an example of a 'perfect' CV for translators here, as this will largely depend on where you are applying.

- What are the cultural expectations concerning the main communicative function of a translator's CV – including the information-to-persuasion ratio – in the country or countries where you are thinking of applying for translation jobs?

Finding that first job 69

A great way to ascertain this is by looking at other translators' CVs if at all possible. However, be careful with online CV templates. Even though they can be a good starting point, they tend to remain too generic overall. Similarly, be wary of CV-writing services as these can be quite expensive for the level of service they offer. A better way around this could be to make the most of your own **translation networks**, whether formal or informal, by asking more experienced translators to let you see their CVs (see Chapter 3 for advice on how you can build such support networks). If you are currently enrolled on a translation programme, your personal tutor and/or your course mates could also help you with this. Looking at other translators' CVs will help you gain a clearer idea of the relevant conventions and expectations. You could also ask them to advise you on the draft version of your CV.

Once you have a clearer idea of CV conventions for the culture(s) in which you are planning to apply for translation jobs, you can start working on the 'master copy' of your own CV. Make sure that you format it and phrase it based on examples of experienced translators' CVs from the get-go. For most countries, your master copy should contain your name, language pair(s) and direction(s) and your contact details as well as all your education, qualifications, training workshops/CPD (i.e. Continuing Professional Development) and work experience (including volunteering and side hustles, which don't have to be directly related to translating) to date. You may also want to include all the language and translation technology you are familiar with and make a note of the context in which you have used it. It will, of course, be much longer than a standard two-page CV, but keeping your master CV up to date will mean that you can use it as a starting point each time you apply for a job.

For each new translation position you are applying for, though, you will have to send a version of your CV specifically **tailored to the job**. Always make sure your CV is specific, clear and concise. This is very important as employers can receive quite a few CVs for each advertised role and they do not necessarily have the time to go through each CV in much detail. Consider, for instance, the research carried out by US job search website theladders. com in 2018, which showed that, on average, employers spend a paltry 7.6 seconds looking at each CV when shortlisting for a role (Lepore, 2020)! This leaves you with very little precious time to convince them that you have a clear understanding of the advertised role as well as possessing all the skills and competences they are looking for. To do so, you should make sure to select only the most relevant information *for this job* from your master copy to keep your CV concise. Every piece of information you select should help you provide evidence that you meet the role's specifications. You should also rephrase parts of your CV by making sure you speak the employer's language. This means re-using the key words that feature in the job advertisement to make it easier for them to see you have what it takes. Again, this is when it may be helpful to think of this as a translation job. You could see the master copy of your CV as your 'source text' or 'start text' that can be translated in many different ways depending on the intended purpose. In this instance, the

70 *Joining the profession*

purpose of the CV you send will be determined by the prospective **employer's** 'needs' (i.e. demonstrating that you have the required skills and experience) and 'preferences' (i.e. using their preferred terms).

In most countries, CVs are accompanied by a **covering letter**. Just like for CVs, conventions around the exact role and purpose of covering letters are largely cultural. In many countries, though, applicants are usually expected to use covering letters to demonstrate their **suitability and enthusiasm for the role** as well as foreground important parts of their CV. Remember, though, that prospective employers often have very little time to sift through a long pile of applications. A general expectation is therefore for covering letters to be clearly structured, tailored to the job and written in the appropriate style. Again, you should try to use your formal and informal translation networks to get a look at some examples of covering letters for translation jobs. This will help you have a better idea of the structure and style you are expected to adopt and the kinds of things you should include. To make sure your covering letter is tailored to the job, not only should you refer back to the published job ad but you should also try to find out as much as you possible can about the company or agency advertising the role. Often, this means having a good look around their website. In some cases, this will allow you to find out more about the company's or agency's culture and its key values ... and whether these align with your own professional values. Should this be the case, you can then use that fact to demonstrate how good a fit you would be for them. If you are not sure about your own values, the activities in 'Topics for discussion and assignments 2.2' (Chapter 2) can help you (re)explore these.

Finally, don't leave any hostages to fortune! Always go through both documents with the finest of all combs to make sure there aren't any typos left. When applying for a translation job, spelling and grammar errors on your CV and covering letter will often prove fatal ... after all, **revision** is key to quality in translation! How can you convince a prospective employer that you have what it takes if you fail to revise your own work to the highest standards?

TOPICS FOR DISCUSSION AND ASSIGNMENTS 4.3

Activity 4.3 Create a master copy of your CV If you haven't got one already, use the guidance above to start working on the master copy of your CV. Even though it will be for your eyes only, getting the communicative function (information-to-persuasion ratio), the style and the formatting right for the culture(s) where you are thinking of applying for jobs is important in your master copy, as this will save you a lot of precious time later on!

Activity 4.4 Tailor your CV to a specific job ad You already have a master copy that is fit for purpose? Then use one of the job adverts you selected for Topics for discussion and assignments 4.2 and follow the guidance above to 'translate' your master copy into a version of your CV that is specifically tailored to meet the 'needs' and 'preferences' of the prospective employer.

4.3.2 Test translations

Once your application has been successfully shortlisted, it is highly likely that you will be asked to complete a **test translation**. Typically, test translations consist of a 200–300 word sample you are asked to translate for free as a way to evaluate your ability to translate. It is worth noting, here, that test translations are not used for recruiting translators to in-house positions only. Translation agencies often ask prospective freelance translators to complete a test translation before adding them to their books, too.

Just a quick word of warning before we start discussing test translations in more detail. Even though it is quite reasonable for translation agencies and companies to ask you to complete a relatively short free test translation as part of their recruitment procedures, be wary of those asking you to complete test translations with a word count greater than the standard 200–300 words. This should always ring some alarm bells. Sadly, some translation agencies and companies notoriously try to source free translation labour by splitting up texts and sending out larger chunks to prospective translators as a 'test translation'. As a rule of thumb, only accept free test translations of 200–300 words. If you are asked to complete a longer test translation, then make sure there is a clear – and legitimate – reason why that is the case and ask for payment (or a reduction in length).

When you complete a test translation, bear in mind that the kinds of test translation employers set and what they are looking for will differ depending on the role they are recruiting for. When recruiting for an in-house position at a translation agency, for instance, employers tend to look for 'all-rounders' with excellent proofreading skills. However, when recruiting a freelance translator, the same agency may well set a test translation in a **specific specialist domain** that corresponds to current demand. Similarly, if you are applying for an in-house position at a commercial company specialising in the production and export of electric bikes, you can expect your test translation to be in that field. Sometimes, test translations can also include a variety of tasks besides translating, such as revision, editing or proofreading.

Marina Ilari, a United States-based translator with experience both in-house and freelance, wrote a very helpful blog post called 'How to Successfully Tackle Translation Tests' for the American Translators Association's online publication, *The ATA Chronicle*. Even though it is mostly aimed at freelance translators who routinely complete test translations to get work from agencies or direct clients, the advice she gives in her post is also very relevant to translators applying for in-house positions. Here is a summary of her top tips (Ilari, 2021):

- *Read the instructions* very carefully to make sure you are clear about the set deadline (if there is one) and any other specific instructions in place (e.g.

72 Joining the profession

formatting and/or character restrictions, reference materials you should consult such as glossaries or style guides etc.). Scour the email exchange for such instructions and double check any Excel files you have been sent as the instructions are sometimes 'hidden' in one of the tabs. Make sure you also consider implicit expectations based on what you know of the direct client, agency or company that has set the test translation;

- If, after a thorough check, you are still in doubt about some aspects of the task, then *ask*! Provided your question is legitimate – meaning you are confident the answer to it is not included in the email exchange, whether explicitly or implicitly – then asking shows how proactive you are. In fact, some will wait for you to ask before they give you a style guide or a glossary ... as another way to test you!
- Do your research and *'research smart'*. If there are no reference materials, do your own online research to check your client's background and their terminology preferences;
- *Proofread* and pay attention to detail. If a sentence or a word is ambiguous due to a lack of context, explain your translation choice in the email containing your work and explain to your client that more context would be required;
- Be *punctual*. First, check the deadline. If there is none, the expectation usually is that you return your work within three to five days for a test translation of 500 words or less;
- Whatever the outcome, always ask for *feedback* as this is the opportunity for you to learn from the whole experience.

Most of us naturally feel reluctant to *ask* the person who set the test for more information when we feel something is missing. We should consider, though, that honest mistakes do happen. One of my graduates once applied for an in-house role at a well-known translation company. As part of the recruitment process, they had to complete both a test translation and a test revision. For the revision task, they were given a target text to improve on. They started doubting their own ability as a reviser when they realised they couldn't find anything wrong with the provided target text. Disheartened, and convinced they'd failed the test, they eventually returned the target text with no amendments. As it turns out, the translation company had mistakenly given them the already revised version of the target text to work on ... no wonder they couldn't find anything wrong with it! They did secure the job in the end, but maybe double-checking with the employer could have spared them some of the angst.

Of course, a certain degree of angst, anxiety or, sometimes, even disappointment are all par for the course with test translations. Without going into the – very legitimate – debate as to whether it is acceptable for qualified and experienced freelance translators to have to routinely complete test translations for free, it is important to recognise that these tests can feel demoralising at times. There is a **psychological dimension** to test translations.

Finding that first job   73

In his article about test translations published on ProZ, freelance translator James Herbert talks about the importance of learning to acknowledge and manage our emotions when a test translation ends up in rejection: 'It's OK', he says, 'to yell (or cry) in front of your computer screen about that idiot agency that can't recognize obvious talent!' (Herbert, 2009). This is because, he explains, 'all losses must be grieved, and having a test rejected is certainly a loss – if nothing else, at least a lost opportunity to work for that agency' (ibid.). However, we should take the time to **acknowledge and process our emotions** before we respond with an angry email. Indeed, 'Nothing much is gained by negativity except reciprocal negativity; do consider sending an email asking for details about the evaluation of your test if you didn't pass. Many agencies will give you some feedback. Even if you disagree, it can be a valuable learning experience' (ibid.). Wise words indeed ... that apply not only to test translations but, in fact, to all job applications.

Never lose heart, though! Most of us will have to apply for many a job before finding the one. **Perseverance** is key.

Further reading

Bowker (2004) investigates the translation profession in Canada in the 21st century. Even though it is now dated, this article still offers interesting insights, and the methodology used by the author can form the basis of useful repeat studies.

Schäffner (2020) discusses translators' changing roles and responsibilities in today's language industry. Rather helpfully, this article also clearly outlines the differences between workflow processes for in-house and for freelance translators.

Chapter 4 in Torresi (2021) shows very clearly how CV and application letters are texts that should be treated as promotional texts in translation. It also gives helpful insights into the cultural elements to take into consideration when (self-)translating such texts.

Part II
On the job

5 Dealing with clients

> **Key questions we will explore in this chapter:**
>
> - What does it mean to see translation as a service and myself as a service provider? Why is it worth finding out who my clients are and what they will expect from me as a translation service provider?
> - Why is trust between me and my clients so important? How can I manage trust effectively in my dealings with clients? How can I make sure I factor in cultural differences, too?
> - What is my professional responsibility to clients as a translation service provider? What about my responsibility to myself, too? How can I make sure I am in a position to cope when and if things go wrong with clients?

One of the enduring myths about translators is that they spend all their time translating away in splendid isolation. There is no denying that being a professional translator involves many hours spent on your own in front of a computer screen. Quite rightly, the ability to work autonomously and to self-motivate are thus valued translator skills.

This is just one side of the coin, though. Today's translation production networks often require professional translators to collaborate with a multitude of other stakeholders in the translation process such as, for instance, fellow translators, project managers, source text (ST) author(s), language informants, subject specialists, IT specialists, graphic designers and so on (see Chapter 3). Translators should therefore possess strong interpersonal skills (also known as 'people skills'), too. In fact, one could argue that the professional success of translators – freelancers in particular, but also in-house translators – depends to a large extent on their **people skills**. This is because translators, who are service providers, constantly have to attract and retain clients. Seen this way, building and managing effective **client relationships** makes business sense. To do so, you will need to understand who your clients are (and what they value) and learn how to use your people skills effectively

DOI: 10.4324/9781003220442-7

78 On the job

when dealing with your clients so that **trust**, which is an essential component of that relationship, can be fostered and preserved.

5.1 Offering your services to clients

First of all, let's go back to the idea that translators are **service providers** (see Kujamäki, 2021). This idea should not be completely new to you. As we saw in Chapter 1, the EMT's 2009 Wheel of Competences placed 'Translation service provision' at the heart of its competence model for professional translators (see also Biel, 2011).

- According to you, what are the concrete implications of seeing translation as a 'service' and translators as 'service providers'?

In her study of clients' expectations of commercial translators, Finnish scholar Nina Havumetsä defines services as '**processes**' which are 'partly produced and consumed simultaneously' and in which 'the customer participates in the production process to a varying degree' (2012: 8). At first, we may find this definition in which services are 'partly produced and consumed simultaneously' at odds with what we know of translation as a process. When you deliver a translation, the translation as 'end product' is certainly produced before it is 'consumed' (i.e. 'read') by the client and the end users!

However, Havumetsä uses an analogy that can help us understand more clearly how this definition applies to translation. When you go to the restaurant, the service you enjoy is not just the food you order (i.e. the tangible end product); it is also the whole experience of eating out, including the welcome you receive, the décor, the atmosphere at the restaurant and so on. The same applies to a client commissioning a translation. What they are buying from you is not just the translation itself, but 'the whole process from the first contact with [you as] service provider to the receipt and use of the actual core of the service [they have bought]' (ibid.). This means that the way you, as a professional translator, act with the client – and make them feel about the whole process – matters. All the more so because 'service provider[s] [are] often unable to differentiate [their] end products from those of the competitors' (ibid.). For both freelance translators and translation agencies, **standing out from the crowd** in the translation industry is therefore often achieved by providing excellent customer service throughout the whole translation process.

For any service provider, standing out from the crowd is something that they have to do from the get-go in their **search for new clients**. Translation service providers should be prepared to devote a sizeable chunk of their time to creating and updating their client base. If you're thinking of going freelance, then you will have the option to offer your services to translation agencies,

Dealing with clients 79

to direct clients or even both (see Chapter 2)! If you decide to work freelance for translation agencies, do not think that sending a couple of CVs will be enough to get you work. Depending on the circumstances (e.g. current market demand for your language combination and/or your specialist domain), you may have to send hundreds of CVs before getting a reply.

This was the case for US translator Corinne McKay, who has since become a very successful freelancer. In her book *How to Succeed as a Freelance Translator*, she explains that one of the reasons some freelance translators fail is because they expect 'too much return from too little marketing effort' (2015: 31). Even if and when you get a positive reply from an agency, don't expect for commissions to materialise straight away. More often than not, the agency will ask you to take a test translation before adding you to their database of freelancers (see Chapter 4). Even if they are happy with the translation, and do add you to the database, you may not hear back from them for another while yet, if at all.

This is because the project managers (PMs) in charge of allocating the work to freelancers usually tend to ask their **'trusted freelancers'** first – the ones they have already worked with and whom they trust to deliver – if they can take on the job before asking new freelancers (whom they see as unknown quantities). This was one of the key findings of an ethnographic study by two UK-based academics, Maeve Olohan and Elena Davitti, which looked at the role of trust in translation project management at translation agencies. Even when none of their trusted translators are available to take on the job, PMs would rather give the job to freelancers that have been recommended by fellow PMs before asking an unknown freelance translator who has been recently added to the agency's database (2017: 399–400). We will explore the importance of trust in greater detail later on in this chapter. In the meantime, to break through this initial wall of reluctance, you should proactively offer and advertise your services to agencies – even once you have been added to their database – by, for instance, 'contacting [them] and offering your availability for short-notice and weekend jobs' (ibid.: 401).

Another potential pool of clients for freelance translators is, of course, **direct clients**. According to the European Language Industry Survey, 45% of freelance translators' business came from direct clients in 2022 (ELIS Research, 2022: 19). Many budding translators choose to work for agencies in the first instance, and then progressively build a pool of direct clients (see Chapter 2). It should be noted, though, that it does not always have to be this way. Some direct clients, for instance, may be more open to the idea of giving a less experienced translator a chance than well-established translation agencies. Either way, you will have to adopt the same proactive approach with direct clients as with agencies by putting your name out there. There are many channels through which you can advertise your services to clients. You could, for instance, have a website advertising your services. A website on its own is not enough, though ... why would potential direct clients visit your website if they don't know who you are and what

80 *On the job*

you do? Networking via both professional associations and social media is therefore crucial to reach out to direct clients (see Chapter 3). This should form part of a well-thought-out **communication/marketing strategy** through which you explain what services you offer as a translator in a clear and consistent way. It should also include getting in touch with (local) businesses that may benefit from your services once you have identified who they may be. This will be an important part of your job as a freelance translator, not just when you start trading (although admittedly you will spend more time searching for new clients then), but also throughout the rest of your career. We will explore the subject of how you can market your business in greater depth in Chapter 8.

You should always seek to **renew and/or expand your client base** so your business does not become over-reliant on existing ones. In fact, this is something agencies do, too, by advertising their services broadly. They also put strategies in place to make sure they retain existing clients. Indeed, an increasing number of agencies now expect their PMs to take on a **relationship management** role as part of the overall service they offer to their clients. Concretely, this means that their PMs pay a lot of attention to how they communicate with the agency's clients both over the phone or by email. The objective is to establish and strengthen a personal relationship between the agency and its clients in order to increase trust and, ultimately, to not lose them to the competition (see Risku et al., 2016 and Olohan and Davitti, 2017). This is something the more successful freelance translators also do effectively, whether it is with their direct clients or with the PMs of the translation agencies that employ them.

5.2 Understanding who your clients are and what they want

As a service provider, you should not just *search* for new clients. You should also **research** them. There are good reasons why both translation agencies and freelance translators should want to look into their new clients, especially when the latter have approached them directly. There is, of course, absolutely nothing wrong with clients offering you unsolicited work. They could be perfectly respectable clients who have come to you as a result of your – evidently successful – marketing strategy. However, you should always do your due diligence, as this could stop you wasting precious time you don't have further down the line. Researching new clients will allow you to form a global impression of whether they are **reliable**, serious about the job and likely to pay you for your services. This is what PMs at translation agencies do; they routinely gather information on new clients by, for instance, researching their online profiles. If a quick internet search indicates that a new client is in financial trouble and is likely to file for bankruptcy, PMs will probably question their ability to pay for the job. Ultimately, they may decide it is not in the agency's best interest to take on the new client's commission.

Dealing with clients 81

Likewise, freelancers should research all their potential clients, whether they are direct clients or translation agencies. Wherever possible, you should use your professional networks to research the translation agencies that offer you work – again, especially when it is unsolicited work – as some of them may already suffer from a bad reputation among fellow freelance translators. Admittedly, if you are a budding freelancer desperate to build your client base, you may not feel that you are in a position to turn anyone down. As the saying goes, after all, beggars can't be choosers. Nevertheless, you may want to bear in mind the following words of advice by Canadian freelance translator Werner Patels: 'It is always better to forgo a potential job [...] than go through the hassle and headaches of chasing after your money later on' (Patels, 2008).

There are many other – more positive – reasons why you should gather some intelligence about your clients. This detective work will allow you to find out more about what they do, how they operate and, crucially, what they will need and expect of you as a service provider. This is, in the end, what will allow you to offer each client a bespoke service. You should also be aware, however, of some of the more universal expectations translation buyers may have. I have already mentioned Nina Havumetsä's study of translation **buyers' expectations** of commercial translators in Finland. Based on a survey of 104 Finnish–Russian translation buyers (excluding translation agencies), it found that clients' criteria for choosing a particular translation service provider were, in order of importance (2012: 125):

- The ability to deliver the job quickly and to meet deadlines (56% of respondents);
- The translator(s)' language skills (50% of respondents);
- The service provider's experience (45% of respondents);
- The fact that the service provider's speciality meets the client's needs (35% of respondents);
- The fact that the service provider has the lowest cost (30% of respondents).

We can all take heart in the fact that cost doesn't come top of the list! However, it is worth pointing out that this study included both freelance translators and translation agencies as translation service providers. In fact, a follow-up question flagged up the fact that translation buyers who choose to go with a freelance translator tend to pay more attention to low costs than those choosing to go through an agency (38% against 21%). Relative to the other criteria, though, this remains encouraging for freelance translators. Havumetsä's study can thus be seen as empirical evidence of what clients in Finland generally rate as important when they hire your services. Admittedly, though, these figures will likely vary depending on **other factors,** such as the country where you operate as well as the domain(s) and language pair(s) in which you specialise. This is why it will be important for you to try and find out what exactly your clients value in your service offer. Beyond the initial

82 *On the job*

research into new clients, this is something a good communication strategy that establishes a trust relationship with your clients will help you achieve.

TOPICS FOR DISCUSSION AND ASSIGNMENTS 5.1

As service providers, professional translators have to both *search* for new clients and *research* them. In fact, researching who your clients might be and what they will expect from you should help you make sure the service you offer matches the market's needs and expectations. This should, in turn, inform your search for new clients. Whether you decide to work as a freelance translator or to set up a translation agency, this will be part of the overall marketing strategy you develop for your business. The following activities aim to make you start thinking about who your potential clients might be, and how to reach them. This is something you will have the opportunity to explore in much greater depth in Chapter 8.

Activity 5.1 Individually, take a few minutes to answer the following questions within the regional and/or national context(s) in which you would like to work as a professional translator. Use what we have just discussed and the industry research you carried out for 'Topics for discussion and assignments 4.1'–which was, in fact, market research – to inform your answers. For each question, list as many different types of customers as possible. Once you are done, get into pairs to discuss your answers with one of your course mates.

- Who are the potential customers who typically engage with freelance translators? What do you think they value the most?
- Who are the potential customers who typically engage with translation agencies? What do you think they value the most?

Activity 5.2 Complete an Internet search for a translation service provider that aligns with your current thinking of how you may want to position yourself in the market as a professional translator (basically, one of your potential 'competitors'). This can be a freelance translator or a translation agency. Use your research to answer each of the following questions:

Who are they?	
Who do they target?	

What do they offer?	
Who are their main competitors?	
Where and how do they promote/sell their translation services?	
Why are they successful (or what keeps them in business)?	
How much do they charge?	
How could their improve their services?	

5.3 Managing trust with a clear communication strategy

As we saw in Chapter 3, the last few decades have seen the emergence of new production networks in the translation industry that are characterised by the **outsourcing** of most translation jobs. In these new production models, each actor is a node interconnected to other nodes. Each node has no choice but to rely on the other nodes to get the job done (see Figure 3.2).

In their seminal paper, 'Managing Trust: Translating and the Network Economy', Kristiina Abdallah and Kaisa Koskinen make the point that trust has therefore become essential for the good functioning of the production networks, in a network economy characterised by 'interaction and mutual dependency' between the different 'nodes' (2007: 677). To be more precise, though, the two Finnish scholars argue that trust is, in fact, one of the weak points of contemporary production networks. This is because trust in such models is often a one-way street due to an imbalance of power. Subcontracted freelance translators, for instance, usually have little choice but to trust the agencies that employ them, as they are not in a position to set their own terms and conditions (ibid.: 678).

Abdallah and Koskinen also show that another related factor that can have a negative impact on trust and, therefore, on the efficiency of the production networks is what is known as 'information asymmetry'. Information asymmetry occurs when one of the actors in the production network possesses more information than the other(s). This happens, for instance, when an agency negotiates a translation commission with their client without involving the subcontracted freelance translator who will produce the translation (ibid.). The fact that the translator doesn't have direct access to the agency's client and was not party to the discussions

84 On the job

around the commission means that they will have to rely on the information the agency is willing to share with them on this, and trust that the information is accurate. Information asymmetry can also be found in situations where you as a professional translator deal directly with clients. In such cases, information asymmetry risks eroding your clients' trust in you as translator. This is because most translation buyers do not have the required expertise to fully understand what is involved in the delivery of a translation project and/or don't have the necessary resources to judge the quality of the 'end product' (i.e. the translation) they are buying from you. Put simply, some might worry that the fact that they don't speak the language you are going to be working with means that you could be doing anything, which could seriously limit or erode trust. It is therefore important that translation buyers feel they can trust you as translation service provider.

When a client first comes to you, be it an agency or a direct client, their trust in you will be limited to what they know about you as a translator based on your CV and, possibly, some recommendations. They may well entrust you with the work, but their trust in you remains mostly **contractual**, and vice versa. This is reflected in the contracts and agreements that are in place to protect everyone's best interests. Over time, though, the objective for you will be to move towards a more meaningful trust relationship, based on first-hand experience of what you know of each other. You will want them to know you can trust them, and they you. This can be achieved by establishing a good communication strategy with your clients.

Establishing a good communication strategy with your clients starts with **honesty** and **transparency**. A good way to achieve this is by being as open with your clients as possible about what you can and cannot do, as well as what you need to do a good job. If, for instance, a client asks you to translate a text that you feel confident you can translate but you know will require more work as it doesn't fall under your usual subject expertise, then you should say so to your client and explain that you will need more time to carry out the necessary research. It is easier to do so at the **negotiating stage,** as it will allow your client to either make allowances for the extra time or commission another translator if they need the work urgently. This being said, if you realise that you won't be able to deliver the translation job at the – either explicitly or implicitly agreed – quality level by the agreed deadline only after you start working on it, then you should still explain the situation to your client.

Honesty as the best policy rests on the assumption that your clients understand – to a point – what it takes to translate a text to a professional standard. However, a lot of translation buyers may be under the misguided impression that a translation is simply the linguistic transfer of a text from one language to the next, and that the work of translators has been made a lot easier and quicker lately by the emergence of machine translation engines. This seems to be confirmed by the fact that, as mentioned earlier, translation buyers tend to prioritise language combination and a translator's ability to deliver the job quickly when choosing a translation service provider (Havumetsä, 2012: 125). Of course, there is an element of truth in all this. But we also know that there is far more to translating than meets the untrained eye. This is why your communication strategy with clients should also contain a **pedagogical dimension** that helps them better understand the ins and outs of professional translating.

Some existing **resources** can help you with this. The UK's Institute of Translation and Interpreting (ITI), for instance, has produced a guide called *Translation: Getting it Right. A Guide to Buying Translation*. Written by freelance translator Chris Durban, the reader-friendly guide starts from the assumption that 'If you're not a linguist yourself, buying translations can be frustrating' (Durban, 2011: 3). It then uses lay language to give translation buyers advice and guidance on a whole range of issues such as, for instance:

- The cost and added value of professional translating (ibid.: 7) as well as the risks of using machine translation (ibid.: 12) and non-professional translators (ibid.: 15);
- The need for clients to think about what, in the source text, will need translating (ibid.: 4), to finalise the source text *before* the translation work starts (ibid.: 11) and to tell the translator what the target text will be for (ibid.: 14);
- The reasons why 'an inquisitive translator is good news' (ibid.: 18).

Since it was first published in the UK, this client-facing, non-country-specific guide has been adopted and promoted by many translator associations across the globe thanks to translations into several languages, including Japanese and Russian. This guide is freely available in several languages on the ITI website: https://www.iti.org.uk/.

The first set of advice on the cost and added value of professional translators could help you develop your own marketing strategy. Similarly, integrating elements of the second and third sets of advice into your communication strategy could help you negotiate the commission by making your client(s) aware of the at-times inevitable tension between the expected quality level, the set deadline and the rate they are willing to pay. Are they willing, for instance, to sacrifice quality for a cheaper and quicker translation? There are cases where this may be fine. What if, though, the text is what Canadian translator Donald Barabé calls a '**prejudicial text**', that is, a text for which 'an incorrect translation is likely to cause severe, irreparable or hardly reparable physical, moral, financial or material prejudice' (Barabé, 2021: 173)? Compromising on quality could result in your translation causing your client or the text's end user prejudice, and you reputational damage. Explaining all this to your clients in a language they understand should help them trust that you have their best interests at heart as well as yours, and ensure that they respect your professional advice.

The second set of advice ITI gives to prospective translation buyers does not always materialise – far from it! This is, once again, linked to

86   On the job

the information asymmetry between you and your direct clients. As opposed to translation agencies, direct clients won't always be fully aware of what translating involves and this may sometimes lead to **unrealistic or unclear commissions**. And yet, you as a translator need to understand their requirements, their objectives and the purpose of the translation project in order to deliver translations that work not just for your clients, but also for other potential stakeholders such as the target readers. This is precisely why 'an inquisitive translator is good news' (Durban, 2011: 18)! On opening a client's translation project, you may find that you don't have enough information about the intended target audience and/or the language variety to be used (e.g. French [Canada] or French [France]? English [Australia] or English [Singapore]?). You may also have questions around your client's preferred file format, their preferred terminology (and whether they can provide a glossary) or the deadline for the job. These questions will likely arise before you start translating, during the project negotiation phase, which makes it easier to ask your clients.

However, what if **further questions** crop up as you are working on or reviewing the translation project? For some of us, our initial reaction may be to avoid asking our busy clients any more questions as we fear this will show us up as ignorant or unprofessional. How can we make sure, we wonder, that our questions come across as professional, that our clients engage with them and that they reinforce the trust relationship we aim to develop with them? In a 2017 article for the American Translators Association called 'How to Deal with Questions during a Translation Project?', Belgian translator and project manager Nancy Matis shared a few tips to help fellow translators achieve just that. Here is a selection of some of her tips (see Matis, 2017):

- **Double-check all the information your client sent you** before you send any of your questions. The last thing you want is to ask them (for) something they have already shared with you, thereby wasting their time and making yourself look unprofessional ... If you are working on a big project involving several translators and there is a shared query file, make sure to consult it first in case your questions have already been answered there;
- **Adapt your communication style to your client.** Always keep the tone polite and professional. However, bear in mind that what is considered polite varies from one culture to the next. Remember to factor in cultural differences! If you are working on a complex multilingual project, 'write your questions in the main communication language' (ibid.). If the language you use for your questions is not your client's language of habitual use, 'adapt all questions to the recipient's language level' as '[p]eople might get frustrated if they need to invest time trying to understand highly technical questions written in a language in which they are not fluent' (ibid.);
- **Do not inundate your clients with emails.** Once you have negotiated all the questions you had during the project negotiation phase, make a list of all

the new questions that crop up as you are working on the project and send them all in the same email. If your direct client or the translation agency uses a question template, make sure to use it;

- **Be as clear and specific as you can be** so that your client understands why you are asking these questions (remember that your direct clients will likely know precious little about translation!). If you are unsure about the interpretation of a term, suggest your own solution that makes your own interpretation of the term clear and ask whether this is correct: 'Proposing your own solution gains your client time and increases the probability that they will confirm immediately rather than postpone (or forget) to write down long explanations' (ibid.).

Whether you are a freelance translator, a PM at an agency or an in-house translator dealing with the company's translation requesters, developing a **clear communication strategy** in which you adapt your communication style to your client(s) should therefore help establish a relationship with them that adds to the perceived value of the service you offer. In their study of the dynamics of trusts in translation project management, Olohan and Davitti observed that both translation agencies at which they carried out ethnographic research had clear communication strategies in place to achieve just that. As well as 'networking' with clients, 'granting [them] discounts [...] or preferential rates', they also used customised quotes 'which can include several pages of additional information about how the [agency] operates and assures quality' as a way to 'convey a trustworthy and professional image' (2017: 406). For both agencies, communicating with clients was clearly a priority, with 'PMs [being] required to devote considerable time to writing targeted letters to clients, phrasing emails appropriately with a personal touch, taking their cue from the client's communication to them when deciding on issues such as levels of formality' (ibid.: 406). For long-standing clients, with whom the PM or agency may have a more established relationship, PMs tended to prefer more direct communication such as telephone calls – provided the clients shared this preference – to allow for a more 'bespoke' and personable communication style that further reinforced trust between both parties (ibid.: 407).

Admittedly, small translation agencies and freelance translators may not always have the resources (or, in other words, the time) to design a **customised communication strategy** for each client. However, there are core elements of what Olohan and Davitti observed (e.g. using quotes to communicate with clients on how they operate and assure quality, taking your cues from clients' communication to them etc.) that could help them develop an effective communication strategy that helps them attract and retain clients. All of the above, one might add, is about using our emotional intelligence to show **empathy** towards our clients by 'recognizing, understanding, and responding to [their] emotions': 'Sensing how [your clients] feel about your requests, or your responses to their requests, will help you interact with them

88 *On the job*

in a personally and professionally satisfying manner, leading both to more work and to enhanced enjoyment in your work' (Robinson, 2020: 106).

TOPICS FOR DISCUSSION AND ASSIGNMENTS 5.2

Imagine the following scenario:

You have just started trading as a freelance translator. You have applied to get on the books of many translation agencies but the rejection letters are piling up, mostly due to your lack of professional experience. The agencies that have added you to their database of freelancers are yet to contact you with work. Fortunately, you have also used your networks and marketed your services on social media and locally in order to get some work from direct clients, too. This is starting to pay off. A very successful local start-up company got in touch with you last month. They had a job for you and they were happy to pay you the standard rate. This job was right up your street; you completed it by the agreed deadline and got paid shortly afterwards. Both you and the start-up were very pleased with this first experience.

A few days ago, the start-up contacted you again. They have another job for you. However, this time round they want you to translate legal contracts. Legal documents are not your area of expertise. They need the translated contracts fairly urgently, since their client needs them for an upcoming meeting. Still, the deadline remains reasonable and you are available. Also, you could do with the money and you're keen to become the start-up's trusted translator. You have a quick look at one of the texts and accept the job.

However, as soon as you open the whole project, you realise it is much harder than you anticipated. The documents are difficult to understand and the terminology is time-consuming to research. The project file contains the source texts to be translated only, and you wonder if one of them may be missing. You are slowly coming to the conclusion that you have a choice between missing the deadline, but feeling fairly confident that the translation is accurate, or meeting the deadline, but knowing that the translation quality is well below your ability. Either way, you are worried about the impact this will have on your client and on your ability to keep them.

Activity 5.3 Identify all the potential issues that could lead to a breakdown in communication between you and your client in this scenario. Are there any ethical issues at play in this scenario? If so, which ones?

Dealing with clients 89

Activity 5.4 Based on your answer to Activity 5.1, explain and justify to a course mate all the different steps you would take to manage trust between you and your client in such a situation. Explain how you would go about communicating your actions and decisions to the client.

5.4 Factoring in cultural differences

An important factor that should also influence the way we, as a professional translators, communicate with our clients is their **cultural background(s)**. As translators, we are all too aware of the way norms and expectations are intrinsically culture-bound when we translate texts. And yet, being only human, we may not always be as good at heeding the potential impact cultural differences can have in our everyday interactions with clients, especially when said clients are from a culture we are not familiar with and communication happens by email (or other channels of electronic written communication).

As professional translators working in the age of '**superdiversity**', however, we will likely encounter both. Superdiversity can be defined as the 'increased linguistic, ethnic and cultural hybridity of our societies and also of the individuals inhabiting them' (Tomozeiu et al., 2016: 261). It has emerged as a result of globalisation and it can be felt, in the translation industry, at all levels of the new production networks discussed in Chapter 3. Figure 5.1, for instance, shows the complex multi-node network of actors and tools involved in the translation of a user guide for a newly developed machine at the translation department of an Austrian technology company that hires five in-house translators. It illustrates how professional translators routinely have to liaise with various different stakeholders. Imagine you are one of the translators working for this department. Some of the other stakeholders you liaise with may well be from a culture you are not familiar with (e.g. project managers, fellow translators, colleagues from the marketing department, colleagues from Research & Development, etc.).

If, as a translator, you want to create long-lasting relationships not just with your clients, but also with other stakeholders in the translation process, then you should aim to develop and maintain high levels of **intercultural competence**. Intercultural competence, here, is understood as a continuum – from low to high – of our levels of 'cultural awareness and empathy, along with curiosity, pro-activeness and [...] awareness [of] social positioning' (Tomozeiu and Kumpulainen, 2016: 275). Gaining greater awareness of social positioning, for instance, can help us see more clearly how a client's cultural background might influence their conception of hierarchy in the workplace, and how this colours the way they interact with us and expect us to interact with them.

Of course, most professional translators already have very high levels of intercultural competence for the source-language and target-language

90 On the job

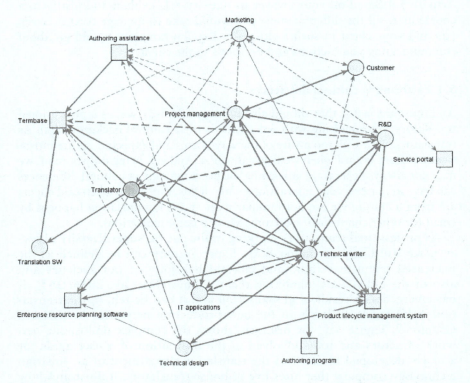

Figure 5.1 Complete network for the translation of a user guide at a translation department (from Risku et al., 2016: 240)

cultures they work with. Most of us proactively engage with them and are very much aware of potential differences in social positioning. However, as translators we cannot be expected to know everything there is to know about the culture(s) of the various different stakeholders we will have to deal with during the course of our careers. I use culture(s), here, because some of the stakeholders may feel that they belong to two or more different cultures, either by birth, by circumstance or by choice. This certainly adds to the richness of the situation, but also to its complexity! This is why the most important words in the above definition of intercultural competence may well be **'empathy'**, **'curiosity'** and **'proactiveness'**.

A good starting point if we want to further develop our intercultural competence is to ask ourselves a few questions that can help us probe our own attitudes and beliefs when it comes to working with people from cultures we are less familiar with. Take a few moments to reflect on the following questions:

Dealing with clients 91

- Am I always open to new cultures I am not familiar with? Do I always believe that interacting with people from new cultures will be an enriching experience?
- Am I always curious to explore different aspects of new cultures, even when these are completely alien to me?
- Do I always remember that we all have different cultural backgrounds that can impact the way we work, and that I can learn from that?

We would all love to answer each of the above questions with a resounding 'yes', wouldn't we? And yet, the use of the word 'always' in each of the questions is enough to make most of us teeter ... Even if we consider ourselves naturally curious and empathetic, do we *always* find working with people from a new culture an 'enriching experience'? Do we *always* proactively try to understand other people's cultures and how their different cultural backgrounds can impact the way they communicate with us?

If we are completely honest with ourselves, very few of us can answer yes to all the above questions all the time. What if we are stressed, or tired, or both? What if communication happens by **email**? This is more than likely, as a recent UK survey that showed that 89% of freelance translators preferred email to other methods of communication (Inbox Translation, 2021). Imagine that a client or another stakeholder in a translation project has addressed you in a tone you find condescending and/or inappropriate in their email. Is it because they are from a different culture with a different understanding of social positioning and politeness, or are they just being rude to you? How can you find out? Do you just check the name at the end of the email? In a world of superdiversity, should a foreign-sounding name make us jump to the conclusion that the person who sent the email is not from the same culture as us?

There are the questions you should ask yourself before you make up your mind about that person's attitude. Most of us tend to react immediately and instinctively when we find somebody else's tone inappropriate, and more often than not we judge them rather harshly. However, we must all learn to take a step back before we do so. Or, in other words, breathing in and taking a step back is the first step to take for improved intercultural competence!

TOPICS FOR DISCUSSION AND ASSIGNMENTS 5.3

People from different cultures can have a different understanding of social positioning. Concretely, this means that they may have a different

92   *On the job*

understanding of the importance – or not – of hierarchy at work, and of what is polite and acceptable when communicating with colleagues, service providers or clients. Although you can't be expected to know everything about every culture, there are resources freely available online that can help you with that.

Activity 5.5 Visit the website https://www.hofstede-insights.com/. Browse the pages of this site to answer the following questions:

- What is the empirical research behind Professor Geert Hofstede's findings on the influence of culture on values in the workplace?
- What are the six dimensions of national culture in the '6-D Model' that emerged from Professor Hofstede's research?
- Imagine that you are a translator on a complex, multilingual project. Which dimension(s) of the '6-D Model' do you think will be the most relevant when dealing with stakeholders from new cultures as part of this project?

Activity 5.6 Now, navigate to the 'Compare countries' tool on the website (https://www.hofstede-insights.com/product/compare-countries/).

- Enter the name of the country where you come from as well as the country where you currently live (if different) and the countries with which you expect to work the most as a translator (e.g. if you are a Chinese > Spanish translator from Venezuela but currently living and working in Spain, then select 'Venezuela', 'Spain' and 'China'). Have a look at the scores for each of the six dimensions. Then, click 'Read more about chosen countries' and look at what is said for each country in relation to its scores. Take a few notes and explain whether this matches your own perceptions of these countries based on lived experiences or regular contacts you have with people who come from these cultures.
- Now, do the same but select a country you know very little about this time. Imagine that a client (or a project manager) from the country you have just selected sent you an email you found either rude or far too informal. Do you feel that reading about the culture of the country this person comes from on this website could help you better understand how culture might have influenced the way they communicated with you? Please explain the ways in which doing so could help change your own initial reaction to your client's email, the opinion you have of them and how you decide to respond to their message.

5.5 Keeping your side of the bargain… without being naïve

So far, I have insisted on the importance of developing a trust relationship with our clients based on a good understanding of who they are and what

Dealing with clients 93

they need, as well as a good communication strategy that shows empathy. However, this alone is not enough.

Let's go back to the scenario described under 'Topics for discussion and assignments 5.2'. Faced with such a difficult situation, it may be tempting for you to deliver the work on time while knowing that the quality of the work will be below your ability and, therefore, below the level of what your client can rightly expect from you. Your client may never realise this, because of the 'information asymmetry' I mentioned earlier. You may well get away with it scot-free and keep your client's trust in you as a professional translator.

This is, however, when **professionalism** and **ethics** come into play. In this scenario, the implicitly agreed quality level for a legal document such as this one is very high. Delivering substandard work could cause serious prejudice to your client and result in reputational damage both for you and the rest of the profession. Behaving in such a way can be seen as unethical, as attested by the fact that most professional associations of translators condemn such a line of conduct in their codes of conduct and/or ethics. As we saw in Chapter 3, most associations have their own code that professional translators must sign up to in order to become a member. Even though there is a slight difference between **codes of conduct and codes of ethics**, both terms are routinely used interchangeably as both offer a set of standards that establish what is considered as acceptable professional behaviour for translators. Indeed, these codes offer guidance on how practitioners should 'conduct themselves ethically for the benefit of the clients they serve, the profession they represent and themselves as practitioners' (Hale, 2007: 103 quoted in Lambert, 2023: 117). Adhering to such a code of conduct/ethics could therefore help you keep your side of the bargain vis-à-vis your clients by helping you uphold professional standards …

What, then, are the **professional standards** we should seek to uphold as professional translators? In her review of a representative sample of seventeen translator associations' codes of ethics/conduct from around the world, Canadian scholar Julie McDonough Dolmaya showed that only two principles are consistently mentioned by all of the codes: **confidentiality** and **competence** (McDonough Dolmaya, 2011: 31). The fact that, apart from confidentiality and competence, translators' codes of conduct/ethics don't always agree on which professional standards translators should uphold should come as no surprise. Professional standards are value-based, and different cultures will prioritise some values over others despite some universals. This is one of the limitations of codes of ethics/conduct. They try to establish a standardised list of common professional standards for a given community, but by doing so they can come across as either too prescriptive or even too limited. What about your own professional values as an individual? As Joseph Lambert puts it: '[W]e are responsible for the choices that we make ethically and cannot simply fall back uncritically on these codes, and both scholars and professionals readily acknowledge that codes offer contradictory and sometimes confusing guidelines' (2023: 116).

94   *On the job*

These – valid – reservations notwithstanding, it is interesting to note that competence and confidentiality are core expectations in translators' codes of conduct/ethics. As we have already discussed the concept of competence (see Chapter 1), let's turn our attention to confidentiality. Maintaining **client confidentiality** means not disclosing any information we have obtained about our clients in the course of our work to any third party without their consent, unless we have a legal obligation to do so. Protecting our clients' confidentiality therefore means that it is our responsibility to ensure that we store all the information we hold about our clients – including, but not limited to, all the documents that form part of the translation project – in a safe space. Before the widespread use of technology, this often meant making sure you kept all the documents safely under lock and key in your (home) office. However, the growing use of technology has also turned this into it into a **data security** issue. IBM defines data security as 'the practice of protecting digital information from unauthorized access, corruption, or theft throughout its entire lifecycle' (IBM, 2023).

Data confidentiality is far too complex an issue to do full justice to this book. However, here are some key questions you should ask yourself in order to protect client confidentiality:

- Do I know what happens to the data I have input into the system when I use a freely available machine translation (MT) tool as part of a translation project? How do I know confidentiality is upheld? (For the many legal and ethical hazards involved in the use of MT, read Moorkens, 2022.)
- What measures can I reasonably put in place to ensure that the online platforms I use to store information on my translation projects, and exchange information with my clients, are not breached by hackers or corrupted by malware or spyware (e.g. emails, online collaboration tools, project management tools etc.)?
- What do I do with the information I hold about a client and a project once the project has been completed? Am I allowed to keep it? If so, for how long? If not, how do I dispose of it safely?

In many countries, data confidentiality is a **legal requirement**. For instance, professional translators based – or working with clients based – in the European Union have to comply with the General Data Protection Regulation (GDPR) while those based – or working with clients based – in China have to abide by the Personal Information Protection Law (PIPL). If you work as an in-house translator, you will likely be provided with the software you need to ensure data confidentiality, and you can also expect some guidelines around the safe use of MT. Bigger organisations may also employ a **Data Protection Officer** whose role it is to make sure that safe and appropriate systems are in place to guarantee data security and adherence to the

Dealing with clients 95

relevant data protection laws. If you are a freelance translator, though, you will have to be your own Data Protection Officer by making sure you don't – accidentally – break the data protection law not just of the country where you work, but those of the countries where your clients are based, too. Should, despite your best endeavours, data confidentiality become compromised for one of your clients (e.g. you accidentally send an email containing information about a client's translation project to another client), then you should inform your client of the situation straight away. You should tell them what measures you will take to try and remedy the situation and to ensure this doesn't happen again. Again, for professional translators working under the European Union's GDPR, this is not just an ethical requirement but a legal one, too.

Similarly, it is important to understand the legislation on **intellectual property and copyright** (also called authors' rights) for both the country where you are based and the countries where your clients are based. The World Intellectual Property Organization (WIPO) defines copyright as 'a legal term used to describe the rights that creators have over their literary and artistic works' (WIPO, 2023). WIPO helpfully gives a list of what is commonly protected by copyright across the world: 'literary works such as novels, poems, plays, reference works, newspaper articles; computer programs, databases; films, musical compositions, and choreography; artistic works such as paintings, drawings, photographs, and sculpture; architecture; advertisements, maps, and technical drawings' (ibid.). However, what exactly is and is not protected by copyright will depend on the intellectual property legislation in place in the country where you are based and/ or where your client is based. There could be more works that are protected by copyright there, such as, for instance, online content. Before you start translating works, or parts of works, that you know are protected by copyright, make sure that your client has secured the copyright holder's permission for the translation. If you are not sure but suspect that something may be copyrighted, then double-check the legislation for the relevant country and ask your client to secure the author's permission if they haven't done so already. If you translate something protected by copyright without the author's permission, and your translation is published, you as translator may be held responsible for breaking copyright law.

As you can see, keeping your side of the bargain and doing right by your clients should not be to the detriment of your own professional interests. Professionalism is **a two-way street**; you should protect your own professional interests by making sure you don't naively accept detrimental terms and conditions. It is with this objective in mind that freelance translator Werner Patels established a list of 'Rules for dealing with translation clients' based on his own experience and that of colleagues. Here is a selection of some of his most noteworthy rules (Patels, 2008):

96   *On the job*

- Make sure your clients have signed a **purchase order** before you start working on a new translation project;
- You as service provider set the terms of payment, not the buyer. Be 'polite, yet firm' about your terms of payment in your initial contact with your clients. Consider charging new clients upfront. For large projects, consider charging a retainer of around 25%;
- Do not sign **contracts** with agencies blindly. Contracts that stipulate that payment to you as translator is dependent on the agency being paid by its end client should be avoided;
- 'Never, under any circumstances, accept work sight **unseen**': You never know what you could be getting yourself into, and may find yourself way out of your depth upon opening the files.

TOPICS FOR DISCUSSION AND ASSIGNMENTS 5.4

Activity 5.7 Use the research you did on professional associations for 'Topics for discussion and assignments 3.1' (Chapter 3) as a starting point. Have a look at the code of conduct/ethics of a professional association you are thinking of joining. Alternatively, if it does not have one, use FIT's 'Directory of members' (https://en.fit-ift.org/members-directory/) to find a professional association relevant to your work that has a code of ethics/ conduct.

- Establish the list of professional standards you should uphold (besides 'competence' and 'confidentiality') according to your selected code of conduct/ethics. Are there any potential gaps or contradictions in the code?
- Go back to the scenario of 'Topics for discussion and assignments 5.2'. Quote all relevant elements from the code you have selected that you feel apply here and explain how they would inform your professional conduct. Are there any potential limitations or 'grey areas' in the guidance provided by your selected code of conduct/ethics? Please explain.

5.6 What if things go wrong?

Finally, what if, despite all your best endeavours, things go wrong? Understandably, most of us don't really want to spend much time engaging with such an eventuality. However, it is important that we prepare ourselves for the fact that things can, and most likely will, go wrong at some stage during our career as a professional translator. Indeed, preparing ourselves mentally for things to go wrong should mean that we are in a better position to deal with issues as they arise.

Dealing with clients 97

What would you do, for instance, if one of your clients got in touch with you to say they are not happy with (aspects of) a translation job you have just delivered? Dealing with **negative client feedback** is never easy, especially when you have put a lot of work into delivering a project or when you feel you were dealing with unrealistic or unclear client expectations in the first place. Nevertheless, it is perfectly legitimate for your clients to give you feedback on your work. If you work for a translation company, there will likely be procedures in place to deal with negative client feedback. If you are a freelancer, though, you will have to manage this yourself. Negative client feedback can focus on relatively minor issues. This is the case, for instance, when a client asks you to make changes not based on objective errors but on their own stylistic preferences. This is never pleasant, but try not to take it personally; always remind yourself that such feedback is not an attack against you or your professional ability as a translator. Stay professional, make the required changes and see this as an opportunity to better understand your client's stylistic expectations for future commissions.

Things can get a bit more complicated when a client wants you to change a term or an expression for something you feel would be incorrect or inappropriate for this commission. In such a case, consider contacting your client to explain the rationale behind your original translation decisions and the reasons why you believe the requested changes may be misguided. If, after reading this, your client still insists on the changes, then you may be left with little choice but to follow your client's instructions while explaining to them that you cannot take responsibility for the said changes. Finally, when you receive negative feedback, do make sure that the feedback is ... for you! A freelance translator recently posted a rather amusing message on LinkedIn in which they explained that a client had sent them an email complaining about their translation. Upon checking the file, they realised that the feedback was not on their work and that it should have been addressed to another translator! *Errare humanum est ...*

What if, however, a client is reasonably happy with your work but doesn't pay you on time or refuses to pay? What would you do then? I have already mentioned some of the pre-emptive measures you can put in place so it doesn't get to that (e.g. researching your clients to make sure they are solvent, having a signed purchasing order before starting work, setting clear payment terms and charging upfront for new clients etc.). Despite all this, **non-payment** is more common that one might like to think. According to a recent survey of UK professional translators, 26% of translators working with agencies and 21% of those with direct clients reported having experienced non-payment (Inbox Translation, 2021). If you are faced with a client who hasn't paid you by the agreed time, then consider sending them a polite reminder with a new deadline in the first instance. It could just be a simple misunderstanding or a clerical error on their part. Consider, too, whether there could be cultural

98 *On the job*

factors at play here, and whether you feel they are relevant. Still, keep a record of all your communications with the client about payment and find out what your rights are. Some countries, for instance, will allow you to charge interest on late payments (Samuelsson-Brown, 2010: 144). Is it the case where you work?

Of course, the fact that you can apply interest doesn't mean that you will want to do so for all your clients; you will need to consider who the client is and the negative impact this may have on your **future relationship** with them. However, if you suspect any kind of foul play on their part, you could tell your client that you reserve the right to start charging interest for late payment if they don't meet the new deadline. If, after all this, your client still fails to pay then it is important that you know what **legal recourse** you have against non-payment. Again, this will vary depending on where you are based. Australia, Brazil, the European Union, Kenya, Nigeria, Singapore, the UK and the USA, for instance, have small claims courts (sometimes called small claims tribunals) that can be used to settle legal disputes where the claim is below a certain threshold. This is a relatively inexpensive and efficient way to try and settle non-payment claims, especially if the amount involved is not too high. However, the country where you are based may not have such a system in place and if so, you will have to balance out the amount you are owed with how much it would cost you in legal fees to try and settle your claim. This is why, in any case, 'prevention is definitely better than cure' (ibid.: 143).

There are many other things that can potentially go wrong in the course of a translator's career, and it would be impossible to think of every eventuality here. This being said, there is one more situation I would like you to consider in closing. What if a client wrongly accused you of having breached confidentiality? This was one of the scenarios we explored in Chapter 3. Let's have another look at this:

- Two weeks after you delivered a translation job to a client, they call you to say that they believe you have breached the agreement of confidentiality you had with them. They ask you to pay a hefty sum in compensation. You did not breach confidentiality, but you don't know how to go about proving you're innocent. You wonder whether it may not be easier to pay the compensation but you also worry about what this would do to your reputation as a professional translator. What should you do?

We have already discussed how belonging to a **professional association** could give you access to a support network of more experienced professional translators who, in turn, could give you invaluable advice on thorny situations such as this one. Some professional associations also offer free legal advice, which could prove really helpful here. However, there are other factors you should consider. Should you be inclined to pay this client the **compensation**, do you have something akin to **professional indemnity insurance (PII)** in place? Even though they are not legally required in most countries, such insurance policies will cover you should a client decide to sue you over alleged professional errors (e.g. negligence, breach of professional duty, breach of confidentiality etc.). It should be noted, though, that despite the financial protection they can offer when things go wrong, only a minority of translators subscribe to such policies. In the UK, for instance, only 24% of professional translators currently hold one (Inbox Translation, 2021).

Finally, when things go wrong for you professionally, this can also impact your **physical and/or mental well-being**. This is why we should all ask ourselves the following question *before* things go wrong:

- Do I have the support and resources I will need to deal with issues such as the ones above effectively, and remain as professional as can be expected of me in my dealings with clients, despite the negative impact these issues may have on my well-being?

This is when, once again, having the support of a professional community and of your own support networks could make a massive difference (see Chapter 3). As the saying goes, 'a problem shared is a problem halved'! Do **share** your problems with fellow translators via your networks. Not only will it halve them for your, but it could also benefit others! Sharing the information you have about clients who won't pay, for instance, could prove useful to fellow translators. To that effect, some freelance translators have set up websites such as www.paymentpractices.net, which seeks 'to provide freelance translators and interpreters with information about the payment practices of translation agencies and other clients for the growing global community of translation service providers' (Payment Practices, 2022). In any case, it will be important to take your own well-being into consideration throughout your career as professional translator so you can face such situations more effectively and continue to thrive as a translator, as we will see in Chapter 9.

Further reading

If you haven't already read it as part of Chapter 3, Abdallah and Koskinen (2007) will help you understand the role of trust, loyalty and social capital in the contemporary network-based translation industry.

Olohan and Davitti (2017) use their ethnographic work at translation agencies to analyse the way trust is developed and maintained between, on the one hand,

100　*On the job*

project managers and the agency's clients, and project managers and the freelance translators on the other. This allows them to observe the important role played by communication in building and maintaining trust.

Kujamäki (2021) draws from the literature in business studies to interrogate the concept of professional service and establish whether the characteristics generally attached to this concept (professional workforce, customisation, knowledge intensity and governance) can be seen to apply to non-literary translation.

6 Managing your translation projects

> **Key questions we will explore in this chapter:**
>
> - What is project management and why should it matter to me as a professional translator?
> - Why is it so important for me to carry out a feasibility study for each new project enquiry I receive? In what ways will this inform my quotation and/or my negotiations with clients?
> - What will I need to do to launch, monitor and close my translation projects in a way that helps me manage them more efficiently and, therefore, more successfully?

We know that professional translators do not *just* translate. As we saw in Chapter 5, translation is a service and, as service providers, professional translators must, among other things, sell their services to and manage their relationships with clients. Arguably, though, client management is just one facet of an even bigger role translators have to play, that of **project manager**. To a varying degree, this is true of all professional translators ... although arguably freelancers are the ones who have to dedicate the most time to this.

6.1 All translators are project managers!

We know from previous chapters that a freelance translator's clients can be either direct clients or translation agencies. However, it would be more accurate to say that most freelancers work for a **constellation** of both direct clients *and* translation agencies (see Figure 6.1). At times, these clients may have competing needs and demands, especially with regard to delivery dates!

DOI: 10.4324/9781003220442-8

102   *On the job*

Figure 6.1 A freelance translator's potential clientele

Box 6.1 Scenario: Project enquiries for a freelance translator

Have a look at Figure 6.1. Now, imagine that on or around the same day …

- 'Direct Client 1' asks you ('Freelance translator X') to deliver a 500-word translation for the following day;
- 'Agency 1' tells you that they need a 15,000-word translation (that is part of a multilingual project involving other translators) delivered within the next two weeks;
- 'Agency 3' wants a 150,000-word project (where you are the only translator) completed within 6 months;
- 'Agency 4' enquires whether you would be interested in completing a 6,000-word translation to be delivered within the next two days;
- 'Direct Client 2' approaches you for a 200,000-word translation project with no specific delivery date.

Take a few moments to ask yourself the following questions:

- How would you determine whether you should accept all six commissions in Box 6.1? If you didn't feel in a position to take on all six, which criteria would you use to decide which project enquiries to accept and which ones to turn down?

Managing your translation projects 103

Admittedly, **client management** will play a part in your decision to accept or turn down some of these enquiries. If, for instance, 'Direct Client 1' is a very valuable client of yours, you may decide to take on the job even though it will not be as lucrative as some of the other commissions. However, other factors – for example **time** (i.e. deadlines), the **resources** you will need to complete each project, the potential **costs** you may incur, the **risks** each project may pose and the **benefits** they may bring to you – should also help you determine whether you feel in a position to take on and successfully deliver on some or all of these competing jobs. Developing solid project management skills will help you integrate these factors into your decision-making process.

At this stage, though, you may well be wondering what is meant by '**project management (skills)**'? In *Translation Project Management*, professional translator and academic Callum Walker explains that project management in general is about 'ensuring that [a project's] unique product, service, or result is achieved successfully and in accordance with the defined specifications' (Walker, 2023: 8). 'Effective project management', Walker continues, 'allows business objectives to be met (e.g. turning a profit), client expectations to be satisfied (which, in turn, generates business goodwill), problems and risks to be resolved in a timely manner, and failing projects to be recovered' (ibid.). Badly managed projects, on the other hand, can lead to 'deadlines being missed, project budgets being exceeded, quality issues, loss of reputation, and dissatisfied clients' (ibid.).

It is clear from all this that the consequences of mismanaging your translation projects could be dire! But what does it take to manage a project efficiently? According to the USA-based Project Management Institute (PMI), which is a professional association for project management, **managing a project successfully** requires project managers to (PMI, quoted in Walker, 2023: 9):

- identify [the] project requirements;
- address the various needs, concerns, and expectations of stakeholders;
- establish and maintain active communication with stakeholders;
- manag[e] resources;
- balanc[e] the competing project constraints.

In his book, Walker applies all of these requirements to the specific context of **translation services provision** in order to provide a 'comprehensive overview of the processes, principles and constraints of project management in the translation industry' (ibid.: xv). The book focuses on the management of translation services by dedicated **project managers** working at translation agencies (which he calls 'Language Service Providers', or 'LSPs' for short). This is because, Walker explains, most translation projects are outsourced to freelance translators via translation agencies in the new production models (ibid.: 7; see also Dunne, 2012: 144 and Chapter 3, 'No translator is an island: Setting up your support networks').

104 On the job

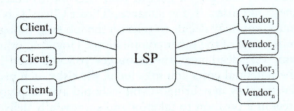

Figure 6.2 Outsourcing model (from Walker, 2023: 7)

Under the **outsourcing model** (Figure 6.2), clients send their translation projects to agencies (**LSPs**) where dedicated project managers select the relevant '**vendor(s)**'–another name for freelance translator(s) that comes from the fact they *sell* their services to translation agencies – from their database of freelancers to help deliver the projects. Project managers are responsible for managing the entire translation service *'from cradle to grave'* (Walker, 2023: 11; i.e. from start to finish) on behalf of the translation agency, which involves liaising with both clients and freelance translators. More often than not, project managers have to manage several projects concomitantly!

- Based on what you have just read, can you identify some of the key tasks a translation project manager will need to complete in order to deliver a translation service that can be seen as successful for all parties concerned (i.e. the client(s), the vendor(s) and the project manager's own agency)?

Using the definitions provided in the international industry standard ISO 17100:2015 'Translation Services – Requirements for Translation Services' as a starting point, Walker shows that the 'service itself is borne from the **translation workflow**' (Walker, 2023: 9). The industry standard ISO 17100:2015 helpfully breaks down this workflow into three distinct phases: **pre-production, production** and **post-production** (ibid.: 5). Using this as a starting point, as well as other sources, I propose the translation service workflow model (Table 6.1) that can be used as a quick checklist for translation project management.

Reading all of this, it could be tempting to believe that translation project management is something only project managers working at an agency or freelance translators working with direct clients need to worry about. Undeniably, professional translators working in-house at translation companies, commercial companies or at institutions such as the UN and the EU often do not have to take on as much of a project management role

Managing your translation projects 105

Table 6.1 Checklist for translation project management based on Gouadec (2007), Matis (2014) and Walker (2023)

	Check
I PRE-PRODUCTION PHASE	
Feasibility study	
• **What does the project consist of?** File type and format(s)? Language pair(s) and (specialised) domain(s)? Number of units? Are there repeated words? Is this repeat work for which you already have a translation memory? etc.	
• **What are the client's expectations?** Deadline? Expected quality level? Are these clear or do they need clarifying with the client? etc.	
• **Are the resources in place to deliver the project successfully?** Human resources (e.g. expertise & availability)? Technical and technological resources (e.g. specific CAT tool?) Provisional schedule? etc.	
Quote	
• **Produce a quote based on the above** that delivers for both the freelancer/LSP and the client?	
Launch	
• **Contracting phase:** sign client-LSP agreement or get a Purchase Order (PO); confirm agreed quality and confidentiality levels and agree payment terms with client.	
• **Organise the human resources:** translator(s) (if other than project manager) as well as revisers, proofreaders, terminologists or harmonisers. Plan who will do what, when, to make sure the project is delivered on time (e.g. project time chart).	
• **Set up the necessary linguistic and technological resources:** • Provide translator(s) (if other than project manager) with source texts and reference materials (e.g. parallel texts, glossaries, term bases, translation memories, style guides if available); • Provide translator(s) (if other than project manager) with access to required CAT tools and other required software; • Give translators (if other than project manager) instructions concerning referred language variety ('locale') etc.	
• **Ask client any outstanding questions** you may still have on the project that haven't been answered (implicitly or explicitly) yet (e.g. specific norms and/or expectations such as a style guide to follow)?	

(*Continued*)

106 *On the job*

Table 6.1 (Continued)

II PRODUCTION PHASE	
• **Manage quality assurance:** Ensure the project complies with what has been agreed with client during contracting phase (e.g. terminology, accuracy, style guides, formatting, Skopos etc.).	
• **Liaise with and coordinate the key stakeholders:** translator(s) if other than project manager, revisers, proofreaders, harmonisers, terminologists etc. Liaise between client and key stakeholders, too.	
• **Monitor the project** to make sure it stays within its initial scope. Additionally, monitor other potential risks that could be associated with the project.	
• **Release the project** to client after completing the appropriate final checks	
III POST-PRODUCTION PHASE	
• Ask for and deal with **client feedback.**	
• **Invoice** client based on agreed payment terms.	
• **Archive** project in line with legal obligations re record-keeping and data protection (applies to administrative documentation as well as task documentation).	
• **Post-mortem:** Reflect on the project. What went well? What didn't go so well and why? Lessons learnt?	

as part of their work. In many instances, most of their time is spent translating ('production phase') and some crucial aspects of translation project management mentioned in Table 6.1 are simply not part of their job description (e.g. quoting and contracting, managing resources, monitoring or invoicing). This notwithstanding, in-house translators can be involved in **feasibility studies** or in the **monitoring of translation projects.** Similarly, freelance translators selling their services to a translation agency do not have to worry about quoting end clients (as this is the job of the agencies' project managers). However, they will still need to undertake their own feasibility study to ascertain whether they are in a position to successfully deliver the project for their own clients (i.e., the translation agencies that hire them). They will also need to **invoice** the agencies. Regardless of their status and their role, all professional translators therefore have to manage

Managing your translation projects 107

key aspects of the translation service workflow in order to deliver their services successfully.

As an overwhelming majority of professional translators work on a freelance basis (see Chapter 2), the rest of this chapter will discuss project management from the perspective of freelance translators. Heavily inspired by Walker's *Translation Project Management*, it will look at key aspects of the translation service workflow that freelancers need to manage efficiently in order to deliver successful translation projects. What follows will no doubt be of particular interest to those of you who are thinking of working freelance. It will also be of interest to those of you considering a career in-house. This is because good translation project management is not just about contracting, monitoring or invoicing. As can be seen from Table 6.1, it is about making sure you as translator have the **resources** you will need to carry out your work effectively, too. Good translation project management is, therefore, *'crucial for [translators'] wellbeing and satisfaction'* (Mitchell-Schuitevoerder, 2020: 18; my emphasis). A key phase in terms of achieving this is before you even start working on the translation project itself, in the pre-production phase.

TOPICS FOR DISCUSSION AND ASSIGNMENTS 6.1

Have another look at Table 6.1, 'Checklist for translation project management.' With a course mate, identify, based on what you know so far, one concrete potential risk for each item on the list, and discuss what you could do as a professional translator to mitigate it.

For example: *Item 1: 'What does the project consist of?'*

- *Potential risk: I don't have the required expertise to deal with this project.*
- *Potential solution: I must make sure I see the project before I accept.*

6.2 Taking on new translation projects: Assessing and quoting

Let's start from the very beginning of the translation service workflow. Imagine that new translation project enquiries have just landed in your inbox (see Box 6.1). As a freelance translator, you will need to carry out what is known as a **feasibility study** for each of them before you take them any further. Should you decide to go ahead and quote a prospective client with a view to winning the commission, then the work you carry out for the feasibility study will form the basis of your **quote**. If the client is an agency and not a direct client, you may not need to quote them. Nevertheless, you should still carry out a feasibility study which, if need be, can form the basis of a (re) negotiation of the rate the agency is offering for the job.

108　*On the job*

6.2.1 *Assessing the feasibility of the project*

Under '4.2 Enquiry and feasibility', ISO 17100:2015 states that a translation service provider (TSP):

> shall analyse the client's enquiry in order to identify the client's specifications for the services and the TSP's capability to meet them, determining whether all the necessary human, technical, and technological resources are available. (International Organization for Standardization, 2015: 7)

Whether they provide ISO 17100-certified services or not, most translation agencies therefore ask their project managers to carry out a **feasibility study** for each new project enquiry. This is because feasibility studies are a crucial stage of the pre-production phase that will set the tone for the rest of the project. Should a translation service provider take on a new project without having all the information they need or the resources to deliver it successfully, then the project will likely soon enter troubled waters.

This applies to all translation service providers, including freelance translators! We have already seen how the question of whether to accept commissions without being confident you can deliver is a very real ethical dilemma ... Should the project fail, this could also cause you lasting reputational damage. One way to avoid this is by carrying out your own feasibility study for each new project enquiry, whether the enquiry comes from an agency or a direct client. Most freelance translators already do so, although they may just carry out a quick 'feasibility study' in their heads without ever formalising the process. They do so on automatic pilot by relying on instinct and/or experience. In some cases, this is enough. A **five-minute mental check** may be all you need before answering Client 1's enquiry with a quote, provided that (1) it is in a language pair and a domain where you have expertise and that (2) it doesn't clash with other work commitments (see Box 6.1).

Instinct, however, cannot always be trusted. What's more, if you are new to the job you will not have the experience you would need to deal with enquiries that are more complex. This is when completing a more 'formal' feasibility study for each new project enquiry you receive can help. Doing so will mean that you start each new project confident that everything is in place for you to deliver the translation service successfully. Your feasibility study needn't be as formal and/or thorough as the ones carried out by project managers at translation agencies. However, you should seek to answer the following **three core questions** as a minimum (see also 'Feasibility study' in Table 6.1).

Managing your translation projects 109

Question 1: What does the project consist of?

You may find the answer to this question rather obvious! As mentioned in Chapter 5, though, you should never take on a new job without knowing what it is you will have to translate. When you receive a project enquiry from a client, the first step is to carry out a brief **document review**. To do so, open all the files to find out what it is exactly the client wants you to translate. If the client hasn't attached any files to the email they sent you, ask them to do so and explain why you need them. If they answer they can't send them to you for confidentiality reasons, ask them to send you a sample and an estimate of the number of units to translate. Again, explain to them that you cannot provide them with a quote without seeing what you will have to translate first. You need to have access to the files or, at the very least, samples of the project in order to carry out the document review.

Once you have the files, you will need to ascertain the following:

- What is the project's **language pair**? More often than not, prospective clients will send you projects in a language pair you specialise in, but you never know… Misunderstandings happen, so you would do well to double-check before you take your feasibility study any further! You may also want to check which **variety** of the target language is required (e.g. French [Canada] or French [France]? English [Australia] or English [Singapore]?). This information may be explicit in the client's enquiry, especially if your client is a translation agency. With direct clients, though, you will often have to try and glean the information from the project enquiry;
- What is the **project type**? Is it a 'documentation', 'software', 'multimedia', or a 'website' project? (Matis, 2014: 11–21)? If is a 'documentation project', are the files in a format you can open (e.g. Word, PDF)? Will formatting be required? Are there illustrations and will the target text(s) need desktop publishing? Also known as **DTP**, desktop publishing is the 'redesign of a translated document using page layout software' (Terra Translations, 2019). This is a time-consuming activity that can require specific software (e.g. Adobe InDesign). This will have an impact on resources, project schedule and the quote;
- What is the project's (**specialised**) **domain(s)**? Do not assume there is just one domain per project. As Nancy Matis rightly points out, a project can cover several domains, such as 'a marketing brochure coupled with a produce license' (Matis, 2016);
- What is the **number of units** you will have to translate? For text-based translations, units are 'typically quantified based on the number of words (for alphabetic languages such as English) [or] characters (for character-based […] languages such as Chinese' (Walker, 2023: 27). For audiovisual translation, it is 'measured in reels (segments of audiovisual content lasting about twenty minutes) or simply in minutes' (ibid.). You will easily find this figure with Word documents. For PDFs, you may have to convert them

110   *On the job*

into Word documents in order to establish it. Alternatively, you can generate the word count by running the project through a **Computer-Assisted Translation (CAT) tool**. A CAT tool will also allow you to see if there are any repetitions in the document and/or matches with existing translation memories (if you have already translated a previous version of the document or if the client provides you with a translation memory attached to this project). This will inform both your project schedule and the quote (see Walker, 2023: 27–28).

Question 2: What are the client's expectations?

As we saw in Chapter 5, as a translator you will need to understand your clients' requirements, their objectives, and the purpose of their translation projects in order to deliver translations that work not just for them, but also for other potential stakeholders such as the target readers. Some key questions you should ask yourself here are:

- Does the client want the project delivered by a specific deadline?
- What quality level does the client expect from the project?

Agreeing on the **required and/or desirable quality level** for a given project can prove more difficult than agreeing on a deadline. It is not uncommon for freelance translators to receive project enquiries in emails such as the one below:

> *Madam/Sir,*
>
> *We need the attached translated into [XXX] by [XXX]. We would be very grateful if you could kindly provide us with a quotation for your services.*
>
> Regards,
> XXX

In order to ascertain the expected quality level, you will need to find out more about the **intended purpose** of the translation. Is the translation meant to be published, or will it be used for information purposes only? If the former, it will require a higher quality level. Similarly, remember that a project's domain(s) will have an impact on the required quality level, especially for '**prejudicial texts**' where 'an incorrect translation is likely to cause severe, irreparable or hardly reparable physical, moral, financial or material prejudice' (Barabé, 2021: 173; see also Chapter 5).

The expected and required **quality level** is an important issue. The higher the quality level, the more expensive it will be for you to deliver the project.

Managing your translation projects 111

Indeed, this will have an impact on the resources you will need to complete the project, the provisional project schedule and, consequently, the quote. As we know, though, some translation buyers are not familiar with the concept of quality level in translation. If you can't make out the expected quality level from the project enquiry, you should **educate** the prospective client about the importance of agreeing a certain quality level. Explain to them that this will be based on the intended purpose of the translation project as well as its domain(s), and ask them any outstanding questions you may have on this (see Durban, 2011; see also Chapter 5). We will discuss how to manage the agreed quality level, which is central to the production phase of the translation service workflow, in greater detail in Chapter 7.

Question 3: Do I have the resources I need to deliver the project successfully?

Once you have a clearer idea of what the proposed translation project involves, and what your client's expectations are, then you need to ask yourself whether you have the **human and technological resources** you will need to deliver it successfully. Of course, not having access to some of the resources you have identified does not automatically mean you should turn a project down. You may find that some of them are desirable, but not essential to the success of a project. Alternatively, you may be in a position to secure access to them before the project starts, should the client accept your quote. However, you can only do so if you have first clearly identified both the human and the technological resources you will need to deliver the project.

Let's start with **human resources**. As a freelance translator, you are your own main resource! The first thing to ask yourself is, therefore, whether you have the **expertise** (language pair(s), domain(s), expected quality level) required for the project. If not, could you refer the client to a fellow freelance translator with the right expertise who is part of your trusted network of colleagues? If you are happy you have the required expertise, you still have to look at your **availability**. This will be determined by both the client's deadline and other, competing work commitments you may already have. In other words, do you have the capacity to take on a new project at this specific point in time?

In order to find out, do a quick **provisional schedule** based on the number of units that need translating and the other services the project might involve (e.g. revision, DTP etc.). To do so, you will need to develop a good sense of what your **daily throughput** is, that is, the number of words or characters you can translate or revise in a day. The average figures often used in the translation industry are around 2,500 words a day for the translation of 'standard texts' and 7,500 for a 'simple revision' (Matis, 2014: 83). However, as Walker points out, a translator's throughput 'will be dependent on a number of [other] factors, such as the language pair, file type, domain, and individual idiosyncrasies (i.e. some [freelance translators] simply work faster or slower

112 *On the job*

than others)' (2023: 28). It will also depend on your experience as a freelance translator (see Chapter 2) and on whether you will use a CAT tool with an existing translation memory and/or machine translation input for the project or not. This is something we will discuss in more detail in Chapter 7.

Let's take the example of 'Agency 1' in Box 6.1. Your prospective client, the agency, would like you to deliver a 15,000-word translation within the next two weeks. Supposing you receive this request on a Monday morning and that the project is due by the Friday of the following week, this leaves you with 10 working days to complete the job (although this will vary depending on where you are based). Supposing, too, that your throughput as a starting translator is 2,000 words a day, then you will need 7.5 days (15,000 ÷ 2,000) to complete the job. However, you may want to add a 10% margin for the **imponderables** of life. This give you a total of just over eight working days overall. Based on this figure alone, you have the capacity to accept the job. However, what if you were already working on another project that will take another three working days to complete? Of course, as a freelancer you could always decide to work seven days a week in order to complete both projects by the agreed deadlines. Bear in mind, though, that if repeated this may prove detrimental to both your physical and mental health. It could, ultimately, have a negative impact on the quality of your work, lead to burnout and make your position as freelance translator unsustainable (see Chapter 9).

An alternative if you don't have the capacity to complete an entire project by yourself by a given deadline could be, once again, to call on your **trusted network** of fellow translators (i.e. other 'human resources'). In a blog post called 'Debunking the Myths about Freelance Translators', Canadian translator Natalie Pavey explains:

> [I]n the case of short turnaround times, many freelance translators call on their colleagues when they are not available so that they can accommodate their clients' needs. In those cases, the lead translator has their finger on the pulse of the project and is aware of all potential issues. (Pavey, 2020)

Of course, you will first need to check that your colleagues are available … and willing! You will also need to let your client know that you are planning to outsource part of the project to trusted fellow freelancers. Finally, you will need to factor in a **harmonisation phase** in the provisional project schedule to make sure that the target texts produced by different translators are consistent with one another (Walker, 2023: 30). However, working collaboratively with other freelancers will allow you to accommodate more urgent and/or more complex – and potentially more rewarding – projects.

What about the **technological resources** you will need to deliver the project? Let's start from the principle that, as a freelance translator, you are equipped with a personal computer, word-processing software such as Microsoft Word or Open Office and reliable Internet access (see Chapter 2). Most direct clients will let you decide which CAT tool to use, if any. If your

Managing your translation projects 113

client is an agency that requires you to use a specific CAT tool, translation memories, termbases or other specific software, then the project manager will usually make sure you are given access to what you need for the duration of the project. If in doubt, though, do double-check with them that it will indeed be the case.

If, however, you are working with a direct client, you will need to make sure you have all the software you need to deliver the project. Imagine, for instance, that you identify the need for specific DTP software as part of your feasibility study. Such software can represent a significant outlay. The main factor behind such an investment should be whether you expect a **return on investment**. This could be based on the size of the project. You could decide, for instance, that direct client 2's project enquiry in Box 6.1 justifies such an investment. Another reason would be that you expect a quick return on investment through future commissions (e.g. you specialise in the translation of marketing materials). In any case, it would be wise to wait for the client to accept the quote before purchasing the software. What's more, should the required initial outlay not be viable for your business, you should seriously consider not pursuing this any further.

TOPICS FOR DISCUSSION AND ASSIGNMENTS 6.2

Ask your instructor to send you a relatively long and complex project enquiry or use the case study on the Translation Studies portal. This will act as your new project enquiry.

Now, imagine that you work as a freelance translator. Select two projects from the list of six project enquiries contained in Box 6.1. These will represent the two projects you have already committed to by the time you receive the new project enquiry.

Prepare a short presentation based on the feasibility study you have carried out for the new enquiry.

6.2.2 *Quoting clients*

Once you are satisfied you have the information and resources you will need to deliver a project successfully, you can start working on a **quotation** based on your findings for the feasibility study. Unsurprisingly, price will be front and centre of your quote. The price you quote has to be right for both you and your client. You will calculate it based on the number of units contained in the project for each of the services you have identified during the feasibility study as necessary for the successful delivery of the project (e.g. translation, revision, DTP etc.).

One of the key questions is how much you can and/or should charge per unit for your translation work. As a freelance translator, you operate in a largely unregulated market in which you compete with other freelancers. Put

114　*On the job*

simply, what you charge will be partly determined by what your clients are willing to pay for the service. This **market rate** is determined by the law of supply and demand. The greater the demand for the translation service you offer, the rarer the supply (i.e. the number of freelance translators in a position to offer this service), and the higher the price! Concretely, this means the greatest factors will be the **language pair(s)** you work with and the **project domain** (Walker, 2023: 131–135). Bear in mind, though, that working with a rare(r) language pair does not mean you can charge a higher unit price if there is little-to-no demand for it where you work. Conversely, working in a common language pair can still lead to a higher price per unit if demand is strong. As for the project domain, having the expertise to provide your translation services in a niche domain that is in high demand will justify a higher unit price. Indeed, according to a recent survey of (mostly) European translators, '[f]reelance translators who narrowly specialise (1–2 areas) charge on average 29% more than those who [...] have no specialist areas' (Inbox Translation, 2021). 'Topics for discussion and assignments 4.1' can help you develop an initial feel for the language pairs and domains currently in demand in the translation industry where you are or where you would like work (see Chapter 4).

Your professional networks can also help you form a better understanding of where the market is for your language pair(s) as well as for specific domains and **other services** besides translation (see Chapter 3). Many professional associations and virtual communities of practice such as ProZ.com or TranslatorsCafé share valuable guidance on current market rates with their members. This is a great starting point, but always assess the relevance of the guidance for your own context when working out your quotes. First, make sure that the advised rates are relevant to the geographical zone where you are based. The translation market may well have become global, but the cost of living continues to vary widely from one country to the next (see Walker, 2023: 136). Your rates should therefore also take into account your own 'overheads' (work-related expenses) such as the cost of your Internet subscription, software and CAT tool(s), or even heating bills if you live in a cold country, for example. You need to be able to pay the rent!

Furthermore, each project is unique and other factors should influence what you charge. The required quality level and the urgency of the project are chief among them. As illustrated by Figure 6.3, **quality**, **time** and **cost** are all interdependent constraints in a project:

If your client requests a **higher quality level**, the project will take longer to complete and costs will go up. You may need, for instance, to outsource quality assurance steps to fellow freelancers (e.g. revision, review and proofreading; see Chapter 7 for a definition of these). This will have an impact on cost; what you charge the client for these services will need to include the fee you will pay fellow translators as well as a reasonable margin for you as de facto 'project manager'. It will also have an impact on time; your project schedule will need to reflect these extra steps of the workflow.

Figure 6.3 Martin Barnes' project management triangle

If your client's request is **urgent**, this will have an impact either on quality or on cost. The client and you may agree on a lower quality level in order to speed up the delivery of the project. If this is not an option, then costs will increase as you call on fellow freelance translators to create extra capacity (as discussed earlier on).

If your client has a set budget for the project, then **costs** will have to be kept down. This can be achieved either by agreeing on a lower quality level (if suitable) or by extending the project deadline.

To sum up, it is perfectly justifiable to quote – or negotiate, if your client is a translation agency – **above standard market rates** for translation projects that are in language pairs or domains that are in demand. Your price will also depend on the agreed quality level, and you should add/negotiate a premium to your quote for urgent work (i.e. tight deadlines).

Understandably, you may worry that doing so will lose you some business. However, you should remember that 'clients enquiring about translations (and related services) are in the market to buy' (Walker, 2023: 141). Clients sending you a project enquiry will already have identified a – sometimes pressing – **need** for translation services; they may find it too time-consuming to ask for and compare multiple quotes (ibid.). Finnish scholar Nina Havumetsä's study of the expectations clients have of commercial translators confirms that cost is not the main criterion for many direct clients; it comes behind translators' ability to deliver the job quickly, their language skills and their experience (2012: 125; see Chapter 5). Similarly, we know from Olohan and Davitti's study that trust is the main factor for project managers at translation agencies when they select freelance translators for new projects (2017: 399–400; see Chapter 5). Obviously, most agencies will have a **predetermined unit price ceiling** for freelancers based on the required language pair and the project domain. This does not mean, however, that you can't (re)negotiate it … especially if you are one of their trusted freelancers!

116   *On the job*

Finally, another factor that could have an impact on your quote is whether you will use a **CAT tool** for the project. In *Translation Project Management*, Walker points out that:

> The main selling point of CAT tools is that they can recycle previously translated segments that are either identical or similar to the segment currently being translated. The theoretical benefit of this is that it saves the translator time (as well as improving consistency); but anything that saves time should also, in theory, save money. As such, it is very common in the translation industry to pay vendors less (and, in turn, charge clients less) for repetitions and higher fuzzy matches (a contentious issue for many vendors [...]. (2023: 37)

If your client is a translation agency, then the project manager dealing with the project will likely run the project documents through a CAT tool, send you a breakdown of the number of **repetitions** and **matches** as identified by the CAT tool and offer you a **reduced unit price** for these. If they give you access to an existing translation memory as part of the project, then there will likely be a greater number of high-level matches in the new project. This, in turn, will make your work on the new project much quicker.

The translation industry is yet to come up with a standardised way of charging for repetitions and (high-level) matches when translating with a CAT tool. This means that each agency will have its own policy on the reduced rate they apply (if any) for repetitions and matches. However, it also means this may be open to **negotiation**. Similarly, as a freelance translator you will have to decide whether you should offer your direct clients a reduced rate for repetitions and high-level matches when using a CAT tool. Your decision should be informed by what is standard practice in your own context, as well as what you believe is right for you and your business. In any case, remember that, at the very least, you will have to check that the repetitions and high-level matches are appropriate in the specific context in which they are used (both at sentence and text level) and that they fully correspond to your client's requirements. This may, therefore, command a unit price not dissimilar to what you would charge for a **revision job**.

Once you have calculated the price for your services for a specific project enquiry – not forgetting to quote for all the '**nonstandard components**', that is, the components besides translating that will be necessary for successful completion of the project such as, for instance, revision and DTP (Matis, 2014: 65)–then you can proceed to write up your **quote**. As expectations around what exactly a quote should include vary from one country to the next, there would be little point in giving you detailed guidance on this here. As a minimum, though, your quote should 'indicat[e] [...] **price and delivery details such as language pair(s), delivery date, format, and medium**' (International Organization for Standardization, 2015: 7; my emphasis). It is always wise to err on the side of caution, which is why you may also want

Managing your translation projects   117

to include the **payment terms** and how long the quote is valid for. Be careful with **currencies**, too. As a professional translator, you will often work across borders. You should therefore make sure you state clearly which currency the quote is denominated in. A good way to avoid ambiguities is to specify both the **currency symbol** (₹) and the **currency code** (INR) in your quote. As for what else your quote should include, you could find it helpful to use your professional networks to see examples of fellow freelancers' quotes for their translation services for the country/-ies where you work.

Remember that, in the face of stiff competition, you will want your quotes to stand out from the crowd! One way to do this is to see them as an important document in your longer-term communication strategy that aims to establish **trust** with your clients (see Chapter 5). As well as their obvious informative function, quotes also have an **operative function** to play; they will aim to convince prospective clients that you are the right person to deal with their projects. A good way to achieve this is by detailing – and, if necessary, explaining – the breakdown of the different elements that make up your final price so your client understands how you came to the final figure (see Walker, 2023: 39–40). Doing so will indicate to your client that, as a professional translator, you understand exactly what is needed for successful delivery of the project. Just as importantly, though, it will also make it clear to them that you didn't pluck the figure out of thin air! Another good way to do is making sure that you quotes are formatted professionally, look clean and tidy, and have a brand image that is consistent with the other client-facing documents you draw up (e.g. invoices, email signature, website etc.). In other words, you should see your quotes as an important part of your **marketing strategy** (see Chapter 8).

Last but not least, what if your client is an agency? Chances are you will not need to quote them. More often than not, agencies will tell you the rate they are willing to offer in the project enquiry, alongside instructions on how to invoice them once you have completed the work. However, you can always decide to see their offered rate as an **opening gambit** ... especially if they need a project delivered urgently and/or if you know you offer a rare-but-in-demand language pair or specialist domain. Should this be the case, then use what we have covered in 6.2 as the basis for an informed rate negotiation with the agency's project manager. Just like with direct clients, don't price yourself out of the market ... but don't sell yourself short either!

TOPICS FOR DISCUSSION AND ASSIGNMENTS 6.3

Activity 6.1 Take the same project enquiry you used for 'Topics for discussion and assignments 6.2' as a starting point. Imagine that, as a freelance translator, you are happy that you have all the information and resources you need to carry out the project and that the enquiry comes from a direct client. Use what you have read in section 6.3.2 'Quoting clients' to prepare a

118   *On the job*

quote for your client. Compare, contrast and discuss your quotes with your course mates.

Activity 6.2 Get into pairs. One of you plays the role of the direct client and the other plays the role of the freelance translator. You will use the quotation prepared by the student playing the role of the freelance translator as the basis for the conversation. The client will pretend that they find the quoted price too expensive and/or that they want the project delivered sooner. The translator negotiates with the client. After five to ten minutes, swap roles. When you are finished, take five minutes to answer the following questions from the perspective of the freelance translator:

- How did negotiating your quote with the client make you feel? Why do you think that is?
- How often did you draw on your feasibility study and the guidance you found on current market rates and so on in your negotiation with the client? How effective did you find it to be? What else could you have used to negotiate with them?

6.3 Launching, monitoring and closing projects

So far, the main emphasis of this chapter has been on just the first two steps of the pre-production phase; the feasibility study and quoting clients. This is because getting these right makes managing the other phases of your translation projects a lot easier. What are the next steps, though, for you as a freelance translator-cum-project manager once a client has accepted your quote? In what follows, we will briefly discuss what it takes to launch and close your translation projects in a way that helps you manage them more efficiently and, therefore, more successfully.

6.3.1 *Final tasks before launching a new project*

Once a client has accepted your quote, you should formalise the agreement between you and the client with what can be called a '**project agreement**':

> Typically, the [project agreement] will take a form similar to the quotation […] and will stipulate precisely the same terms and conditions set out in the quotation: the names, addresses, and contact details of the client and [you as service provider], project reference numbers, delivery date(s), total fee (and currency), etc. (Walker, 2023: 41)

This is an important part of the **contracting phase**, which should seek to clarify your own **legal obligations** as well as your client's. The project

Managing your translation projects 119

agreement should thus mention the agreed quality level for the project and whether you are expected to follow specific rules regarding confidentiality (e.g., if you have to destroy some or all of the project data after completion) (ibid.: 43). Rather importantly, it should also stipulate the payment terms for the project. Bear in mind that what can be considered as a legally valid agreement will depend on the legislation of the country where you are based. As a rule of thumb, though, you should hold off starting work on a new project until some form of agreement between you and your client has been signed off (or confirmed in writing, albeit in an email) or, at the very least, until your client has raised a purchase order for your services (see Chapter 5).

Once you are happy with the contracting phase, you can start **organising the resources** you will need to complete the project successfully, as identified in the pre-production feasibility study (see Table 6.1). Let's first consider the **human resources** needed for the project. Often, this will seem very straightforward as you will be the only person working on the project. This being said, you still need to have a concrete idea of how long each step of the project workflow will take so you can meet the contractual deadline. Similarly, if the project involves fellow freelancers as co-translators or revisers, you will need to make sure everyone knows when exactly they will be expected to complete their part of the project. This is why it is important to finalise the project schedule based on the different steps needed in the production workflow and with the project's deadline firmly in mind.

Before launching the project, it is also helpful to identify who, in both your professional and personal support networks, you might be able to turn to for advice as '**informants**'. Informants can be source-language informants or target-language domain-specialist informants. They don't necessarily help you in an official capacity on the project; they are the people you know you can turn to if, after having exhausted every other avenue, you find yourself stuck with specific aspects of that project. Source-language informants can therefore advise you on your interpretation of a source-language term. Target-language domain-specialist informants, on the other hand, will advise you on the suitability of a target-language term you have selected in a given context. Your informant could be, for instance, an air-conditioning engineer whom you know, and who will advise you on the suitability of specific terms for the translation of the assembly instructions of your client's latest air-conditioning system.

In parallel to this, you will also need to organise the **linguistic resources** required for the project. If you use a CAT tool and your client has provided you with an existing **translation memory** and/or a **termbase**, you will need to integrate them into the project. This may involve converting them to a suitable file format. It could be that the client has provided you with a **glossary** (e.g. as an Excel spreadsheet) instead; you will have to convert it into a termbase for your CAT tool. What if you haven't been provided with

120   *On the job*

a glossary (or a termbase)? In such a case, it is helpful to try and identify suitable **parallel texts** in order to create your own (whether you use a CAT tool or not!). There are different types of parallel texts that can help you. Ideally, you will find translated texts published by your client on the same or a similar topic (on their website etc.). These texts will allow you to identify their preferred terms for specific concepts. However, make sure you review them and that you find the proposed translations appropriate for the project you are working on. If you work with a CAT tool, you may decide to spend some time using your CAT tool's **alignment function** to align source-text segments to matching target-text segments. It can be time-consuming, but this will allow you to create a relevant translation memory for the new project. The length of the project will be a key factor in deciding whether this is a worthwhile undertaking. If you can't find such existing translations, then you should try and identify texts on the same or a similar topic that were originally written in the target language. These will allow you to identify the most commonly used terms for your project's key concepts that you can then feed into your glossary. Finally, make sure you review your client's **style guide** if they gave you one and that you know which **target-language variety** they expect you to use. If, after an initial review of the linguistic resources, you still feel you are missing some resources and/or information that you need to complete the project successfully, then you should get in touch with your client to ask them for the missing documents or information. Remember, though, that you should only do so once you have carefully double-checked all the information and documents sent by the client (Matis, 2017; see Chapter 5).

TOPICS FOR DISCUSSION AND ASSIGNMENTS 6.4

Activity 6.3 Spend some time searching the Internet to find out what translation project agreements tend to look like and contain in the country where you'd like to work as a translator. Some professional associations have some advice on this on their websites and/or discussion forums. You may also find guidance on this in translators' blogs, but make sure you check the validity of the claims they make.

- What is considered as a legally valid agreement? Are formal agreements usually signed or do less formal agreements prevail?

Activity 6.4 Imagine you are a freelance translator and that your client has accepted the quote you gave them in 'Topics for discussion and assignments 6.2'. Identify who, in your personal and professional networks, could act as informants for this project.

Managing your translation projects 121

6.3.2 Monitoring your projects

All pre-production jobs done! Congratulations, you are ready to launch your new project. As you enter the '**production phase**' (see Table 6.1), you will need to continue 'addressing the various needs, concerns, and expectations of stakeholders' (PMI, quoted in Walker, 2023: 9). You will do so by ensuring that the quality of the project complies with what you have agreed with your client during the contracting phase. In order to give **quality management** all the attention it deserves, we will cover this crucial phase of the translation service workflow separately in Chapter 7.

According to the Project Management Institute, another key requirement of successful project management is to 'maintai[n] active communication with stakeholders' during the production phase' (ibid.). As translator-cum-project manager, you will therefore need to develop an effective **communication strategy** that will inform not only how you communicate with your clients (whether a direct client or a translation agency's project manager), but also how you liaise with and coordinate all the other fellow freelance translators who may be involved in the delivery of the project during the production phase. Please have another look at Chapter 5 if you feel you need a refresher on this.

This leaves us with one final important aspect of project management for us to consider during the production phase: 'balancing the competing project constraints' (ibid.). This is best achieved by monitoring the project to make sure it stays within its initial **scope** during the production phase (see Table 6.1). The notion of scope in project management is very closely linked to that of quality. Indeed, as highlighted by Walker:

> scope and quality cannot be fully disentangled [...]. [S]cope refers more to deciding *what* needs to be done and how, while quality refers more to how to evaluate the output (and, indirectly, the process undertaken to achieve the defined quality standard). **Scope management**, therefore, concerns developing an understanding of the items that need to be produced and the tasks to be carried out, the quantity and varieties needed of a particular product or service [...], and how all of these considerations are linked to questions of time and resources. (2023: 145–146)

As you can see from the above definition, the scope of your translation project (or, in other words, the 'commission') should have been carefully negotiated with your client in the pre-production phase of the project. However, it sometimes happens that the scope of the project changes during the production phase. This is what PMI calls '**scope creep**', that is, the 'uncontrolled expansion to product or project scope without adjustments to time, cost and resources' (PMI, quoted in Walker, 2023: 150).

There are two main reasons behind scope creep in translation projects. The first one is that your clients decide to **move the goalposts** only once

122 *On the job*

you have launched the project. This happens, for example, when clients add 'just a few documents' to the project without adjusting the deadline (or the quoted price), when they ask you halfway through a project to use a different termbase (again, without adjusting the deadline) or when they decide they want you to produce target texts at a higher quality level than what had been agreed, for example. These changes are often caused by the fact that your client doesn't really fully understand what it takes to deliver a translation service; this can often be resolved by integrating a pedagogical dimension into your communication strategy with clients (see Chapter 5). In any case, you will need to explain to them that any changes to one of the three constraints of the project management triangle – quality, time or cost (see Figure 6.3)–will inevitably have a knock-on effect on the other two constraints and should, therefore, lead you to **renegotiate** (aspects of) the commission.

The other main reason behind scope creep can be us as translation service providers. Sometimes, we are eager to please our client by **going the extra mile** for them. We decide, for instance, to provide complementary services such as carrying out extra quality assurance checks, revising or updating a client's glossary, providing free DTP work, and so on. Of course, there is nothing intrinsically wrong with this. As we have already established, freelance translators compete with each other in an unregulated market and it can therefore be tempting – or even necessary?–to go above and beyond in order to stand out from the crowd. However, this clashes with the concept of effective scope management, which is about 'avoiding undertaking any tasks that are not explicitly asked for or included in the project brief by the client' (Walker, 2023: 154). Ultimately, it will be up to you to decide how to balance (positive) client retention with (negative) scope creep. This is something you will therefore need to review carefully for each new project. One way to do so is by asking yourself the following questions:

- Is providing free services an effective client-retention strategy in my specific work context? What about this specific project? Will it add value to the project for my client?
- How much is it going to cost me? Is it sustainable for me and my business medium-to-long term?

If, after answering these two questions, you decide to go ahead and do it, don't assume that your clients will necessarily notice that you provided free services. In fact, most won't! A good way to draw their attention to that fact is to include these services in your final invoice followed by 'free of charge'.

Managing your translation projects 123

6.3.3 *Delivering and closing projects*

In her description of the 'Main Steps of a Translation Project', Nancy Matis warns us that:

> Delivering a translation project is not always merely a matter of sending a file via email. You might also have to run a last check before delivery, double-check that all instructions have been followed, use a special media for delivering the project, rename the target files, send to people other than the initial requestor, etc. Moreover, the delivery of the target files does not necessarily mean that the project is fully finished. The client might send some feedback, a post-mortem could be requested, or, after a while, some archiving might become essential. Invoicing and profit calculation will also be part of this last step. (Matis, 2016)

Once you have completed the production phase of the project, the first thing to do is, therefore, to undertake some final checks before returning the project to the client. This is what ISO 17100:2015 calls '**Final verification and release**' (International Organization for Standardization, 2015: 11). These final checks aren't particularly time-consuming, but they are important in that they will help you make sure you don't accidentally send the wrong files or omit something that could dent your reputation with the client. Walker provides a very helpful **checklist** that can help to ensure your project meets all the agreed specifications before you release it. Please note that, depending on the nature of the project, only some of the questions below may apply (see Walker, 2023: 76–78):

- Are all the required files present?
- Are the files to be delivered all in the target language (so you don't end up accidentally returning source-text files to the client)?
- Are the files to be delivered in their final 'deliverable' form (i.e. ready for the client to use)?
- Have all the required quality assurance steps been carried out?
- Are the files compliant with the project specifications (e.g. adherence to style guides or terminology lists)?
- Which files need to be delivered (i.e. do you need to return provided translation memories, termbases or glossaries)?
- Has the client specified a particular naming convention for files?
- Does the client require a specific delivery mode?

Once you have carried out these final checks, you can deliver the project to your client. You should then seek **feedback** from them. We have already discussed how to deal with client feedback in Chapter 5. However, I would like to stress the importance of *actively* seeking and handling your

124 *On the job*

clients' feedback as freelance translators. Dropping your clients an email or, depending on their preferred communication style, picking up the phone to ask them whether they are happy with your work (after giving them some time to review the project) should form part of an overall communication strategy whereby you aim to establish trust between you and clients. Let your clients know that you value their feedback and that, wherever possible, you will act on it to make sure that you fully deliver the service they expect from you. Ultimately, handling feedback well could mean not losing your clients to the competition. More selfishly, though, another reason for actively seeking client feedback is that it will likely benefit your own **professional development** as a translator. Even though some of your clients' feedback will be very project specific (e.g. use of terminology, format etc.), some of it may relate to your management of aspects of the translation service (e.g. time management, communication with client etc.). Such feedback can be a very valuable way to find out what you can improve (further) in your management of the translation service you provide, and thus benefit your work on future projects.

If, after seeking – and dealing with – your client's feedback, you are satisfied that they are happy with the service you have delivered, you can **invoice** them for your work. A lot of the information in your invoice will be similar to the one contained in your quote. However, scope creep might meant that it needs updating to reflect the exact nature of the service you have provided to your client. Just as for quotes, the content of invoices varies from one country to the next. You should note, too, that in some countries it is a **legal requirement** to include some key information in your invoice. Again, you should use your professional support networks to find out what exactly must appear in your invoice, as well as the other pieces of information freelance translators customarily include, for your own work context (see Chapter 3 for support networks and Walker, 2023: 95–97 for invoices).

Finally, you can start completing what ISO 17100:15 calls the '**closing administration**':

> *The TSP shall have a process in place to ensure full project archiving for an appropriate period and to meet all legal and/or contractual obligations regarding the preservation or deletion of records and data protection.* (International Organization for Standardization, 2015: 11)

This draws our attention to an important element of translation project management: What do you do with all the data generated by a project upon completion? As we saw in Chapter 5, data confidentiality and, therefore, **data management and archiving,** is something we need to take seriously as service providers.

First, though, it is important to have a clear understanding of the kind of data translation projects generate. Walker helpfully distinguishes between

Managing your translation projects 125

'administrative documentation' and 'task documentation' (2023: 99). A translation project's **administrative documentation** is made up of the 'files relating to the management of the project in broad terms (including agreements, financial documentation such as purchase orders and invoices, and general project records)' (ibid.: 98). It also includes email threads with clients and payment receipts. In some countries, it is a legal requirement to keep some of this data for a certain period of time for accountability or regulatory purposes (ibid.: 99). Similarly, you may want to keep hold of some of this data if you expect repeat business from your client. However, it remains your responsibility to store it safely and to dispose of it when it is no longer needed (see Chapter 5).

The same applies to the project's **task documentation**, which consists of 'files related to the translation itself (including the source and target files, as well as other linguistic resources such as style guides, [translation memories], glossaries, etc.)' (ibid.: 98). Again, there can be good reasons to want to hold on to these files for a while after completion of the project. It may, for instance, be wise to retain all versions of the source-text files and target-text files up to six months after completion, in case it takes your client a few months to identify issues with aspects of the project (ibid.: 99). Past that point, you may only want to keep the final versions if there is no confidentiality clause stopping you from doing so. What about the reference files and the style guides provided by clients? These are only worth keeping if you can foresee some repeat business with your client. Similarly, you may ask yourself which versions of a project's translation memories, termbases and glossaries you want to keep (if any), provided you are allowed to keep them. In any case, you will need to come up with a curated filing system that allows you to safely manage and store all the data generated by your projects.

Sifting through past projects' files can be an opportunity for you to reflect on the lessons learnt from past projects. This is what is known as a '**post-mortem**' in project management speak. During a project's post-mortem, you look back and reflect on what went well and what didn't go so well in all three phases – pre-production, production and post-production – of the translation service (see Matis, 2014: 206 and Walker, 2023: 106). A project's post-mortem should therefore be based on your client's feedback, but not only that. It should also include the feedback you have received from other relevant stakeholders, too (e.g. a project manager's if your client was an agency, or fellow translators involved in the project delivery). Crucially, though, it should also include your own thoughts and reflections on the project. In order to help you formalise these, you could complete a very brief '**Start, Stop, Continue**' exercise after each project (see Box 6.2).

126   *On the job*

Box 6.2 Start, Stop, Continue Exercise

This reflective exercise should take less than 20 minutes, and it will help you generate lists of action points that should help you further improve how you manage future translation projects. Use Table 6.1 as a starting point.

- **START:** Based on the feedback you have received, and your own evaluation of the success of the translation project, is there anything you did not do in your management of the translation service workflow that you should do next time?
- **STOP:** Based on the feedback you have received, and your own evaluation of the success of the translation project, is there anything you did in your management of the translation service workflow you feel you should not do in future projects because it didn't add any value?
- **CONTINUE:** Based on the feedback you have received, and your own evaluation of the success of the translation project, do you feel you managed specific areas of the translation service particularly well? What made what you did so effective? Could this be reinforced and/or adopted to other areas of the translation service workflow?

You can complete this exercise as an in-house translator, too. Admittedly, implementing changes is rarely as straightforward in a corporate environment. Depending on your position and/or the culture of the company, you may not feel in a position to volunteer your thoughts on ways to improve the quality of the translation service the company delivers. However, some companies have systems in place to capture such feedback. This may also be the opportunity for you to gradually play a more active part in the management of your company's translation service provision. Whatever your status as a translator, becoming a **reflective practitioner** will ensure you continue to grow as a professional translator (see Chapter 9).

TOPICS FOR DISCUSSION AND ASSIGNMENTS 6.5

If you have taken part in a simulated translation project as part of your course, or if you have already worked professionally on the delivery of a translation project outside your course, review your management of the translation service by completing the 'Start, Stop, Continue Exercise' in Box 6.2.

Managing your translation projects 127

Further reading

Published as part of the same Routledge Introductions to Translation and Interpreting series as this textbook, Walker (2023) gives an excellent overview of translation project management in the translation industry in its chapter 1. For those wanting to find out more about this topic, you can also read chapters 2–4 of Walker. Finally, Walker's chapter 7 on scope and scope creep is an excellent introduction to some of the issues discussed in the following chapter of this book (Chapter 7).

Also published as part of this Routledge Introductions to Translation and Interpreting series, Rothwell et al. (2023) offers accessible step-by-step guidance on how to choose suitable tools for translation projects. Chapter 1 will introduce you to the principles of CAT tools. Read chapter 4 for a very helpful introduction to terminology management in CAT tools.

Chapter 1 in Mitchell-Schuitervoerder (2020) offers an excellent step-by-step overview of the translation project management workflow and the CAT tools that are used in the process.

7 Managing translation quality

> **Key questions we will explore in this chapter:**
>
> - What are the different competing definitions of translation quality? Concretely, how can they help me manage quality on my translation projects?
> - How can I determine, and manage, the right level of translation quality for each new translation project?
> - What is the impact of translation tools and technology on translation quality and how I manage it?

Talking about translation quality can be a bit daunting … not least because, as pointed out by Belgian scholar Ilse Depraetere, this is undoubtedly the single most important issue in translation. Indeed, according to her, '[t]here are three issues that are important when it comes to translation: quality, quality and quality' (Depraetere, 2011: 1). For decades now, academics in translation studies have therefore been obsessively trying to **define and measure translation quality**. And yet, they are still to agree on what makes a 'good' translation. Across the divide, in industry, most translation service providers try to stand out from the crowd by – ironically – all making the same repeated claim that they deliver 'quality translations'. But what does this mean? Can the quality of a translation be guaranteed, measured and evidenced, or is there a more subjective side to it?

As many pages have already been written on the topic, our objective will not be to come up with the ultimate definition of translation quality but, instead, to explore what is commonly meant by translation quality, especially in industry. Taking a pragmatic stance, we will focus primarily on translation quality assurance (QA) over translation quality assessment although, as we will see through our definition of quality in this chapter, the former inevitably involves aspects of the latter. We will look at what we can do, as professional translators, to ensure we produce translations that meet our clients' **quality expectations**. This is, of course, something we already started discussing in

DOI: 10.4324/9781003220442-9

Managing translation quality 129

Chapter 6. If you take another quick look at Table 6.1 'Checklist for translation project management', you will soon notice that quite a few of the steps professional translators should take to manage their projects aim to guarantee the quality of the translations they deliver to clients. Examples of this can be found in the pre-production phase (e.g. understanding client expectations; setting up resources), the production phase (e.g. ensuring compliance with what was agreed in the contracting phase; monitoring the project) and the post-production phase alike (e.g. dealing with feedback; reflecting on the project).

As we have already discussed the QA steps of the pre-production and the post-production phases in Chapters 5 and 6, the present chapter will home in on **QA in the production phase**. It will help you form a better understanding of the measures you can put in place to make sure that you manage the quality of your translation work appropriately and effectively during that phase. As many professional translators now use computer-assisted translation (CAT) tools and machine translation (MT) to produce their translation work, we will also discuss the interplay between these tools and technologies and translation quality.

7.1 What do we mean by translation quality?

7.1.1 *Defining translation quality: From* good *to* good enough

Before we start, please take a couple of minutes to try and answer the following question:

> • How would you define translation quality?

Not easy, right? Even if you have a fairly good idea of what translation quality means to you, it is likely that your conception of translation quality will not be shared by everyone on your course ... And even if you all agree on what translation quality means and looks like on your course, you will likely find that local translation service providers have a very *different understanding* of this concept. This is because, to quote Depraetere again:

> Be it in the context of translation training or in a business context, irrespective of whether we are dealing with human translation or machine translation, we continually struggle to get a grip on the concept of 'quality' and search for an adequate methodology to gauge and improve the quality of the translation output. (2011: 1)

In an article called 'Translation Quality Assessment Demystified', Iranian academic Behrouz Karoubi agrees with Depraetere that we first need to 'get

130 On the job

a grip' on the concept of quality before we can attempt to define translation quality. To him, 'there is little to be gained in a discussion of quality if it is not clarified what is meant by the term' (2016: 257). In an attempt to do so, Karoubi therefore borrows a categorisation of the different possible conceptualisations of quality found in the field of education (see Harvey and Green, 1993) to see how these definitions can help us make better sense of the different **conceptions of quality in translation** (see Table 7.1). As you will see from Table 7.1, there is a notable difference in the way academics and industry professionals think about quality in translation.

On the one hand, **translation scholars** have, until relatively recently, mostly defined translation quality as meaning exceptional. Focusing largely on translation (often, literary translation) as an end product, the key question their research into translation quality has long sought to address is: *'How do we know a translation is good?'* (House, 2001: 2; my emphasis). A reason for this could be that, as part of their job, most academics are routinely required to assess the quality of their students' translation work in a way that is seen to be as objective as possible. This has led them to develop – at times, complex – models of translation quality assessment. One of the best known among them is undoubtedly the one developed by German academic Juliane House (see House, 1977).

However, **industry professionals** have rarely – if ever – adopted the translation quality assessment models that have emerged from academic research. This is something Joanna Drugan observed while carrying out empirical research for her book *Quality in Professional Translation*: 'During hundreds of interviews and research visits to LSPs for this book, not a single academic model was mentioned as a way of assessing translation quality in the real world' (2013: 36). This is because professional translators tend to prefer more pragmatic definitions of translation quality such as 'perfection (or consistency)', 'value for money' or 'fitness for purpose'. Put simply, the question industry professionals are most interested in is not 'How do we know a translation is good?' but, rather: *'How do we know a translation is good enough?'* (ibid.: 43; my emphasis).

In the translation industry, quality is no longer an absolute or, in other words, a set of (impossibly high) standards that a translation as end product must conform to. Instead, translation quality is primarily seen as a *process* that is functionally defined by the purpose of the translation, that may need to conform to particular specifications and that should remain as cost-effective as possible, within the limits of Martin Barnes' (1988) project management triangle (see Chapter 6). For professional translators, quality is therefore something that can be 'improved and achieved efficiently and consistently at all stages of the process' by putting the appropriate QA procedures in place (ibid.: 70). Following these should, in turn, help guarantee the quality of the translation as end product.

Table 7.1 Harvey and Green's categorisation of the different conceptualisations of quality and their application(s) in the field of translation based on Karoubi (2016: 258–261)

Conceptualisation of quality	Application(s) in the field of translation
1. Quality as exceptional	1. **Exceptional as in 'special' (elitist view):** This definition of quality as distinctive and inaccessible can be found in the translation studies approaches that emphasise 'untranslatability and the impossibility of achieving the quality of the original […] in translation', for example the translation of holy books such as the Koran, or the Bible in the Middle Ages (Karoubi, 2016: 258). 2. **Exceptional as in 'conforming to high standards':** In this variant, the different components of quality are defined but they are still seen as almost unachievable. In translation studies, this variant can be found in 'the prevalent conception of quality in the early linguistic theories of translation such as Catford's (1965) and Nida & Taber's (1974), in which achievement of the full equivalence of some sort is set at the ultimate standard for making a judgement about the quality of a translation' (ibid.). 3. **Exceptional as in 'passing a set of required standards':** In this variant, excellent is understood as 'passing a set of quality checks that, unlike high standards, are based on attainable criteria'. In translation studies, this definition of quality as exceptional can be found, for instance, in Juliane House's translation quality assessment model (ibid.: 259).
2. Quality as perfection (or consistency)	With this definition, quality means **conforming to particular specifications** instead of (high) standards. Quality, here, is no longer defined as 'something special and hard to achieve' (as was the case with the conceptualisation of quality as exceptional). It is, instead, 'something that everybody can achieve depending on how the specification is defined' (ibid.). Industry standards such as ISO 17100:2015 'Translation Services – Requirements for Translation Services', which are 'a set of expectations the fulfilment of which could certainly have a positive impact on the quality of translation' (ibid.), reflect this conceptualisation of quality as perfection (or consistency).
3. Quality as value for money	Here, quality is viewed from the perspective of the translation buyer, for whom 'the satisfaction of his requirements at an affordable price is the most important factor' (ibid.). Quality is therefore defined as the **cost-effectiveness** of the translation service. As observed by Karoubi, 'this extremely market-oriented interpretation of quality has not been paid so much attention in academic discussions, probably because it reduces translation just to a commodity that is offered for sale' (ibid.).
4. Quality as fitness for purpose	In this conceptualisation of quality, quality is 'defined functionally in terms of the extent to which the object of assessment fits its purpose' (ibid.: 260). In the context of translation, you will likely recognise this pragmatic definition of quality as fitness for purpose from the **functionalist approach** to translation. Please have another look at '3.1. Translators in the age of networks' in Chapter 3 if you need a refresher on this.

132   *On the job*

7.1.2 *Benchmarking translation quality: Industry standards*

As a translation student, handing in translation assignments in which you conformed to one of the three definitions of quality as 'exceptional' may have been the way to achieve the top marks (see Table 7.1). In some ways, becoming a professional translator can therefore involve learning to rid yourself of some of the **perfectionist tendencies** that served you so well during your studies. Quality can sometimes compete with cost or time. As we saw in Chapter 6, it would be unsustainable for you as a professional translator to aim to produce exceptional translations all the time ... unless you catered exclusively for a niche translation market where rates reflected the fact that top quality was an essential requirement. And even if you did cater for such a market, you would do well to adopt the definition of quality as 'perfection (or consistency)' over the more academic view of 'quality as exceptional'. This is because this conception of translation, in which quality is something you can achieve by conforming to particular specifications, can offer you more pragmatic means of controlling key quality factors throughout the production process and, as a result of this, guarantee the quality of your translation service to clients.

As we have already seen in previous chapters, **industry standards** represent such an attempt to benchmark quality. They do so by setting specifications that, if followed, should have a positive impact on the quality of the service provided. In the translation industry, ISO 17100:2015 'Translation Services – Requirements for Translation Services' is a good example of this. First published in 2015, ISO 17100:2015 contains specifications for the entire translation service from cradle to grave, and not just the translation phase. For instance, as the professional competence of the people carrying out a translation service will affect the quality of the translation as end product, ISO 17100:2015 contains specifications about the professional competences of translators (and their qualifications), as well as those of revisers and reviewers (see International Organization for Standardization, 2015: 5–7; see also Chapter 1). Similarly, the international standard contains specifications on aspects of the pre-production phase ('4.2 Enquiry and feasibility', '4.4 Client–TSP agreement', '4.6 Project preparation'; ibid.: 7–8) and of the post-production phase ('6.1 Feedback'; ibid.: 11) that are seen as crucial in order to guarantee the quality of translation projects. We have already discussed all these as part of Chapter 6, which looked at translation project management. In what follows, we will focus on part 5 of the standard, '**Production process**' which details the QA steps to take during the translation phase in order to be ISO 17100-certified.

As you will see from Figure 7.1, the ISO 17100:2015 translation process requires up to **five QA steps** to be taken after the first step of the phase, translation itself, so as to manage quality during the production phase. They are as follows:

Managing translation quality   133

Figure 7.1 ISO 17100:2015 translation process

1. **Translation:** Although not a full QA step, translation already forms part of the QA process, as the translator must make sure they produce a target text that complies with 'the purpose of the translation project, including the linguistic conventions of the target language and the relevant project specifications' (International Organization for Standardization, 2015: 10). This is something we discussed in Chapter 6;
2. **Check:** This is the first, *compulsory* QA step of the production phase. Also called 'self-revision', this task is carried out by the translator themselves, who checks the produced target text for 'possible semantic, grammatical and spelling issues, and for omissions and errors, as well as ensuring compliance with any relevant translation project specifications' (ibid.: 10);
3. **Revision:** This second *compulsory* QA step is essential for all ISO 17100:2015-certified translation projects. Revision is the bilingual examination of the target text by somebody other than the translator – often a fellow translator – against the source to make sure it is free of errors and suitable for its intended purpose (ibid.: 10). This step must be carried out by someone 'with translation and/or revision experience in the domain under consideration' (ibid.: 6);
4. **Review:** This is the first *optional* QA step to take place after revision, as it only needs to take place if it was included in the project specification (i.e. it was specifically asked for by the client or, alternatively, is something that is required given the text's purpose and domain). Review is the monolingual examination of the target text by a domain specialist (who is not necessarily a translator or a reviser). Its purpose is to 'asses[s] domain accuracy and respect for the relevant text-type conventions' (ibid.: 10);
5. **Proofreading:** This is the *second* optional QA step after revision. According to the ISO standard, proofreading is about checking for 'defects' in the target text (ibid.: 10). A helpful way to look at this QA step is, therefore, to think of it as 'a final stage of checks often focusing on very technical (and sometimes visual) issues in the TL content' such as, for instance, 'punctuation marks', 'dates formats', 'adherence to style guide', 'pagination', 'layout and appearance' and so on (Walker, 2023: 74). This step should take place after the desktop publishing (DTP) phase if required;
6. **Final verification and release:** This compulsory last QA step can be seen as a last final check before returning the project to the client. Again, this should take place after DTP (see '6.3.3 Delivering and closing projects' in Chapter 6).

134　*On the job*

Even though there is no obligation for translation service providers to adhere to ISO 17100:2015 and, consequently, to follow all its compulsory and/or optional QA steps, being ISO 17100-certified can be a way for them to demonstrate that they meet widely recognised, high-quality professional standards. In any case, the ISO 17100:2015 translation process is a useful way for us professional translators to think about the QA steps we may need to integrate into our workflow in order to meet our client's quality requirements.

This, in turn, leads us to an important point. One of the requirements for all ISO-certified translations is that the target text be revised by somebody who is not the translator. As we know from Chapter 6, however, completing this QA step will necessarily drive up the cost of a translation project. Depending on the intended function of the target text(s), this may not be needed, or be what the client wants ... which is a problem for us translators as service providers (see Chapter 5). Indeed, according to seasoned professional translator Geoffrey Samuelsson-Brown: 'The only true benchmark if you are translating for a living is whether you provide what your client wants' (1996: 134). This, in fact, partly echoes the wording of the international standard ISO 8402:1995 'Quality management and quality assurance', which defines quality as 'the totality of characteristics of an entity that bear on its ability to satisfy stated and implied needs' (International Organization for Standardization, 1995: 5). However, it is interesting to note that, unlike in Samuelsson-Brown's quote, in ISO 8402:1995 the **'needs'** to be satisfied to achieve quality are not necessarily limited to the client's (although, admittedly, they play an important part), and they **can be implied**. In any case, though, ISO 8402:1995 tells us that following the QA specifications found in ISO 17100:2015 blindly for all new translation projects – or, for that matter, in other relevant industry standards – is not the way to achieve quality. This is because translation quality, here, is understood as 'fitness for purpose'.

TOPICS FOR DISCUSSION AND ASSIGNMENTS 7.1

In 2021, Austrian academic Madeleine Schnierer identified 18 (inter)national industry standards relevant to German and Austrian translation service providers besides ISO 17100:2015 (see Schnierer, 2021: 111–113):

- **11 international standards:** for example, ISO 2384:1977, 'Documentation – Presentation of translations'; ISO 704:2009, 'Terminology work – Principles and methods'; ISO 26162:2016, 'System for the management of terminology knowledge and content'; ISO 18587:2017, 'Translation services – Post-editing of machine-translation output' and so on.
- **7 national (German and Austrian) standards:** for example ÖNORM D 1210:2004, 'Requirements for technical communication and documentation services'; ÖNORM D 1201:2009, 'Translation services – Translation

Managing translation quality 135

contracts'; DIN 16511:1966, 'Correction marks'; DIN 2340:2009 'Short forms for terms and names' etc.

Activity 7.1 What about your own situation? Browse the Internet to identify all the national and/or industry standards relevant for translation service provision in general, and quality management in particular, in the country or countries where you would like to work as a professional translator.

Activity 7.2 When you are done, prepare a short presentation in which you explain which standard(s) will be most relevant to you as a translator in your desired professional context. Say how it/they will influence the way you manage translation quality throughout the production process, and why.

7.2 Ensuring the right quality level in your translation projects

7.2.1 What is the right quality level?

Those in academia and in industry who continue to define quality as exceptional tend to believe that translation quality defined as '**fitness for purpose**' is shorthand for lower quality. However, one could argue that this is based on a misunderstanding of what is meant by quality as fitness for purpose. The conceptualisation of quality as fitness for purpose simply means that the required and/or desirable quality level of new translation projects – and, therefore, the QA steps you will put in place – should be assessed based on the target text's intended purpose. In other words, the produced target text should be good *enough* to serve its intended purpose. What it is does not mean, though, is that everything should be translated on the cheap, with few-to-no QA steps, in order to save time or money. In fact, in some cases, producing a target text that is 'good enough' to serve its purpose can still require a very high level of quality assurance.

Should a client, for instance, want you to translate a patient information leaflet for a new drug, then the translation process will need to follow all five post-translation QA steps of the ISO 17100:2015 translation process to be deemed fit for purpose (whether the translation is ISO 17100-certifed or not). This is because, with such a text, there is an implied need to be accurate and accessible to a wide readership (including, potentially, members of the general public with reading difficulties etc.). Not ensuring the highest level of QA could therefore result in translation errors that, in turn, could endanger the lives of the drug's users. This could be seen as an abdication of our social responsibility as translators and, therefore, as **unethical** (Lambert, 2023: 139–141). From a legal point of view, we could also be held **liable** for any prejudice caused by a translation error. There are times where it is just not worth scrimping on quality.

Conversely, though, one could argue that applying all five post-translation QA steps blindly when your client has no intention of publishing the target

136   *On the job*

text(s), and when the domain means that errors aren't likely to cause prejudice, will unnecessarily extend the time it takes to deliver the project as well as inflate the price. This, over time, is likely to lose you clients who might prefer cheaper, quicker or, in other words, more 'fit-for-purpose' alternatives.

In this functionalist approach, the translation brief should therefore contain information – whether implicitly or explicitly – that allows you to infer the **right quality level** for a project based on the intended purpose (or function) of the target text. Yet, we know that translation buyers are not always clear about what translating involves and that, regularly, translation briefs contain little-to-no information that can allow us translators to infer what the appropriate quality level might be. On other occasions, translation buyers can be under the misguided impression that a translation project can be carried out to a lower quality standard than we, as professional translators, are comfortable with. All this can lead to what Samuelsson-Brown has called '**quality gaps**' between the quality level our client expects and what we as translators understand that they want, or between the quality level they want and what we feel is required (2010: 42). In such instances, it is our role as professional translators to advise our client(s) on the right quality level, or to (re)negotiate it. Please have another look at Chapters 5 and 6 for more guidance on this.

7.2.2 *The right QA steps for the right quality level*

Once you and your client have agreed on the right quality level for a project, you will need to put in place **appropriate and commensurate** QA steps to deliver it. Surprisingly, though, a recent large-scale survey of largely freelance translators found that a staggering 35% of them had no QA processes in place whatsoever to manage the quality of their work (Doherty et al., 2018: 101). Considering that errors in translation can cost you both your reputation and business, this is a very expensive mistake to make!

As we know, the question of the right quality level for the texts of a given project – and, therefore, which post-translation QA steps you will put in place – is largely determined by two key factors: their **intended purpose** and whether they can be seen as 'prejudicial texts' or not. As a quick reminder, prejudicial texts are texts for which 'an incorrect translation is likely to cause severe, irreparable or hardly reparable physical, moral, financial or material prejudice' (see Barabé, 2021; see also Chapter 5). A text's domain is what makes it a prejudicial text or not. What follows is a proposed list of common applications for translations and the QA steps they are likely to involve. While it is based on Samuelsson-Brown's categorisation (2010: 106–112), this list also takes into consideration whether we are dealing with (non-)perishable and prejudicial texts:

- **Translating part of a text information ('abstracting')**: This is the case when, for instance, a company considers taking over a foreign company and wants to know all the relevant or essential financial data about the

Managing translation quality 137

target of the takeover bid under a time constraint. Your client may ask you to scan through the financial documentation and 'pick out all the information of importance' (ibid.: 106). In such an instance, quality is 'being able to extract the information that is of real use to the client' (ibid.). A careful check and final verification should be enough in such an instance;

- **Translating a complete text for information:** This is what is required for most translations produced for information purposes. In such a case, style does not matter as much as for translations for publication. When translating for information, a simple QA check and final verification may suffice ... This being said, you may need to consider revision as an extra QA step for prejudicial texts, even if you are translating for information only. Indeed, 'major decisions may be made on the basis of the information you provide in your translation' (ibid.: 108). As a result, you may be held liable for any prejudice caused by a translation error. A more pragmatic way around this is to agree with your client that revision is not necessary, but add a disclaimer explaining that all due care has been taken to produce an error-free translation and that you cannot be held liable for any outstanding errors. In a similar vein, Samuelsson-Brown suggests that, should you translate a legal text for information purposes, you add a statement at the end of your work along the following lines (even if it has been revised): 'Although due care and attention has been given to this translation, it should not be considered a legal document and the original language document takes precedence over this translation in any dispute concerning interpretation' (ibid.: 112);
- **Translating a text for publication:** This is when the translation is meant to be published, whether it be for a restricted or a wide audience. Usually, translating texts for publication will require more post-translation QA steps than translating for information. This is because a translation that doesn't conform to the target-readers' stylistic expectations for a certain text type could damage your client's reputation (e.g. scientific texts) and/or hurt their bottom line (e.g. marketing texts or tourist texts). The number of post-translation QA steps you decide to implement when translating for publication will thus be based on both the text domain and the intended target audience (e.g. large audience vs restricted audience; lay audience vs expert audience etc.). Another useful dimension to take into consideration here is whether the texts you are translating are 'perishable' or 'non-perishable' (Doherty et al., 2018: 100). **Perishable texts** are 'texts for immediate consumption with little or very little purpose thereafter' such as online travel reviews or social media posts (ibid.). These texts often do not require extensive QA evaluation. **Non-perishable texts,** on the other hand, are 'typically careful texts' that are 'crafted so as to possess aesthetic value and/or to clearly convey important, often durable messages' and that require, therefore, robust QA procedures (ibid.). Prime examples of non-perishable texts are literary and marketing texts. Finally, prejudicial texts translated for publication will also require high levels of QA.

138 *On the job*

In legal texts, for instance, '[t]he position of a comma could change the verdict!' (Samuelsson-Brown, 2010: 111). This means that, just like some non-perishable texts, prejudicial texts translated for publication will likely require all post-translation QA steps to be taken during the production phase (i.e. check, revision, review, proofreading and final verification before release).

Even though this list can help you choose which post-translation QA steps to implement to achieve the right quality level, it leaves you with quite a bit of room for interpretation. This is because each translation project is different. In fact, within the same translation project you may find that not all documents can or should be translated at the same quality level and that, therefore, some specific documents may require extra QA steps. If you work in-house, you will have to follow the quality assurance procedures in place at your workplace. As a freelance translator working with direct clients, though, you will be the judge of what are the right amount of QA checks for each new project. In most instances, it will be a matter of deciding whether revision – which is sometimes called 'other-revision' (Jakobsen, 2019: 69)–is necessary to achieve the right quality level.

TOPICS FOR DISCUSSION AND ASSIGNMENTS 7.2

Imagine you are a freelance translator and that your client has accepted the quote you gave them in 'Topics for discussion and assignments 6.2' (see Chapter 6). Based on the above, discuss with a course mate what the agreed quality level is for this project and the QA steps you will put in place to manage it throughout the production phase.

7.2.3 A few words on revision ...

Apart from checking – or, in other words, 'self-revising'–your work and the final verifications before release (which should both come as standard), **revision** is undoubtedly the most common post-translation QA check of the production phase. If, as a freelance translator, you have identified revision as a necessary QA step for a new project, then you will have to hire a fellow freelance translator with the right language pair as a reviser for the project (which is why professional networks are so important; see Chapter 3). Similarly, whether you work freelance or in-house, you will likely be asked to revise the work of fellow translators as part of your job as a professional translator. It is therefore important that you have a clear understanding of what revision is about.

Echoing what we discussed at the beginning of this chapter, Brian Mossop (2019: 9) makes the point in *Editing and Revising for Translators* that: 'The concept of quality under which revisers work may vary from country to

Managing translation quality 139

country, or from language pair to language pair'. The logical consequence of this is that, just like there is no universal agreement on what translation quality is about, there is *no universal understanding of what the role of reviser entails*. Concretely, what does this mean for you as a professional translator? First of all, always make sure you know exactly what is expected when you are asked to revise a document. Conversely, communicate clearly to colleagues what you expect them to do if you hire them as revisers. In both cases, the specification of the role of reviser in ISO 17100:2015 can act as a starting point. According to the international standard, a reviser shall:

> examine the TL content against the SL content for any errors and other issues, and its suitability for purpose. [...] As agreed upon with the project manager, the reviser shall either correct any errors found in the target language content or recommend the corrections to be implemented by the translator. (International Organization for Standardization, 2015: 10–11)

Based on this, in order to act as a reviser you will therefore need to:

* **Be given a 'revision kit'** that includes the source text(s), the relevant resources (e.g. terminology, style guides etc.) and the self-revised version of the target text(s) (see Gouadec, 2007: 78);
* **Know what the purpose of the text is.** It is important for the reviser to know the purpose of the text(s), as this will influence what the reviser chooses to focus on. Depending on a text's purpose, accuracy may either be extremely important (e.g. published legal text) or not (in-house employee newsletter of a multilingual company);
* **Know who has final responsibility for the revisions.** The person in charge of the translation project 'must provide clear instructions to the reviser as to how [...] corrections are to take place and who will have responsibility for approving and/or implementing them' (Walker, 2023: 70).

Provided these conditions have been met, you can start checking the quality of the target text(s) paying particular attention to (see Mossop, 2019: 137):

* Transfer issues (accuracy; completeness);
* Content issues (logic; facts);
* Language and style issues (suitability for text type and end users; terminology; idiom; linguistic correctness; compliance with style guides);
* Presentation issues (layout; typography; organisation).

Please note, however, that your role as reviser is to 'find [and fix] problems', but not to 'make changes' for the sake of it (ibid.: 116). Indeed, a real danger for revisers is that of '**over-revising**' by making corrections based on their own preferences when, in fact, the quality of the original target text would have been good enough (see Nitzke and Gros, 2021). There are

140   *On the job*

two main issues with this. First, making unnecessary changes is 'costly in terms of time and consequently money' (ibid.: 22). Second, it does nothing good for interpersonal relationships. Remember that you will be asked to revise the work of colleagues, who are professional translators just like you ... To avoid unnecessarily changing their work, Mossop therefore advises you to think of yourself as a *reader* – and not a writer – when you revise a text and to always ask yourself '*Can I justify this change?*' (e.g. dictionary meaning, client instructions etc.) before making any changes (Mossop, 2019: 201).

TOPICS FOR DISCUSSION AND ASSIGNMENTS 7.3

Pair up with a course mate who shares the same language pair as you; you will revise each other's work. Each of you will send the other a short (~200–300 word) translation project you have carried out for one of your practical translation classes. Please note that this should be your own work, not the version that integrates your tutor's feedback. Once you have revised each other's work, and you have had time to read each other's revisions, arrange to meet up to have a 30-minute conversation in which you reflect on the revision process. Use the following questions as prompts:

As a reviser:

- Do you feel you were given all the information and documentation you needed to revise effectively? If not, what do you feel might have been missing?
- How easy did you feel it was to make a distinction between 'objective errors' and preferential changes? Why (not)?
- Looking back, what do you feel you might do differently next time in order to be more efficient as a reviser?

As a translator/revisee:

- Do you feel you set your expectations clearly to the reviser? If not, what do you feel might have been missing?
- How do you feel about the suggested changes? Are there instances where you think some of the changes might be more preferential than purely objective? Do you agree with all of them? Why (not)?
- How do you feel about the way the reviser made/indicated the changes? In other words, do you feel the way the reviser went about

Managing translation quality 141

> revising the document (e.g. gave positive feedback as well as negative feedback or just negative feedback; their level of politeness etc.) might have influenced the way you felt about the whole revision process in this instance?

For both:

> • Based on this experience, what would you say is needed for revision to be both efficient and constructive?

7.3 Translation tools and technology and quality management

If you work as a freelance translator, part of your role as project manager will be to make sure you have both the necessary human and technological resources in place to manage quality for each new project (see Chapter 6). If, for instance, revision is a required QA step to achieve the right quality level, then you must make sure that you can call on a fellow freelance translator to complete this step. Similarly, it is your role to assess which **tools and technology** to use to deliver on the agreed quality level for a given project. In what follows, we will briefly discuss how translation tools and technology can help you with QA, as well as the new processes they create and some of the challenges they may pose.

7.3.1 Computer-assisted translation (CAT) and QA

In the last couple of decades, CAT software such as Trados Studio, MemoQ, Phrase TMS, Déjà Vu, Wordfast, Smartcat and so on 'has grown from relatively simple tools that often worked alongside a text editor such as Microsoft Word, to become feature rich (and often inexpensive), networked environments within which translation jobs can be managed, carried out utilising a range of different inputs, and checked' (Rothwell et al., 2023: 6).

As can be seen in Figure 7.2, when you upload a translation project into CAT software, it slices up the source text(s) into segments. Unlike MT (machine translation) engines, though, CAT tools won't carry out the translation work for you. What they do, though, is make your work as a translator arguably easier by bringing together essential **quality assurance resources**:

> CAT leaves all the linguistic and cultural decisions in the hand of the translator, but exploits [...] key strengths of the computer to prompt them with useful information [...]. Computers are better than people at storing, comparing, searching for, and accurately recalling items from potentially huge

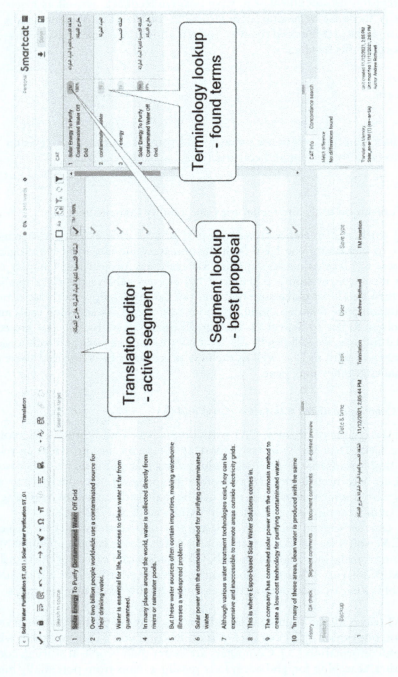

Figure 7.2 Online CAT interface (Smartcat) from Rothwell et al. (2023: 21)

Managing translation quality   143

volumes of data, and it is above all these qualities, applied to linguistic resources created during previous translation assignments, that CAT was developed to exploit. Assuming suitable **legacy translation** data is available, a CAT tool will typically present you with sentences of the source text (ST) for translation one at a time (segments), automatically looking up each word in a customised glossary or termbase and simultaneously checking a different data resources, usually a translation memory (TM), to see if the sentence, or sentences similar to it, has been translated before. (ibid.: 11–12)

As a translator, it remains your job to type in the corresponding translations in the target segments with the help of additional resources designed to make the process quicker while increasing consistency. The decision of which resources to use, however, is up to you and will largely depend on what you are trying to achieve for a given project.

Translation memories (TMs), for instance, are a core feature of CAT software that can help you manage quality on your translation projects. TMs are databases of stored translation units made up of legacy source-text segments and their corresponding target-text segments saved from previous translation work. TMs thus allow you to recall your own past work or that of fellow translators at any time. When you open an existing translation memory in a new project, the CAT software will scan the TM's stored translation units to find legacy source segments that match the new project's source-text segments. Whenever it finds a match, it retrieves the whole translation unit from the TM (i.e. the legacy source segment as well as its corresponding target segment). It then suggests the target segment to you as a possible translation alongside a match score that indicates how similar to the new source segment it believes the retrieved legacy source segment to be. Put simply, the match score 'shows the translator where the legacy translation needs to be adapted to the new context' (Rothwell et al., 2023: 36). All you need to do, then, is review the proposed segment to make sure that it works in its new translation context; your role here is similar to the role of a **reviser**.

Alongside TMs, **termbases (TBs)** are another core feature of CAT tools for quality management. TBs are multilingual electronic glossaries about domain-specific concepts and the terms used to designate them. When you add a TB to a translation project, the CAT software scans it for existing terms. Whenever it recognises terminology from the TB, it indicates the found term(s) to you as translator. Provided the information has been entered into the TB, it can also indicate your client's preferred terms and/or the terms that you should be using. Just like a TM, a TB can be updated live as you work on a given translation project.

Undoubtedly, both TBs and TMs can help professional translators manage consistency more efficiently, which is an important aspect of quality management for most projects. As you can imagine, these two features will be all

144 *On the job*

the more important on larger, collaborative projects where it may be hard to maintain consistency across translators otherwise. This is why both are routinely used by in-house translators working at big institutions such as the European Union or the United Nations. Besides TMs and TBs, CAT software also includes a number of other features that can help you with quality management during the translation phase:

- **Placeable tags**: The CAT software identifies 'non-translatables, such as numbers, proper names, URLs, email addresses' and, for each of them, 'present[s] the translator with a list of placeables from which the correct one can be inserted' in the target-text segment (Rothwell et al., 2023: 18). As the translator doesn't have to retype these in the target segment, there is a reduced risk of errors (typos etc.);
- **Localisable tags**: a type of placeable that ensures the target text matches local conventions, for example, 'dates (French DD.MM.YYYY becomes MM.DD.YYYY in US English but remains as DD/MM/YYYY in UK English) and decimal separators (e.g. English 1,999.75 is written 1 999,75 in French and 1.999,75 in German)' (ibid.);
- **Quality assurance function**: Designed to support the translator with QA checks, this function can be used at any time (either while you are translating or once you have finished). It is an error spotter that will draw your attention to any perceived anomalies: 'QA checks that your numbers are correct, that you have not typed two spaces, that you have used your client's preferred terminology in a custom TB, that you have been consistent, that you did not miss or misplace tags' (Mitchell-Schuitevoerder, 2020: 95). It will also check for identical source/target segments, missing target segments (no translation) and so on. QA can thus make the process of carrying out the two QA steps required of all translation jobs (i.e. 'check' and 'final verification') much quicker and more efficient. This is why many language service providers (LSPs) 'make it a requirement to perform a QA check before delivering the target file' (ibid.). However, it cannot ensure the linguistic or cultural appropriateness of the target text. This is why you have the final say as translator: '[I]f the warning error is inappropriate, you can tick an ignore box' (ibid.).

CAT tools can therefore facilitate the management of the agreed quality level on your translation projects not just while you are translating (e.g. terminology management with TMs and TBs), but also during the ensuing **QA steps** (e.g. 'check' and 'final verification'). Should this QA step be required, CAT can also facilitate 'revision' by allowing the reviser to revise the texts in the same digital work environment as the translator, thereby giving them access to all the necessary resources and eliminating the need for multiple file versions (see Rothwell et al., 2023: 23–25).

Given how widely accessible it has become, and how it can help manage quality more efficiently on translation projects, it is hardly surprising that

Managing translation quality 145

an increasing number of professional translators now use CAT software to complete their translation projects. A 2020 worldwide survey of translation professionals, for instance, found that 66% of respondents used CAT tools for most of their projects (Pielmeier and O'Mara, 2020: 42). Similarly, a recent European survey showed that the number of respondents reporting that they never used CAT tools had fallen from 23 to just 12% between 2017 and 2022 (ELIS Research, 2022: 23). According to the survey organisers, this can be interpreted as a sign that 'CAT technology is slowly but surely [being] implemented in all use cases, including those for which the technology used to be considered less useful' (ibid.).

Yet, it remains important to assess the usefulness of CAT tools for new translation projects on a case-by-case basis. In some cases, the time it will take you to set up the right parameters in your CAT tool, create a new TM using an alignment tool (if you don't have access to an existing, relevant TM) or convert a glossary into a TB may just not be worth your while for relatively short documents. Besides, you should also consider that using a CAT tool can create *new challenges* with regard to translation quality itself. As mentioned earlier, translators working with CAT software translate in segments instead of full sentences and paragraphs. This, in turn, can have a negative impact on the overall cohesion of the produced target text. Indeed, one can easily lose oversight of the whole text when translating in segments. This is something we all need to keep in mind when using CAT technology. Depending on what you are trying to achieve, there are times, therefore, where it may be easier – and quicker – to work directly in a word processor for shorter texts.

TOPICS FOR DISCUSSION AND ASSIGNMENTS 7.4

Imagine you are a freelance translator and that your client has accepted the quote you gave them in 'Topics for discussion and assignments 6.2' (see Chapter 6). Consider the following questions to discuss the advantages and disadvantages of using a CAT tool for this project (see Rothwell et al., 2023: 30–31):

- Will using CAT technology help you manage the agreed quality level more efficiently on this project? (see 'Topics for discussion and assignments 7.4' for the agreed quality level)
- Based on what we covered in Chapter 6, could there be other benefits to using a CAT tool for your management of the translation project overall besides quality management during the production phase?
- Do you think that the benefits of using CAT technology (e.g. increased production speed, more efficient quality management etc.)

146   *On the job*

> will outweigh the additional cognitive demands using the technology will make on you as a professional translator?
> • Do you know who will own the resources created by the CAT tool upon completion of the project (e.g. TM, TB)?

7.3.2 *Machine translation (MT) and QA*

Unlike CAT software, **machine translation (MT)** engines 'attemp[t] to produce a complete draft translation automatically' (Bowker, 2023: 92). Even though this form of technology first emerged after the Second World War, it only started becoming more popular in the mid-2000s when Google Translate made it accessible to everyone with the launch of its first free online tool (ibid.: 93). In *De-Mystifying Translation*, Canadian academic Lynne Bowker shows that the popularity of machine translation has since grown exponentially, especially with the adoption of **neural machine translation (NMT)** from the mid-2010s. NMT, she explains, is:

> a data-driven approach to machine translation that uses an artificial intelligence technique known as machine learning. [This] requires that an extremely large sample of texts and their human translations be provided to the MT system as training material. In the case of NMT, the tool contains an artificial neural network that consults this training corpus and, based on the patterns identified in the training data, learns how to translate new texts. Although the translations produced by NMT systems are not perfect, they are usually of much higher quality than texts produced by [previous MT systems]. (ibid.: 96)

Despite these improvements, and the fact that an NMT system learns continuously, the quality of the output of an NMT tool can only be, in reality, as good – or as poor – as the quality of its training material. This is what is known as the **'GIGO effect'** (Garbage In, Garbage Out), which makes some translators wary of machine translation (Drugan, 2013: 31). Google Translate, which is undoubtedly one of the most popular free NMT engines at the time of writing, is a good example of this; it uses all the existing translations it can find on the Internet as training material, regardless of their actual quality. This also explains why some NMT engines are better for some language pairs than others, as this is also based on the availability (or not) of electronic texts that can be used to train the NMT system (Pym, 2020: 441). Another criterion that will affect the quality of MT output is the 'relative standardization' of the texts that need translation; 'highly technical texts with fixed terminologies and a limited repertoire of verbal relations' for instance, tend to perform better (ibid.). To remedy this, some major translation services, such as the European Commission's Directorate-General for Translation (DGT), have started developing their own **bespoke MT systems** ('eTranslation' in DGT's case) that they train on their own, curated and domain-specific data in the language pairs that they need. As they are trained on more limited data, however, some of these bespoke NMT systems are sometimes found not to be as effective as open models such as Google Translate or DeepL. What's more, the quality of the system's raw output cannot be fully guaranteed, as NMT cannot fully take a translation project's context, its purpose or even the source text(s)' implicit information into consideration.

These limitations notwithstanding, there is no denying that the quality of NMT has continued to improve for the last ten years. This certainly helps to explain why, over the last decade or so, MT has been 'increasingly **integrated into CAT environments** [...] where the human translator is presented with translation proposals from (human-produced) translation memory matches, together with MT outputs' (O'Hagan, 2020: 3; my emphasis). More and more, whether you use a CAT tool or not, part of your job as a professional translator will therefore be to 'post-edit' the raw output of MT to guarantee its quality or, in other words, to make sure that it is 'fit for purpose'. The language industry describes this as the 'human-in-the-loop'–or, more flatteringly, 'expert-in-the-loop'–model, whereby translation tools are combined with human intelligence with the aim of increasing quality, productivity and job satisfaction.

The jury is still out on whether these aims are always achieved, as some professional translators worry about the impact of these changes on their own **agency** and on the **quality** of their work (see Pym, 2022: 446–447). Still, according to a 2022 report by Slator, the 'expert-in-the-loop' model (i.e. the integration of MT into the production workflow) is fast becoming the dominant translation method in the language industry (see Slator, 2022: 8–12). Interestingly, the number of freelance translators who use MT as part of their production workflow is also on the up. According to a 2022 Europe-wide survey, around 70% of freelance translators used MT to some extent, although only just over 30% used it 'daily' or 'regularly' while the remainder used it 'occasionally' only (ELIS Research, 2022: 23). These findings seem to be confirmed by a 2020 CSA Research survey, according to which only 22% of respondents used MT 'on most projects' while 33% used it only 'if a client request[ed] it' and 45% never used it at all (Pielmeier and O'Mara, 2020: 42). These figures confirm that, despite the increasing number of free-lance translators who integrate MT into their workflow, most freelance translators refuse to use MT indiscriminately for all new projects. Some factors that may influence your decision to use MT for a given translation project are (adapted from Nitzke and Hansen-Shirra, 2021: 67):

- The **availability** of an MT system in your own professional context and the **costs/benefits analysis** for the project (see Chapter 6, section 6.2);
- The perceived **performance** – and therefore **usefulness** – of MT for the project's language pair and domain;

148   *On the job*

- The **benefits versus risks ratio** for the project (i.e. do the benefits of MT + post-editing (PE) outweigh the risks?);
- Potential **confidentiality issues** caused by the use of MT for the project (i.e. will the data be shared? How many people will have access to the translation?);
- The **required quality level** for the project (i.e. the right quality level based on the client's needs and the risk level the text(s) represent(s));
- What you perceive your **role** as a translator to be and the potential 'cognitive friction' that becoming a post-editor of machine translation can cause (see Mitchell-Schuitevoerder, 2020: 21).

Admittedly a more personal one, the last factor remains very real to many translators. Recent studies have shown how a production model based on **PEMT (post-editing of machine translation)**, which is often driven by cost-saving intentions, can be seen as a form of 'Digital Taylorism' that can make some professional translators feel alienated – or, in their own words, feel like 'robots' themselves (Courtney and Phelan, 2019: 108; see also Moorkens, 2020). If not managed properly this, in turn, may well become a threat to the sustainability of the translation profession (see Chapter 9).

While recognising the strength of these feelings for some, it is important for all of us to consider, too, that:

> Given the full range of use-cases that are present nowadays, [...] it is self-evident that those translators who argue that there is only one level of quality – namely 'flawless' human translation – are stuck in the dark ages. A big driver behind the adoption and development of translation-oriented solutions – from raw MT to fully managed translation, editing and proofreading – will be the ability to offer a range of services which are flexible enough to meet these different quality requirements. (Way, 2013: 2)

Concretely, what this means is that we may want to consider using MT as part of our workflow provided it is available, it is appropriate for the translation project, it is ethical for us to do so and it helps keep the cost down. Admittedly, the last point remains *controversial*. Why, one might ask, would a freelancer necessarily want to keep costs down? The answer could be that they feel they ought to in order to remain competitive in what is often a highly competitive market (see Chapter 8). As we will see in our final chapter, however, ultimately translators have a responsibility to themselves, too. This could mean that, as a freelancer, you decide to use the tools available to facilitate your work while remembering – and charging for – the fact that:

> [T]ranslation (and related services) is a *professional service*, requiring not one lengthy (and costly) training in the form of university degrees, accreditations and continuing professional development, but also a wide

Managing translation quality 149

range of skills and competences not that dissimilar to those required by lawyers, accountants, and other highly paid professionals [...]. (Walker, 2023: 39; my emphasis)

If you do decide to integrate MT into your production workflow, then you will need to post-edit the raw output of the MT tool to check that it is fit for purpose. PEMT is often done within a CAT environment, although it doesn't necessarily have to be the case. As the objective when using MT is to save time and money, the nature of the tasks you should carry out when post-editing should be based on the quality requirement for the translation project. You should therefore follow the **TAUS (Translation Automation User Society) guidelines** on post-editing that distinguish between 'light post-editing' (Light PE) and 'full post-editing' (Full PE), which you will find on www.taus.net:

- **Light PE:** This is primarily for texts that are for information, perishable and/or non-prejudicial. The aim of light PE is therefore to 'produce a sort of minimum viable (translation) product, removing offensive material and aiming for a semantically correct translation, without making stylistic changes' (Rothwell et al., 2023: 110). This can be seen as equivalent to the 'check' QA step we discussed earlier on in this chapter;
- **Full PE:** This is primarily for texts that are for publication and are non-perishable (whether they are prejudicial or not). Full PE 'adds consideration of grammar (including hyphens and punctuation), syntax, formatting, and terminology' (ibid.: 31). This can be seen as the equivalent to the 'revision' QA step we discussed earlier. Just as with revision, the recommendation is that you make the fewest possible changes to the raw MT output.

Given that more and more professional translators are adopting the 'expert-in-the-loop' production model, not considering integrating MT into your workflow where it is relevant may make it more difficult for you to compete in the open market. This is why I felt it was important to discuss it as part of this chapter on quality management. According to Anthony Pym, '[t]here seems little doubt that translation will increasingly become pre-editing and post-editing, and the translator's role will be to correct and authorize texts that have been produced electronically' (2020: 448). The impact of automation will continue *redefining* what it means to be a professional translator. *If you can't beat them, join them* ... as they say. Yet, this threatens to leave swathes of professional translators feeling alienated by the whole process as they reluctantly adopt MT + PE to survive. It doesn't have to be all doom and gloom, though. 'That kind of task', Pym continues, '*can* involve high-level, satisfying intellectual work, relieved of the donkeywork that much manual translating involves. It is up to translators and their employers to ensure that that kind of work-process quality is appreciated and rewarded' (ibid.). Very wise words indeed!

150 *On the job*

Further reading

As well as giving an excellent overview of the contemporary translation industry in Chapter 1, Drugan (2013) offers a thought-provoking discussion of the different understandings of what quality means in translation across the academy–industry divide in chapter 2.

Mossop (2019) is a clear and thorough introduction to 'editing' and 'revising' for professional translators. Chapters 2 and 3 give very helpful, concrete advice on how to carry out copy-editing and stylistic editing respectively (both concepts are defined in the book). If you have a bit more time to dedicate to this, you may also find chapter 9, on computer aids that can be used for checking, as well as chapters 10 to 16 on revision, helpful too.

Chapter 8 of Walker (2023) offers a very accessible introduction to quality management as part of translation project management. Even though they were written with translation agencies in mind, his concluding comments about the potential cost of poor quality management should resonate with all professional translators.

Chapter 11 in Rothwell et al. (2023) gives an excellent overview of both the benefits and risks of using CAT tools for quality assurance purposes.

Part III

Continuing to grow as a professional translator

8 Understanding your market and marketing your business

> **Key questions we will explore in this chapter**
>
> - What is entrepreneurship and why does it matter to me as a professional translator?
> - Why is it so important to identify my primary target market as part of my marketing strategy? How do I use this information to develop a USP and value proposition that will allow me to stand out from the crowd in what can be a saturated market?
> - Which marketing mix should I adopt to deliver my value proposition to potential customers? How can social media and personal branding help me with this?

According to successful freelance translator Corinne McKay, one of the main reasons some freelance translators fail is because they expect 'too much return from too little marketing effort' (2015: 31). If, as a professional translator, you want your business to grow – and, in fact, to continue to grow – then you need to take the time to engage with marketing seriously.

Similarly, Philip Kotler, who is seen by many as the father of modern marketing, once famously remarked that '[m]arketing takes a day to learn and a lifetime to master' (Kotler, n.d.). Marketing is thus both a science to be learned and a difficult art. This chapter will give you some of the fundamentals you need in order to learn to **position** and **market** your translation business. Admittedly, it will be of particular interest to those of you wishing to embark on a freelance career. This notwithstanding, it should also be of interest to those of you thinking of an in-house career either as a translator or a project manager. Indeed, part of your role may involve customer acquisition and retention. What is more, we will see how both freelance and in-house translators can benefit from marketing themselves and their profession on social media.

DOI: 10.4324/9781003220442-11

154 *Continuing to grow as a professional translator*

This chapter will thus help you develop a **marketing strategy** for your translation services. However, as Philip Kotler also famously said: 'Markets always change faster than marketing' (ibid.). This is certainly true of the contemporary language industry, where technologies and automation, for instance, are disrupters that constantly reshape the market. Your marketing strategy will therefore need to evolve over time to reflect these external factors, but also to integrate your own growth and evolution. Indeed, as a professional translator you will continue to learn, develop and acquire new skills through gaining experience and engaging in continuing professional development (see Chapter 9). This, in turn, should have an impact on what you can offer clients, and how you position yourself in the market. This is why the last stage of your marketing strategy should be to constantly '**evolve your value proposition**' (see Figure 8.2). Fortunately, though, regularly reviewing your marketing strategy to integrate these changes should prove easier, and a little less time-consuming, than developing it from scratch as you start to become a master of the difficult art of marketing.

8.1 Translators as entrepreneurs

Yes, you have read this right. I have just used the 'e-word', which, to some of us, can sound a bit intimidating. Professional translators really are entrepreneurs, though. Let me explain. If you feel the label of entrepreneur doesn't apply to you as a professional translator, then it may have something to do with the way you think of **entrepreneurship**. Let's use this as our starting point. In the last couple of decades, research into entrepreneurship has shown the important role that national cultures can play in the way people think of entrepreneurship (see Hayton et al., 2002; Heilbrunn et al., 2017 and Valliere, 2019). National media, for instance, convey social representations of entrepreneurship that reflect the differing cultural norms and expectations societies hold regarding that concept (Anderson and Warren, 2011). Depending on your own national culture(s), therefore, you will have developed your own unique understanding of and attitudes towards entrepreneurship. Please take a few minutes to answer the following question before you read on:

- How would you define entrepreneurship?

In many Western countries, the term entrepreneur is often associated with rich and famous individuals who have had a bright idea and managed to commercialise it very successfully. Bill Gates (the founder of Microsoft) or Mark Zuckerberg (the founder of Facebook) are two perfect examples of such **entrepreneurial success stories** who reinforce the long-standing Western perception of entrepreneurs as people who innovate, start a business to capitalise on their idea and create (immense) wealth in the process. If you share

Understanding your market and marketing your business   155

this understanding of entrepreneurship, then you may struggle to see professional translators as entrepreneurs.

However, since the 1990s our understanding of entrepreneurship has shifted as a result of Howard Stevenson's seminal redefinition of the concept. According to the Harvard professor, entrepreneurship is better understood as '[t]he process by which individuals – either on their own or inside organizations – pursue opportunities without regard to the resources they currently control' (Stevenson and Jarillo, 1990: 23). **Opportunities,** Stevenson explains, must be seen as relative as they will vary not just *between* individuals, but also *for* individuals over time. They should therefore be defined as 'a future situation which is deemed desirable and feasible' (ibid.). Similarly, a person's desires '[will] vary with current position and future expectations' and their capabilities '[will] vary depending upon innate skills, training, and the competitive environment' (ibid.). A person's willingness to pursue opportunities regardless, however, or, in other words, to 'find a way', is key to entrepreneurship.

Seen that way, being an entrepreneur is not restricted to individuals who start a new business. It is, instead, about seeing opportunities where others see problems, with the creation of new services and solutions. Hence it is a mindset that can be found 'anywhere that individuals and teams desire to differentiate themselves and apply their passion and drive to executing a business opportunity' (Allen, 2012: 5). This does not only apply to those of you aspiring to work freelance. Indeed, the only characteristic that is intrinsic to all entrepreneurs is passion, i.e. 'the drive to achieve something' (ibid.). With the right mindset, in-house translators can be entrepreneurs, too – or, as they are sometimes called, 'intrepreneurs'–as they help recognise (new) business opportunities, gather the necessary resources to act on them and drive them to completion.

As a budding professional translator, you are about to enter a fast-changing industry that is increasingly being disrupted by new technologies, automation and artificial intelligence (AI) (see, for instance, Drugan, 2013; Moorkens, 2017; Larsonneur, 2019; Schmitt, 2019 and Lambert and Walker, 2022). Adopting an **entrepreneurial mindset** could therefore be key to your professional success. Fortunately, this mindset can be learned and practised (see Barnes and de Villiers Scheepers, 2018). The first step will be for you to wave goodbye to all the unhelpful stereotypes you may hold about what it takes to be an entrepreneur, such as, for instance: 'Entrepreneurs are all visionaries', 'I need a great idea to be an entrepreneur', 'Entrepreneurs are reckless' or 'Entrepreneurs are in it for the money' (Allen, 2012: 27–32; Burns, 2018: 7).

This last **stereotype** is particularly interesting for us. In an eye-opening article that explores the translation profession from a sociological perspective, Israeli scholar Rakefet Sela-Sheffy shows that many professional translators tend to see passion – for foreign languages and cultures – as a more 'worthy' driver than money:

> Translators tend to demonstrate economic 'disinterestedness' [...] and avoid discussing remuneration and other material expectations in describing

their profession [...]. Instead, they stress the non-material gratifications – satisfaction, freedom, interest, perfection or cultural impact – which they gain, at least in theory, from their work. (Sela-Sheffy, 2022: 170)

Yet, translation is not a hobby for professional translators but something they do for a living. Even though they are not necessarily 'in it for the money', professional translators can – and *should* – expect appropriate financial rewards for their work, just like any other entrepreneurs. Being passionate about something doesn't mean you should do it for free! Having a positive balance sheet remains, after all, key to the sustainability of any **business venture**. Again, developing an entrepreneurial mindset could be the key.

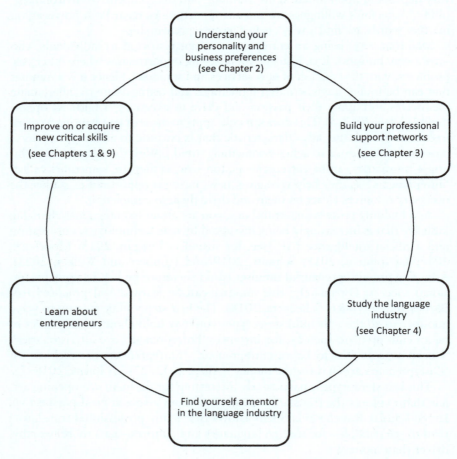

Figure 8.1 Preparing for entrepreneurship in the language industry (adapted from Allen, 2012: 36)

Understanding your market and marketing your business   157

Figure 8.1 illustrates some of the concrete steps you can take to prepare for entrepreneurship in the language industry. As you can see, we have already covered quite a few of those steps in previous chapters. Chapter 3, for instance, aims to help you start building your professional networks. Similarly, we have already discussed the importance of researching the language industry in Chapter 4. Two other steps, however, are new: 'Find yourself a mentor in the language industry' and 'Learn about entrepreneurs'. Your professional networks will be the ideal place to find yourself a **mentor**. He or she should ideally be someone from the language industry who has the career you aspire to have and who can be 'your guide and sounding board as well as [your] champion and gateway to contacts' (Allen, 2012: 37). You should also try to find out as much as you can about **successful entrepreneurs** – both within and outside the translation industry – by reading magazines, articles, books, blogs and so on, and, if possible, by talking to the entrepreneurs themselves. This will help you develop a better understanding of the entrepreneurial mindset you will need to develop to position and market your translation business – and, as the market continues to evolve, *re*position it – in the language industry market.

TOPICS FOR DISCUSSION AND ASSIGNMENTS 8.1

Activity 8.1 Find a newspaper article or a blog post about a successful entrepreneur. The article or the blog post can be from your own or another culture. Read it carefully, and then answer the following questions:

- Which social representation(s) of entrepreneurship does your chosen article or blog post reflect?
- Based on the article or the blog post, what contributed to the entrepreneur's success that could also contribute to yours as a professional translator?

Activity 8.2 Get into pairs. In this activity, you will have the opportunity to reflect on whether you have an entrepreneurial mindset by taking and discussing the results of a psychometric test developed by a UK university: the General Enterprise Tendency (GET) test. The GET test is freely available at http://www.get2test.net/, where you can also find information on how it was developed and how it has been empirically tested for validity and reliability. Of course, a test such as this one should always be taken with a pinch of salt. However, it does provide an indicative – but by no means definitive – measure of your enterprising tendency, which we will use as a starting point for reflection. Please follow the next couple of steps:

158 *Continuing to grow as a professional translator*

- **Individually:** Go to http://www.get2test.net/. Take the test (this takes about 10 minutes)–there are no right or wrong answers!–and save the generated GET test report at the end of the test. Read it carefully;
- **In pairs:** Meet up to discuss your GET test reports. No need to share all the details – just what you are comfortable with sharing. Consider the following questions during your discussion:

- How do you feel about your overall score? Do you believe it is a fair representation of your entrepreneurial tendency? Why (not)?
- In which areas ('autonomy', 'creativity', 'risk' or 'locus') did you score highest? How could this help your career as a professional translator (taking into consideration the context in which you would like to work)?
- Similarly, in which areas ('autonomy', 'creativity', 'risk' or 'locus') did you score lowest? What measures could you take to make sure this does not stop you achieving your objectives as a professional translator (in the context in which you would like to work)?

8.2 Positioning yourself in the language industry market

8.2.1 *Identifying potential customers through market research*

Developing an entrepreneurial mindset is about learning to see existing needs and problems as business opportunities by coming up with solutions for them through new or improved services. To do so, one first needs to develop an excellent understanding of the market in which one operates by using **market research**. After all, you can be the best at what you do, and have a great website and a fantastic social media campaign ... but you will still be in a sticky situation if nobody needs or wants what you have to offer!

As you will see from Figure 8.2, the first thing you need to do as a professional translator entering the market as a freelancer is, therefore, to understand who has the problem of needing something to be in a different language while lacking the skills to translate it themselves. This group will become your **target market**, and identifying this will be the foundation of your business development.

For many professional translators, this target market, however, will remain unwieldily large ... especially when working in a common but sought-after language pair (e.g. English to Chinese or Spanish to English). In the first instance, you will therefore want to identify from your target market those groups of customers that most need your solution to their problem, because other solutions are not as satisfactory. This group's '**problem**' will necessarily be more specific than just needing to have a document translated, although it

Understanding your market and marketing your business 159

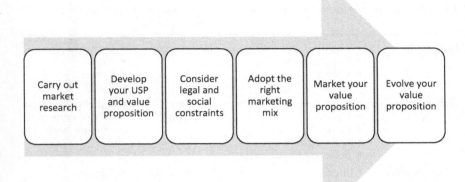

Figure 3.2 Developing and marketing your translation business

will have to be sufficiently widespread for your market segment to be viable. Bear in mind that some of your prospective clients' needs and problems will be context specific. The research into the language industry you have already carried out as part of the Topics for discussion and assignments 4.1 (Chapter 4) and 5.1 (Chapter 5) should help you with that. It may be, for instance, that you identify a group of customers who need translations into a specialist subject domain with which you are familiar, or who need translation-related services you feel you can offer. Of course, all potential clients will all have specific needs and/or problems. However, while customers are all unique, 'it is possible to group them in some way that is useful in terms of targeting, for example, by identifying their group needs or problems' (Burns, 2018: 144). These groups are called **market segments**.

There are many different ways to go about market segmentation. This being said, you should make a distinction between **business-to-consumer (B2C)** and **business-to-business (B2B)** segmentations when, based on your research, you start organising prospective clients into market segments. B2C refers to the process of offering your services directly to consumers as end users. This is the case, for instance, when a translation service provider (TSP)–be they a freelance translator or an agency – translates an individual's birth certificate. B2B, on the other hand, is about businesses offering their services to other businesses. This is the case when a freelance translator translates for a translation agency or for a local small or medium-sized enterprise (SME). In most instances, it is easier to find and access the information you will need for B2B segmentation. This is fortunate for us, as for many freelance translators B2B

160 *Continuing to grow as a professional translator*

Table 8.1 Examples of descriptive factors included in B2C and B2B market segmentation

B2C (business-to-consumer) segmentation		B2B (business-to-business) segmentation	
Geographic	• Location • Region • Urban • Rural	**Geographic**	• Location • Region • Urban • Rural
Demographic	• Age • Gender • Education • Occupation • Socio-economic group	**Industry sector(s)**	• Industry sector(s) they operate and/or work with
Psychographic	• Lifestyle • Attitudes	**Business size**	• Start-up • SME • Large corporation
Behavioural	• Level of usage • Benefits sought • Loyalty	**Behavioural**	• Level of usage • Benefits sought • Loyalty

represents their greatest market segment, whether in the form of translation agencies or commercial end-clients (Pielmeier and O'Mara, 2020: 32). There is no golden rule about where to look, though. Once again, it will all depend on your own circumstances and the context in which you work. Table 8.1 gives you an idea of the descriptive factors you may find useful to include in your B2C and B2B segmentation of the market.

Segmenting your target market will allow you to more clearly identify not only your prospective customers, but also their shared needs and problems, and to classify them into groups that are easier to target. Indeed, you can then use your market segmentation to create **customer profiles** (also known as 'buyer personas' or 'user profiles') for each of the market segments you have identified. Customer profiles are used in both B2C and B2B. They are a way to describe consumers categorically so they can be grouped for marketing and advertising purposes. If you already have clients, you can base your customer profiles on existing clients. However, when you start developing your translation business you will likely need to base them on your market segmentation. Bear in mind that customer profiles are not real, but constructed from your market research around the idea of a *typical* customer for your translation services. In other words, they are 'personas'. You can come up with a name for each persona that encapsulates their identity as one of your typical customers. If, as identified by your market research, some of your typical customers are businesses, then you can create an imaginary profile for a person working for this type of company. This should be the person most likely to make the decision to hire your translation services (e.g. a PM for

Understanding your market and marketing your business 161

Table 8.2 Example of descriptive factors included in a customer profile

	B2B or B2C?
Customer's name:	
Demographics	B2C: Age? Gender? Education? Occupation? Socio-economic group? Income? etc. B2B: Consider also industry sector or area(s) of specialisation, business size (start-up, small and medium-sized enterprise (SME) or large corporation?).
Psychographics	Lifestyle? Attitudes? Values? Interests? 'Values' is probably the most important factor here, for both B2C and B2B. What does this customer value?
Important details	Anything not captured by demographics and psychographics that you feel is relevant for the customer profile (e.g. for B2B: ambition to enter new foreign markets? etc.)
Goals	What is this customer trying to achieve? What is important to them?
Pain points	What challenges does this customer typically face that could stop them meeting their goals?
Needs	What are their current translation needs? Do they have any additional translation-related needs (e.g. proofreading)? Do you anticipate that their needs will evolve in the coming years? Where do you fit into this evolution?
Customer benefits	What benefits will your translation services offer to this customer? How will they provide value to them?
How they currently engage	How does this customer currently go about finding and hiring translation service providers? Which media do they use?
How to reach them	Which channels/media are best suited to reach out to this customer? (e.g. do they typically prefer to be approached directly and in person or via LinkedIn?)

translation agencies, a CEO for small businesses, a marketing manager for medium-sized companies etc.). Table 8.2 illustrates the kind of information you may want to include in your customer profiles.

Creating customer profiles based on your market research will allow you to **visualise** who your typical customers are. It will give you an enhanced understanding of your customers; *who they are, what they do, what they are trying to achieve, the challenges they face, what they need, what they value, how they engage with translation services and how to reach them.* This, in turn, will allow you to refine your own translation service offer and put in place a suitable marketing strategy that uses the right channels and media to engage with prospective clients.

TOPICS FOR DISCUSSION AND ASSIGNMENTS 8.2

Imagine that you are a freelance translator trying to identify your primary target market, or a PM at a translation agency who has been tasked with profiling the agency's primary target market in order to understand – and engage – clients from this market segment more efficiently.

- Based on your chosen scenario, select the relevant information from the research work you have carried out for 'Topics for discussion and assignments' 4.1 and 5.1 (Chapters 4 and 5)–which was, in fact, market research!–as a starting point. Carry out a bit more research if necessary.
- Use what we have just discussed to segment your/the agency's market, identify your/the agency's primary target market and create a typical customer profile for this primary target market.

8.2.2 Developing your USP and value proposition

Once you have identified potential customers through market research, you should use your market segmentation and customer profiles to develop your **USP ('unique selling point' or 'unique selling proposition')**. As can be seen from Figure 8.3, your USP will be what sets you apart from your competitors as a translation service provider:

When you start working on your USP, your first reflex might be to emphasise your qualifications, your professional membership of translator

Figure 8.3 USPs for translation service providers

Understanding your market and marketing your business 163

associations and your experience as a translator. Quite rightly, too! These are all extremely valuable; you should definitely foreground them as evidence that you can offer 'high-quality translation services'. As mentioned in Chapter 7, however, this alone will not be enough to help you stand out from the crowd. Indeed, many of your competitors with equivalent credentials will likely make the exact same claims! In an age-old business like translation, it is easy to get lost in a sea of competitors ... especially if you work with a relatively common language pair. This is why it is so important that your USP focuses on the qualities of your translation business that set you apart from other TSPs.

When developing your USP, you should therefore focus on what you can offer prospective clients that is unique to you. These will be your **competitive factors.** Table 8.3 below gives you examples of potential tangible and intangible competitive factors for TSPs. This list is just indicative, and it is far from exhaustive! As can be expected, the language pair(s) you can offer can be one of your competitive factors alongside subject domain specialism and specialisation. You should note, though, that working with a rare(r) language pair is not necessarily a major competitive factor if there is little-to-no demand for it where you work (see Walker, 2023: 133). Other competitive factors, which are not unique to TSPs, are price, quality and delivery speed. We have already discussed these in Chapter 6 (see Figure 6.3: Martin Barnes' project management triangle). Finally, strong technical skills and/or other translation-related services you can offer (e.g. desktop publishing) can also be tangible competitive factors for you as a professional translator. Most of these factors are in fact linked to the 'hard skills' you can offer your clients (see Chapter 1).

Table 8.3 Examples of tangible and intangible competitive factors for TSPs

Tangible competitive factors	*Intangible competitive factors*
Language skills (language pair(s))	Image
Specialist subject domain(s)	Communication style
Specialisation (e.g. transcreation, video-game localisation, AVT etc.)	Reliability
Price	Customer service
Quality	Convenience
Delivery speed	Ease of use
Location	Reputation
Qualifications	Consultancy/advice to clients
Endorsements	Creativity
Past professional experience	Flexibility
Other translation-related service offered (e.g. DTP, revision, back translations, etc.)	Cultural understanding
Strong technical skills	Values (e.g. sustainability, social justice etc.)

164   *Continuing to grow as a professional translator*

If you look at the examples of intangible competitive factors listed in Table 8.3, however, you will soon realise that most of them are linked to your own personality traits, values and so-called 'soft skills' (see Chapter 1). Hence the importance of **knowing yourself** – not least your strengths!–well. In other words, your own identity will be reflected in the identity you create for your business.

> Your values and visions are tools that create identity for your business – an identity that should be reflected in your value proposition. And if this identity is attractive to customers it can create value. At the very least, a clear identity for the business means that customers know what they are buying and, if they like it, [it] facilitates a repeat purchase. (Burns, 2018: 147)

Despite being universal, the way we define and understand values such as 'honesty', 'integrity', 'creativity', 'loyalty', amongst other examples, remains **culturally oriented** (see Katan and Taibi, 2021: 254–259). As individuals, our personal histories also influence which values we choose to adopt. This is largely a subconscious process, which is why it is important to take the time to reflect on one's own values with value exercises such as the one contained in Activity 2.4 (see 'Topics for discussion and assignments 2.2' in Chapter 2). Doing so will help you identify the values that currently matter most to you. You may then decide to integrate them into your USP, provided you feel they are relevant to your target market.

Of course, if you take them individually, the examples of competitive factors listed in Table 8.3 will hardly be unique to you. However, by selecting the ones that you can offer (tangible factors), that are particularly strong for you (intangible factors) and that align with what you know your customers need and value from translation services (see Figure 8.3), you will create a **unique blend** that will become … your very own USP! As you finalise your USP, you should aim to answer the following three questions for each of the market segments you have identified from your market research (see Burns, 2018: 146):

- How will your translation service solve a problem for typical customers from this market segment?
- What benefits – tangible and intangible – can your customers from this market segment expect?
- Why should customers from this market segment hire you over one of your competitors?

As a final step, you may find it helpful to summarise your answers in a brief, memorable statement that outlines to your customer groups why they should hire your translation services, and how you are different from competing TSPs. This statement will be your **value proposition**, which you can then use as the foundation of your marketing strategy.

Understanding your market and marketing your business 165

TOPICS FOR DISCUSSION AND ASSIGNMENTS 8.3

Activity 8.3 Have another look at your answers to Activity 5.2 ('Topics for discussion and assignments 5.1' in Chapter 5), which asked you to research one of your potential competitors.

- Based on your answers and what we have just discussed, what would you say is their USP?

Activity 8.4 Imagine that you are a freelance translator trying to develop your USP, or a PM at a translation agency who has been tasked with (re) defining the agency's USP.

Think about Activity 8.3 and what you said about this translation service provider's USP:

- How does this influence your own/your agency's USP? Is there a gap you/your agency can fill?
- What are most of your future competitors highlighting? How can you/ your agency be different?

Use Table 8.3 as a starting point to establish your own list of competitive factors. Then use the market research, segmentation and customer profiles you carried out for 'Topics for Discussion and Assignments 8.2' to identify where what you can offer as a translation service provider matches that which your primary target market needs and values (see Figure 8.3).

Activity 8.5 Write your value proposition. Once you have completed Activity 8.4, use the following template to write a brief value proposition with your/the agency's primary target market in mind:

Because as a TSP I offer/my agency offers [*competitive factors that match what primary market needs and values*], **it will** [*problem solution*] **for** [*customer profile or primary target market segment*] **meaning that** [*customer benefits*].'

8.3 Marketing your translation business

8.3.1 Developing your marketing strategy

Now you have developed your USP and your value proposition, you need to communicate it to your customers via a clear and impactful marketing strategy. But what do we mean by marketing exactly? According to the UK's Chartered Institute of Marketing, marketing is 'the management process

166   *Continuing to grow as a professional translator*

responsible for identifying, anticipating and satisfying customer requirements profitably' (CIM, 2015: 2). As you can see from this definition, marketing is bigger than just promotion and advertising. For professional translators, it is about 'understanding the competitive marketplace and ensuring [we] can tap into key trends, reaching consumers with the right [service] at the right price, place and time' (ibid.: 3). This means that you started working on your marketing strategy the minute you started researching your target market. The next phase of your marketing strategy should be to promote your value proposition to potential customers in a way that will attract new business, retain existing customers or build loyalty to your services.

The first step to achieve this will be to adopt the right **marketing mix** for your translation business. As explained by Paul Burns in *New Venture Creation*:

> [A] marketing mix is a combination of factors about your service [...] that you can use to influence customers. It is the vehicle that delivers your value proposition to your target customer segments. It should help you to create your brand identity and will support it. (2018: 176)

As shown in Table 8.4, a common model for marketing mix is the '5 Ps' model, namely: Product (in our case, an intangible product – a service), Price, Place, Promotion and People.

Answering the questions contained in Table 8.4 will help you develop the right marketing mix for your translation business. You need to make sure, though, that you develop a marketing mix that is fully **consistent** with your value proposition so you reinforce the overall benefits your prospective clients are looking for. All components of the marketing mix must be consistent among themselves, too. For instance, if, in line with your value proposition, you decide to charge a high price for a high-quality, niche translation service, then you need to make sure all the other aspects of your marketing mix – place, promotion and people – reflect this, too. Just like your USP, your marketing mix will be unique to your translation business.

Once you have adopted the right marketing mix as the best vehicle to 'delive[r] your value proposition [...] to your target customer[s]' (Burns, 2018: 176), you will want to start actively promoting your value proposition – and, if you have one, your brand – to prospective customers. Your answers to the questions relating to the fourth P ('Promotion') in Table 8.4 should already give you a fair idea of where – and when – you can best reach your primary target market. This should help you select the most adequate **marketing channels** for your market ... and there are many of them to choose from! For example, you may decide that more traditional marketing channels are more consistent with your value proposition. In this case, word of mouth, professional associations' directories, email marketing, newspaper ads, web ads, trade shows and so on will be your preferred way to promote your translation business. Conversely, you may decide that these are not the best way to

Understanding your market and marketing your business 167

Table 8.4 Example of questions you can ask yourself for each of the 5 Ps to develop the right marketing mix as a TSP

Product (or service)	• What does your typical customer want from the translation service? (e.g. quality, convenience etc.) • How will the customer use it? • What features must the translation service have to meet the customer's needs? • What is the name of your translation service? • Are there different quality levels/types of service available? • How is the translation service you offer different from your competitors'?
Price	• How much does it cost you to deliver the translation service? • What is the customers' perceived product value? • What is your current pricing strategy? • How much room is there for negotiation? • Do you think that providing discounts (volume, loyalty etc.) and/or having special offers could increase your market share? • Can your pricing strategy keep up with those of other TSPs? • Are you clear on how well your pricing strategy maps onto your customers?
Place	• Where do customers look for your translation service? (e.g. if online, which website(s)? if on social media, which one(s)? etc.) • Do you need to have an online presence? • Does face to face remain a good way to sell your translation services in your own context? How about over the phone? • What do other TSPs do? How can you learn from that and differentiate yourself?
Promotion	• How can you reach customers with your marketing messages? • Is it best to use social media in promoting the product? • Will you reach your audience by advertising online, in the local/ national press or on the Internet? • How important is word of mouth for promoting your translation services? If it is, what can you do to make sure it happens? • When is the best time to promote? Is there seasonality in your market? • How do other TSPs promote their business? And how does that influence your choice of promotional activity? • What is your brand?
People	• What does the customer expect from you in terms of communication as part of the service you offer? • What is the role of communication with clients in the service you offer? • How much emphasis do you as a TSP place on advice, support and/or relationship management (trust) as part of the service you offer to clients? • What is the customer's perceived value of advice, support and/ or relationship management (trust) in the service you offer?

168 *Continuing to grow as a professional translator*

reach your primary target market and opt for newer channels instead, such as social media (LinkedIn, Facebook, X (formerly Twitter), Instagram and, more recently, TikTok), online communities or even podcasts.

When deciding which channel(s) to adopt to market your services, you should also take into consideration other factors besides where your clients are. Indeed, if you have another quick look at Figure 8.2, you will notice that the next step after 'Develop your USP and value proposition' is '**Consider legal and social constraints**'. What is legal and socially acceptable in one country may not be in another. As already mentioned, data protection, for instance, is a legal requirement in many countries. Laws such as the EU's General Data Protection Regulation (GDPR) will limit what you can or cannot do with the data you hold on existing or potential customers, which in turn will have implications regarding the channels you may or may not use. It is your responsibility to find out which laws may limit your ability to use some marketing channels in the country or countries where you would like to work as a professional translator. Similarly, make sure you only use marketing channels that are deemed socially acceptable where you work. You may end up offending prospective clients otherwise, which would be utterly counterproductive. If in doubt about the legality or social acceptability of the marketing channels you are thinking of using, ask your support networks for advice and guidance first (see Chapter 3).

8.3.2 Social media and personal branding

With already 4.26 billion social media users worldwide and this number predicted to grow to approximately 6 billion by 2027, it is no wonder that **social media** is fast becoming a major marketing channel for businesses (Statista, 2023). In the words of Franziska Iseli, the founder of the marketing mentoring agency Basic Bananas:

> The purpose of [social media marketing] is for you to connect with your customers, network with potential strategic partners, attract prospects, build relationships, collaborate with brands, create communities and share brilliant content to build authority, which leads to trust and increased sales. (2021: 1)

Among some of the main benefits listed by adopters of social media marketing are exposure, traffic and direct communication with prospective clients (Statista, 2023). As an added bonus, you can achieve all this at **no financial cost**. All you will need to do is to create accounts on your chosen social media channels, which is often free.

Quite understandably, social media marketing is thus becoming increasingly popular with professional translators, too. A large-scale survey conducted by CSA Research in 2020, for instance, shows that a majority of prospective direct clients (65%) still typically find a translator or an interpreter

Understanding your market and marketing your business   169

through word of mouth (Pielmeier and O'Mara, 2020: 31). However, a non-negligible number of them also find these professionals on marketplaces such as Proz.com (27%) or thanks to the translator's 'presence on social media' (25%) (ibid.). Perhaps unsurprisingly, the same survey also shows that the more traditional channels of word-of-mouth (57%) and in-person marketing (40%) remain the most common ways for freelance translators and interpreters to 'proactively pursue' direct clients (ibid.). However, these are closely followed by **'social media networking'** (33%) (ibid.). In fact, according to the survey, social media marketing seems even more effective when it comes to proactively pursuing translation agencies (39%). These figures thus confirm the growing importance of social media as a marketing tool for professional translators. Despite all the obvious benefits of social media, however, your decision to add it to your marketing mix should primarily depend on your answers to three key questions:

- Is social media the best way to deliver your value proposition to your typical customers (as identified by your market research)?
- Are you comfortable with using/learning to use social media to market your services to your typical customers?
- Are there legal or social constraints in place that could limit your use of social media – and/or of some specific sites – as part of your marketing mix?

If your answer to the first two questions is yes, and provided you have checked that there are no legal and/or social limitations to the use of social media as a marketing tool in the context in which you are thinking of working, then you should seriously consider adding it to your marketing mix. As alluded to by Franziska Iseli, professional translators can use social media for a variety of marketing purposes. First of all, social media can be a great way to 'attract new customers' (Iseli, 2021: 1). Indeed, with its ability to make content go viral, social media can spread word-of-mouth recommendations quickly (**referral marketing**). Professional translators can also use social media to 'network' with partners, to 'connect' with customers, to 'create' communities, and to 'share' content that 'builds' authority and, as a result, trust (ibid.). In other words, social media will allow you to 'establis[h] a presence and creat[e] a community around your service' (Burns, 2018: 214). This is what is also known as **content marketing**, a marketing approach whereby you use blogs, articles, videos or webinars or similar to create valuable content that generates attention and, ultimately, builds a community of interest around your services: 'The key to success is getting people to "talk about" your site or share resources such as videos that you produce' (ibid.). This should be balanced, though, with the need for professional translators to '[u]se social media responsibly for professional purposes' (EMT, 2017: 10; see also Chapter 1).

170 *Continuing to grow as a professional translator*

A 2020 survey of professional translators on the subject of 'Social media and translators' showed that the social media sites professional translators most commonly used for professional purposes were LinkedIn (88.2%), Twitter (53.8%), Facebook (44.1%), WhatsApp (21%) and Instagram (14%) (Loock, 2020). Which sites you decide to use as part of your marketing mix will depend on the context in which you work, the social media your typical customers engage with and the platforms you are comfortable with, as well as your marketing purposes (e.g. referral marketing vs content marketing). For most of us, a key objective on social media is to 'buil[d] and maintain [our] **online reputation**, both within and outside the translation industry' through referral and content marketing (Adams, 2013: 3; my emphasis). As pointed out by professional translator Nicole Adams, however, '[t]he flipside of online reputation building is that your reputation can be ruined just as quickly as it is built, particularly if there is no clear line between your business and personal use of social networks' (ibid.: 4). Her advice is, therefore, to 'always present yourself professionally' on social media (ibid.: 3). This means never publishing anything you wouldn't say in real life or that is not suitable for public view (ibid.: 4). She also advises professional translators to create separate profiles for personal and business use on the social media sites they also use for personal purposes (ibid.: 5). This is to keep both spheres separate, as '[p]ictures of your pets or children, for example, may look lovely on your personal website or profile but are not appropriate to display on your professional pages' (ibid.: 3). Even though Adams's advice on keeping a clear line between the personal and the professional will still ring true to many of us, we must note that the idea of such a strict divide between the spheres has been increasingly challenged in the last few years. Some freelance professional translators, for instance, have started exploring the use of more unexpected social media platforms such as TikTok to create content marketing that also focuses on their own personality and values as part of their marketing strategy.

This is the case for professional translator Kelsey Frick, who produces regular posts and videos not just on LinkedIn, but also on TikTok, in order to push her '**personal brand**'. Personal branding is about creating content on social media that consistently markets yourself and your career as brands. Originally used by influencers, personal branding is a marketing strategy that can also benefit professional translators. As explained by Frick, developing their personal brand on social media is a way for freelance translators to sell not just their service, but also their values and the kind of person they are to prospective customers (Roberts, 2021). To achieve this, though, it is important that your personal brand be visible in all your interactions with customers, and across all the social media sites you use. Your personal brand is not just about the font you use or the colour of your logo (if you have one!). More importantly, it is about the tone you use in all your interactions with your clients. By adopting personal branding as part of her marketing mix, Frick explains, she no longer has to actively look for clients. Instead, she

Understanding your market and marketing your business 171

is in the privileged position of having clients come to her. Personal branding is not just for freelance translators, though. Indeed, in-house professional translators who want to promote themselves in the language industry can also benefit from developing their own personal branding strategy while continuing to promote the company/agency for which they currently work.

Besides all the potential marketing benefits of maintaining a social media presence, there is another reason why all professional translators should consider engaging with social media. In her book exploring *Translation and Social Media*, Canadian scholar Renée Desjardins uses the example of LinkedIn to argue that professional translators' digital presence on social media can benefit the profession as a whole. Indeed, social media can both give individual translators a **renewed sense of agency** and make the whole **profession more visible** to other professions. In other words, the digital content professional translators create on social media is a way for professional translators to market not just their own services, but also their entire profession – *what it is professional translators do, and why it matters* – to all potential stakeholders:

> perhaps more fundamentally, the profiles of professional translators on LinkedIn underscore that translators are no longer invisible. In the way that translators can now promote their freelance practices, in the way that they can now network with other professionals, in the way that they can self-describe what they do and how, [social media channels] have given contemporary translators a voice and an unprecedented level of agency. Translators' notes and prefaces have historically given translators a means to be read or 'heard', but this was only for the readers of a specific translated text. Because [social media] has a significantly wider reach, what translators say about translation, their profession and their process on [social media] has a higher likelihood of making an impact in other professional circles and beyond. (Desjardins, 2017: 110)

TOPICS FOR DISCUSSION AND ASSIGNMENTS 8.4

Activity 8.6 Imagine that you are a freelance translator trying to develop your marketing strategy, or a PM at a translation agency who has been tasked with helping (re)develop the agency's marketing strategy.

Based on your answers to 'Topics for discussion and assignments 8.3' (especially Activity 8.5), use Table 8.4 as a starting point to develop the right marketing mix to deliver your/your agency's value proposition to your primary target market. Under 'Promotion', say exactly which marketing channels you will adopt and why (please be as specific as possible).

Activity 8.7 As mentioned, the EMT Competence Framework lists the ability to '[u]se social media responsibly for professional purposes' as one of the competences professional translators should have (EMT, 2020: 10).

172 *Continuing to grow as a professional translator*

To that end, it is important for you to be aware of the legal and social constraints around social media use in the context(s) where you would like to work as a translator. Spend some time searching the Internet for potential legal limitations on the use of social media in general, and of specific sites in particular, for marketing purposes, in the country or countries where you would like to work as a professional translator. Does this apply to referral marketing, content marketing or both?

Then research social media etiquette for the same country or countries. How will the do's and don'ts affect the way you market yourself on social media there?

Activity 8.8 In this last activity, you are encouraged to find out more about personal branding. First of all, have a look at the website of Franziska Iseli, the founder of the marketing mentoring agency Basic Bananas: https://franzis kaiseli.com/. Then, check out as many of the social media channels she uses that you have access to (Facebook, LinkedIn, Instagram, YouTube, Apple Podcasts). You will find links to them on her website. When you are done, please discuss the following questions with a course mate:

- How does Franziska present–'brand'–herself on her website and her social media? Pay attention not only to the font, pictures and videos she uses, but also to her tone. Is she consistent–'on brand'–across all social media?
- Based on this, how does she come across? What are her values, as portrayed by her social media?
- How comfortable are you with the mix between personal and professional on Franziska's social media?
- If you are from a culture or cultures different to Franziska's, are there any elements of her personal branding you believe could be seen as socially unacceptable in your own culture(s)? Which one(s) and why?
- Overall, in what ways would you say Franziska's personal branding can help her with her business and career? Are there elements of this you could adopt as a professional translator?

Further reading

Chapters 5–7 in Burns (2018) offer aspiring entrepreneurs clear, step-by-step guidance on how to develop their value proposition, decide on a marketing mix and communicate that value proposition.

Chapter 5 in Desjardins (2017) explores the relationship between online social media (OSM) and professional translators. While emphasising the benefits of greater

Understanding your market and marketing your business 173

social media visibility for professional translators, it also mentions some of the challenges that can come with it.

Listen to Roberts's (2021) podcast 'Personal Branding with Kelsey Frick' to find out more about the ways in which personal branding can help freelance professional translators grow their business: https://www.dotrobertstranslation.com/meet-the-translator/episode/4ddba8d2/personal-branding-with-kelsey-frick.

9 Keeping it sustainable

> **Key questions we will explore in this chapter:**
>
> - What is CPD and why is it important for me as a professional translator?
> - How can self-care help me ensure that my work as a professional translator remains sustainable over time?
> - What can I do to help ensure the sustainability of translation as a profession?

In 1987, in its seminal Bruntland Report, the United Nations' World Commission on Environment and Development first defined **sustainability** as 'meeting the needs of the present without compromising the ability of future generations to meet their own needs' (UNWCED, 1987). Understood in such a way, sustainability is primarily about managing economic and social development in a way that avoids the 'exploitation', 'depletion' or 'irreversible alteration' of our resources and environment (Chiesa et al., 2018: 3).

More recently, however, as a result of global changes in the labour market that have led to 'an increased spreading of non-standard forms of employment, such as temporary employment contracts' (ibid.: 1), which can be a source of stress and of 'psychological and physical illness' (ibid.: 2), scholars have started approaching the concept of sustainability from a psychological perspective, too. This approach is known as the **psychology of sustainability**. As explained by Chiesa et al. in the journal *Sustainability*: 'The psychology of sustainability and sustainable development is concerned with understanding how it is possible [for individuals] to establish meaningful lives and meaningful work experiences despite the numerous challenges, transitions, and changes that characterize the current career paths' (2018: 2).

As we have already mentioned elsewhere in this book, translation as a profession is not without its very own numerous challenges! So much so that in his seminal book *Becoming a Translator*, Douglas Robinson observes that:

DOI: 10.4324/9781003220442-12

Keeping it sustainable 175

One would think that burnout rates would be high among translators. The job is not only underpaid and undervalued by society; it involves long hours spent alone with uninspiring texts working under the stress of short deadlines. One would think, in fact, that most translators would burn out on the job after about three weeks. [...] That most don't, that one meets [...] translators who are still content with their jobs after thirty years, says something about the operative of the greatest motivator of all: they enjoy their work. (2020: 44)

The psychology of sustainability could help us understand what, in Robinson's words, makes it possible for us translators to still be 'content with [our] jobs after thirty years' (2020: 44; see also Hubscher-Davidson, 2020).

What can we do to facilitate our own continued **professional growth** and **well-being** while working in an industry that is as challenging as it is complex? This is what we will explore in this chapter.

9.1 Keeping on top of your game to keep on top of the game: CPD

9.1.1 Why CPD matters ... a lot!

As previously discussed, change in the translation industry is both constant and fast-paced. In fact, change has been so intense and so far-reaching in the last two decades that German academic Peter Schmitt came up with a new term for the industry, **Translation 4.0**:

Analogous to the established concept of 'Industry 4.0', the philosophy of an emerging new translation industry can be called 'Translation 4.0'. Challenged by a continuously growing demand for translations, increasingly volatile markets, fierce global competition and aggressive pricing, the translation industry is responding with fully digitalized data handling, real-time project management, strictly organized processes, quality control, short response times and comprehensive added-value services for clients. [...] Due to the closing gap between the quality of human translations (HT) and neural MT (in particular DeepL), MT will cover a growing share of the low-end translation market volume, with the consequence that translators who cannot offer a substantially better value (i.e. quality/price ratio) than MT will become obsolete. (Schmitt, 2019: 193)

Recent advances in **artificial intelligence (AI)** seem to confirm Schmitt's intuition about MT as a major disrupter in the language industry. Built on large language models (LLM), generative AI – such as, for instance, OpenAI's ChatGPT, Google's BARD or Adobe's FireFly – has already started reshaping the translation workflow (see Slator, 2022). LLMs, for instance, now allow for 'text adaptation via prompting, dynamic application of glossaries and

176 *Continuing to grow as a professional translator*

style guides during translation, cleaning and maintenance of translation memories, [and] quality estimation' as well as 'error detection, generation of variations of target text for expert linguists to choose from, automating manual tasks (e.g. tag placement), automated post-editing, and synthesizing parallel texts to train other MT models' (Stasimioti, 2023).

As a result of these new developments, the role of professional translators will undoubtedly continue to evolve rapidly in the coming years. Of course, nobody knows with certainty what the future holds for the translation profession. However, when asked in a survey which new roles they expected to see emerging in the near future, a majority of translation service provider (TSP) leaders mentioned roles that 'require a combination of linguistic and AI-interaction expertise' such as 'Prompt Engineer', 'Post-editor of LLM MT Output', 'AI Editor', 'Language Engineer', 'Source Language AI Copy Editor' or 'Translation AI Reviser' (Stasimioti, 2023). As predicted by Peter Schmitt, it looks like the future will indeed belong to translators who manage to **adapt to the changing translation ecosystem**' (2019: 193, my emphasis).

All this means that, as professional translators, we can never stop learning. In order to continue thriving, you will therefore need to find room in your sometimes-heavy workload to regularly engage with **CPD activities** that enable you to 'maintain, develo[p] and broade[n] [your] knowledge, skills, experience and understanding' (Dastyar, 2019: 67). This is also the view of the International Federation of Translators (FIT) in its 2022 position paper on Continuing Professional Development (CPD). 'Enhancing personal skills and capabilities', FIT rightly argues, 'is indispensable in these times of rapid changes' (FIT, 2022: 1).

The benefits of engaging with lifelong learning are thus now widely acknowledged, as attested by FIT's 2022 position paper. For freelance translators, 'CPD qualifications clearly offer them competitive advantages in the fiercely contested marketplace' (FIT, 2022: 1). As for in-house translators, CPD 'ensures that [they] keep abreast of changes in their respective industry' (ibid.). On its website, the UK's Institute of Translation and Interpreting (ITI) lists some of the main potential **benefits of regular CPD** for all professional translators (ITI, 2023). It

- Provides evidence of your commitment to your career and profession;
- Boosts your profile with existing and potential clients;
- Enhances [your] understanding of your specialist field;
- Gives you the potential to earn more;
- Helps you improve your productivity, efficiency and confidence by learning new skills;
- Enables you to learn a new specialism;
- Keeps you up to date with your source language;
- Leads to greater job satisfaction.

Keeping it sustainable   177

This list shows how your engagement with CPD benefits your clients and/ or your employer as you maintain and enhance your skills (not least your language skills). It also demonstrates your **commitment** to the profession. As can be seen from the rest of the list, though, ultimately you will likely be the main person to benefit from your engaging in CPD. It could help enhance your professional profile, increase your productivity and potentially boost your earnings through specialisation.

Some of you, however, may feel a bit puzzled by the last item, which states that CPD 'leads to greater job satisfaction'. Recent studies into the impact of CPD among healthcare professionals can help us understand this a bit better. Despite what ITI's list might lead us to believe, these studies have shown that CPD is not just about 'acquiring knowledge and skills, but also [developing our] professional identity, which leads to success as a professional' (Allen et al., 2019: 1088). In other words, CPD is not just about *what we know*, but also about *who we are* as professionals. This is because CPD allows us professionals to engage with a community of practice that shares a mutual interest, which in turn can help us develop support networks that may lead to future collaborations (ibid.; see also Chapter 3). This process can lead to 'improved job satisfaction, reduced burnout and increased retention' (ibid.: 1096). This can be seen to apply to professional translators, too. In a recent article, for instance, the head of the Training Unit at the European Commission's Directorate-General for Translation, Merit-Ene Ilja, stressed the importance of CPD for staff motivation (2023: 224).

All this should convince you of the importance of CPD for you as a professional translator. Keeping on top of your game by engaging with CPD will help you ensure that your role as a professional translator remains sustainable long term with regard to both *what you offer* (your skills and competences) and *how you feel* about the job (your motivation levels). Given these known benefits of CPD, many professional translator associations' **codes of conduct and/or ethics** now make it a requirement for their members to engage with it (see, for instance, the Bundesverband der Dolmetscher und Übersetzer's (BDÜ's) Code of Conduct article 1.9 in section 1, 'Main professional obligations', in Germany, or AUSIT's Code of Ethics '8. Professional Development', in Australia). Some associations, like the UK's ITI, even state a recommended number of hours that members should dedicate to CPD activities (in ITI's case, 30 hours per year). Others also state the kinds of activities members should prioritise during their CPD time. However, most avoid being too prescriptive, as they see CPD primarily as a matter of personal responsibility. This is because CPD is, essentially, a process by which one should: 'take control of [one's] own learning and development, by engaging in an on-going process of action and reflection' (Megginson and Whitaker, 2007: 3).

178   *Continuing to grow as a professional translator*

TOPICS FOR DISCUSSION AND ASSIGNMENTS 9.1

Activity 9.1 Have another look at your answers to 'Topics for discussion and assignments 3.1', which asked you to identify the professional association that will be the best fit for you as a professional translator.

- If your chosen association has a code of professional conduct and/or ethics, does it set CPD requirements for translators? If so, which ones?
- Have a look at the association's website, too. Does it contain any information, advice and/or requirements for members about CPD?
- Based on your findings, how important do you think your chosen association finds it that its members engage with CPD? Why do you think that is?

Activity 9.2 What about you? How do you feel about CPD for professional translators? To help you find out, discuss the following questions with a course mate:

- What could the benefits of engaging actively with CPD be for your career as a professional translator?
- Conversely, what do you think the consequences of failing to engage actively with CPD could be for you as a professional translator (if any)?

9.1.2 *Starting to plan your CPD as a professional translator*

9.1.2.1 *What should CPD look like for me as a professional translator?*

You may find the Megginson and Whitaker's definition of CPD inspiring, if a bit vague, too. Convinced as you are of the benefits of CPD, you might like to start 'taking control'–or, in other words, planning – your ongoing learning and development as a translator … but perhaps you don't know where to start. What should CPD look like for us as professional translators? In what follows, we will have a look at the kinds of CPD activities professional translators can engage with to stay on top of their game, while trying not to fall into the prescriptive trap. This is because **your own development needs** should be at the heart of your CPD, and nothing else. You, and you alone, are in control … so please read what follows as pointers that are only meant to help you get started on your journey. Before we start, take some time to reflect on the following questions:

> - What should the main objectives of CPD be for professional translators?
> - What kind of CPD activities should professional translators undertake to achieve these objectives?

According to Ehsan Taebi and Mir Saeed Mousavi Razavi, the main focus of CPD for professional translators should be on the continuous development of **translation competence** as defined by competence models such as PACTE's or the EMT's (Taebi and Razavi, 2020: 312). Consequently, the two Iranian scholars define CPD for professional translators as the process of:

> constantly preparing the right conditions for the gradual, coordinated, and balanced emergence of translation sub-competences over time and in the larger mould of translation competence, in such a way that [professional translators] [are ...] prepared to optimally and autonomously perform [their] responsibilities in [their] unique (or desired) professional ecology. (ibid.: 319)

If you can't remember what is meant by translation competence in these models, have another quick look at Chapter 1. To put it simply, translation competence is your overall competence as a professional translator, which itself is made up of various specific sub-competences. As suggested by Taebi and Mousavi Razavi, the CPD activities you undertake as a professional translator should ideally help you (further) develop aspects of the **sub-competences** that feed into your overall competence as a translator. As you will see from Table 9.1, competence models can therefore be a great way for you to start identifying specific areas you feel you should develop (further) in order to advance your career as a professional translator.

As part of your CPD, you may therefore find it more relevant to prioritise your 'language sub-competence' by attending regular language classes, either to enhance your command of a source language you already offer or to learn a new source language you would like to add to your service offer. Or you may, instead, find it more beneficial to complete a massive open online course (MOOC) in a specialist subject domain (e.g. on cybersecurity, electric cars etc.) in order to familiarise yourself with the terminology and some key concepts ('Cultural sub-competence'). You could also decide to attend a series of workshops delivered by your professional association on transcreation ('Translating sub-competence') or on LLMs ('Translation tools and technologies sub-competences'). Or, as a budding translator, you may find it makes more sense to start your CPD journey by reading online articles and/or attending webinars on the latest trends in the language industry in order to (further) develop your marketing strategy ('Language industry sub-competence').

180 *Continuing to grow as a professional translator*

Table 9.1 Examples of CPD areas contributing to professional translator competence (based on PACTE, 2003: 60 and EMT, 2022)

Examples of CPD areas specific to professional translators that contribute to professional translator competence ('hard skills'):	Language sub-competence Cultural sub-competence (includes subject-domain knowledge) Translating sub-competence Translation-related specialist sub-competence (e.g. AVT, transcreation) Translation project management sub-competence Translation tools and technologies sub-competence Language industry sub-competence
Examples of CPD areas not specific to professional translators but that contribute to professional translator competence ('soft skills'):	Time management sub-competence Entrepreneurial sub-competence Interpersonal sub-competence (e.g. teamwork skills, leadership skills) Emotion management sub-competence Ergonomics sub-competence Reflective practice sub-competence

If you have another look at Table 9.1, you will notice that all the examples of CPD activities we have just mentioned primarily fall under the umbrella of **hard skills**. These are the skills, (mostly) specific to professional translators, that contribute to your translation competence. They are all crucial skills but, as part of your CPD, you should also engage with activities that can help you (further) develop some crucial **soft skills** for translation competence (see Table 9.1; see also Chapter 1). If we go back to our last example, you may find that reading about the language industry and talking to fellow translators has allowed you to refine your own USP (see Chapter 8) but that you still lack the knowledge and the skills to develop your business plan and/or your marketing mix ('Entrepreneurial sub-competence'). You may therefore decide to complete a MOOC or to attend workshops/webinars on this. A bit later on in your career, you may find it difficult to manage your work-related stress and might therefore want to engage with CPD activities that help you with that ('Emotion management sub-competence'). A bit later on still, you might land yourself an in-house job as a senior translator that involves coordinating a team of more junior translators. As this is a leadership role, you may benefit from attending CPD workshops that will help you work on your leadership skills ('Interpersonal sub-competence').

You should note that, just like the (sub-)competences of the PACTE and EMT models, the sub-competences listed in Table 9.1 'are interrelated, but do not necessarily develop in parallel or sequence' (Taebi and Mousavi Razavi, 2020: 320). As I have tried to make clear throughout this book, each of them is 'like a cog in a wheel of a sophisticated system' (ibid.). The – constantly

Keeping it sustainable 181

evolving – needs of **your own translation ecosystem** should therefore dictate which sub-competences you decide to prioritise at any point in time.

9.1.2.2 *Which areas of my CPD should I prioritise?*

As a professional translator, you will have precious limited time to dedicate to CPD activities. You will therefore have to decide which areas of your CPD you want to prioritise. According to freelance translator Lloyd Bingham, the thing to bear in mind is that CPD is about **future-proofing your career.** 'We need to continue working on our skills', he explained in a podcast, 'in order to do what machines can't' (Roberts, 2022). Even though Bingham agrees it is important to continue developing both hard and soft skills through CPD, he therefore believes novice translators should prioritise two specific hard skills; specialist subject-domain knowledge ('Cultural sub-competence') and target-language writing skills ('Language sub-competence'). Both, according to him, are crucially important in the age of machine translation (MT).

The first one, **specialist subject-domain knowledge,** is about our ability to understand our clients' sector and the domain-specific source texts we translate for them. In the age of Translation 4.0, 'our main (and maybe only) advantage over MT is our ability to understand what we translate' (Schmitt, 2019: 224). It is this ability that allows us to 'produc[e] meaningful and functionally adequate translations of homogenous quality' (ibid.: 223)– something MT cannot always do. Nobody can be an expert in everything. However, specialist subject-domain knowledge doesn't mean you need to become an absolute expert. You just need to develop enough expertise in a topic to understand your clients' source texts and be familiar with the terminology and style requirements in your target language. If you have a first degree in a field other than translating or modern languages (e.g. architecture, art history, biomedical sciences, business, computing sciences, law etc.), then you may want to specialise in that field ... provided this also answers a market need as identified in your market research (see Chapter 8). If you are from a modern languages background, though, you will likely enter the language industry with no area of specialisation – apart from modern languages and/or translating, that is! In that case, CPD will help you develop the required expertise in the specialist subject domain(s) you have identified as promising in your market research. Indeed, '[s]pending several months immersing oneself in a technical subject [...]–such as wind turbine rotor blade production, roof constructions in the USA and Germany, knitting and weaving machines – provides a solid knowledge basis and an excellent starting point for a successful career as a specialized technical translator' (ibid.). As can be seen from the examples given by Schmitt in this quote, a professional translator's area of specialisation can be very specific. One could even talk about 'sub-specialisations'. This means that, even if you have some expertise in a broad field such as law, medicine or similar, CPD can allow you

182 *Continuing to grow as a professional translator*

to sub-specialise by helping you develop the necessary knowledge about specific areas of that field (e.g. contract law or intellectual property law for law, and infectious diseases or oncology for medicine). Reading articles, attending courses/webinars/conferences, listening to podcasts or taking a MOOC are examples of CPD activities you can do to develop the necessary expertise in these sub-fields to truly tailor your service offer to your clients' needs.

The second sub-competence Bingham believes novice translators should prioritise as part of their CPD is **target-language writing skills**. This is about making sure that you produce content that is fluent and respects the style and conventions of the target text's genre. As linguists, our efforts are traditionally focused on our mastery of our foreign language(s). However, as a professional translator you also need to ensure sure that you have impeccable command of your target language (which, for most of us, is also our L1). Whether we live abroad or not, this is a challenge for all of us. A possible solution is to attend writing skills workshops as part of your CPD; many professional associations organise such workshops these days. A cheaper – and very efficient – way of working on your target-language writing skills, however, is … reading! Indeed, reading is a 'valid and valuable professional development activity for professional translators' (Fulford, 2012: 276). What you read should include 'material and works dealing not only with language and translation related topics, but also geographical and cultural matters, business, information technology, general literature (including fiction), and current affairs/news, as well as materials related to the translator's own specialist subject' (ibid.: 277).

All this applies to budding in-house translators, too, as attested by the results of a 2021 survey of professional translators working in-house at member organisations of the International Annual Meeting on Language Arrangements, Documentation and Publication (IAMLADP). The survey found that, compared with the 2010 results of the same survey, **three skill sets** have become increasingly valued in the last decade (Lafeber, 2023: 40):

- [K]nowledge of the subject of the translation […], and understanding of the authoring and intended use of the source text;
- [A]bility to make effective use of CAT tools, including recycled content and MT output;
- [H]aving the target-language skills to convey detailed levels of meaning when required.

The survey thus confirms that specialist subject-domain knowledge, target-language skills and translation tools and technologies skills are three sets of hard skills that are increasingly valued for all professional translators.

However, this should not make us forget the importance of continuing to develop our soft skills as part of our CPD. In fact, the same survey also found that 'flexibility', 'a willingness to learn' and 'an ability to work both independently and with others' are 'as important as linguistic skills' for in-house

Keeping it sustainable 183

translators working in an institutional setting (ibid.: 39–40). The first of these soft skills, 'flexibility', is defined as the 'adaptability to cope with unpredictable workloads, [or] changes in procedures or working methods' (ibid.: 39). As the professional translator's role becomes increasingly more complex and multifaceted, **flexibility**, one could argue, is becoming a crucial attribute for all those translators who, in the context of Translation 4.0, regularly have to 'cop[e] with difficult conditions and inappropriate roles yet still deliver work that fulfils customer expectations' (Risku and Schlager, 2021: 20).

Recognising the risks these challenges pose to translators' mental well-being, the UK's ITI published a position statement on translators' mental health and well-being in 2021. In its statement, ITI advises that 'translators' continuing professional development needs to include a commitment to acquiring and improving psychological skills alongside specialist knowledge as a means of responding and adapting to external events' (Hubscher-Davidson, 2021). The author of the ITI's position statement, Séverine Hubscher-Davidson, is an academic who researches the role of emotions in translation. Based on her work with professional translators, she suggests that developing your **emotional efficacy** as a translator should enable you to 'become more skilled in dealing with emotion-laden and difficult issues in [your] work, to be less stressed and depleted after emotional work, and to respond more effectively to environmental demands' (Hubscher-Davidson, 2018: 203). Further, greater emotional efficacy 'may enhance performance in ambiguous situations' and 'facilitate the resolution of complex emotional decision-making' (Hubscher-Davidson, 2018b: 94). Focused emotional intelligence (EI) interventions, such as CPD workshops dedicated to EI, can help you further develop your emotional efficacy. Such workshops, with group discussions and interactive participation, have been shown to have 'real effects on behavioural modification' (Hubscher-Davidson, 2018b: 94). Considering that EI interventions can help you respond better to stress and improve your general well-being (see Dave et al., 2021), and that translators with greater EI are more likely to report higher job satisfaction (Hubscher-Davidson, 2018a: 196–197), embedding EI training into your CPD could be a good way to ensure your role as professional translator remains sustainable in the long run.

TOPICS FOR DISCUSSION AND ASSIGNMENTS 9.2

When we talk about CPD, we often think of attending CPD events such as courses or workshops organised by professional bodies or universities or similar. This is what is known as formal CPD. There are, however, other types of CPD. On its website, the UK's ITI therefore makes a helpful distinction between three types of CPD for translators: 'formal CPD', 'self-directed CPD' and 'contributing to the profession'. I have already mentioned a couple of self-directed CPD activities, such as reading or listening to podcasts.

184 *Continuing to grow as a professional translator*

Spend some time searching the Internet for advice from professional associations, as well as translator blogs on CPD activities you could engage with as a professional translator. Select the ones that you feel could be most relevant for your own context and sort them into three categories, as follows:

- **Formal CPD:** e.g. courses, workshops, webinars
- **Self-directed CPD:** e.g. reading, listening to podcasts
- **Contributing to the profession:** e.g. committee work in a professional association, mentoring

9.2 Keeping in good form to stay in the game: Self-care

9.2.1 Well-being matters: Potential physical, cognitive and organisational stressors for translators

In 2020, a UK survey identified personal, health and well-being concerns as some of the issues faced by language professionals (CIOL, 2020). We can all easily imagine how physical ill health can affect our ability to perform as professional translators. What about our well-being, though? The World Health Organization (WHO) defines well-being as:

> a positive state experienced by individuals and societies. Similar to health, it is a resource for daily life and is determined by social, economic and environmental conditions. Well-being encompasses quality of life and the ability of people and societies to contribute to the world with a sense of meaning and purpose. (WHO, 2021: 10)

If we agree with WHO that our well-being is 'a resource for daily life', then we must consider that this resource can run dangerously low or even become exhausted. This, in turn, could hamper our ability to contribute to society through our work. Where does this leave us professional translators? According to Canadian scholar Maureen Ehrensberger-Dow, 'the added value of human translation (i.e. over MT solutions) relates to uniquely **human traits** such as creativity, discourse awareness and understanding of the target audience' (2020: 151). Poor well-being, she believes, could have a negative impact on our ability to bring this 'added value' to our translation work. She therefore argues that: 'the well-being of translators should be a priority for employers and clients' (ibid.). Similarly, ITI's position statement on translators' mental health and well-being makes it clear that professional translators need to look after not just their physical health, but also 'their mental health and wellbeing' so they can 'carry out their assignments safely and effectively' (Hubscher-Davidson, 2021).

What can we do to protect our well-being at work, then? First, we can develop our awareness of what, in our role as a translator, could affect it. Let's start by taking a few moments to think about the following question:

> - According to WHO, well-being is 'determined by social, economic and environmental factors' (WHO, 2021: 10). Think about these factors in relation to the work of professional translators in your chosen context. Concretely, what would you say could affect their well-being?

As argued elsewhere in this book, professional translating is best seen as a context-specific, **situated activity**. Indeed, professional translators work 'in a context of personal interactions, in a given place and time [...], in connection with other processes and with an organizational structure' (Kuznik and Miquel Verd, 2010: 26). This is why, in the last fifteen years, an increasing number of researchers have decided to look at the ways in which professional translators' regular interactions with both their physical and their social environment can influence not just their decision-making, but also their well-being (see Ehrensberger-Dow, 2019). This is what is known as the ergonomics of translation.

Many of us tend to associate the concept of **ergonomics** with our physical environment and, accordingly, our physical well-being. However, ergonomics is about much more than that. On its website, the International Ergonomics Association (IEA) defines ergonomics as:

the scientific discipline concerned with the understanding of interactions among humans and other elements of a system, and the profession that applies theory, principles, data, and methods to design in order to optimize human well-being and overall system performance. (IEA, 2023)

In a work context, ergonomics can help 'optimise' people's well-being – and, ultimately, their performance – by informing the design of systems and environments that are 'compatible with people's needs, abilities and limitations'. The main idea is, therefore, to limit potential sources of strain, stress or tension (also known as 'stressors') during interactions with 'other elements of a system' (ibid.). Quite an endeavour! To achieve this, IEA therefore recommends adopting a holistic approach that involves looking at three different areas of ergonomics:

- **Physical ergonomics**, which is 'is concerned with human anatomical, anthropometric, physiological and biomechanical characteristics as they relate to physical activity';
- **Cognitive ergonomics**, which is 'concerned with mental processes, such as perception, memory, reasoning, and motor response, as they affect interactions among humans and other elements of a system';
- **Organisational ergonomics**: which 'is concerned with the optimization of sociotechnical systems, including their organizational structures, policies, and processes.' (ibid.)

186 *Continuing to grow as a professional translator*

Table 9.2 Main physical, cognitive and organisational stressors for professional translators (based on Ehrensberger-Dow, 2019, Ehrensberger-Dow and Jääskeläinen, 2019 and Ehrensberger-Dow, 2020)

Physical	• Inadequate workplace • Inadequate workstation
Cognitive	• Challenging nature of documents to translate • (Imposed) use of translation tools and technologies
Organisational	• Little-to-no opportunity for collaboration and exchanges with other translators and/or stakeholders in the translation production networks • Unreasonable productivity expectations • Limited job security, status, trust and agency

In her work on ergonomics in translation, Maureen Ehrensberger-Dow uses IEA's approach as a framework to identify the environmental factors that can influence the translation process (see Ehrensberger-Dow, 2019, Ehrensberger-Dow and Jääskeläinen, 2019 and Ehrensberger-Dow, 2020). As you will see from Table 9.2 above, we can use her work as a starting point to identify, for each of these three areas of ergonomics, some of the main **potential stressors** that could affect our well-being as professional translators and, consequently, jeopardise our ability to work effectively.

First of all, as professional translators we may experience **physical stress** in our work environment that can affect our well-being (see Table 9.2). Stress, here, should be understood as the pressure or tension we may experience as a result of our interactions with our work environment as translators. Due to the sedentary nature of the job, one rarely thinks of translation as a physical activity. However, professional translators tend to spend long hours in the same workspace typing at a computer. Working in an inadequate space, where some environmental factors such as the room's layout, the temperature, the light and/or the ambient noise are not right – and we have no control over them – can be a potential source of physical unease that could have negative consequences for our ability to concentrate as well as our health (Ehrensberger-Dow, 2020: 151). Another major source of physical stress can be our workstation, namely our computer screen(s), keyboard, mouse/other input devices and the desk chair we use. According to the European Agency for Safety and Health at Work, a workstation that is not right for us and/or the work we do will lead to poor posture, especially 'awkward limb and neck positions' (EU-OSHA, 2017). If this situation is prolonged, it 'will accelerate or exacerbate the development of musculoskeletal symptoms' such as 'neck, upper limb and back pain' (ibid.). Over time, this may have a detrimental impact on our ability to carry out our work effectively.

As well as these physical stressors, we should also be aware of the potential **cognitive stressors** that have the potential to affect our well-being as professional translators. As can be seen from Table 9.2, how we react to, and

Keeping it sustainable 187

interact with, some of the documents we have to translate may be a potential source of cognitive strain. Indeed, we may react emotionally to a source text's 'subject matter', its perceived 'quality' and/or its perceived 'terminological, conceptual and linguistic complexity' (Ehrensberger-Dow, 2019: 39). Let's start with a text's subject matter. Some of us can find the content of some texts emotionally challenging to translate. Recently, for instance, UK-based professional translator Clare Suttie posted the following message on LinkedIn (Suttie, 2022):

What's the saddest job you've ever had?

There are a few jobs that stick in my mind. Many years ago, an elderly lady came to our office when we were based in London. We were down a hidden alleyway, up many flights of stairs. The lady had a certificate in Arabic, with some documents needing translating. It turned out to be the death certificate of her son, who had died on a holiday, and some accompanying reports. I made her tea, we had a chat and I have always remembered her.

These days we don't always meet the people we are translating for, but they can still make a lasting impression. In recent months, we have provided translations for a couple who have had two babies who have died. [...]

The many responses to Suttie's post made it clear that, even though we all react in our own unique ways to a source text's content, some texts have the power to make us experience **negative feelings** such as sadness, for instance. At times, the emotion elicited may simply be boredom. As pointed out by Hubscher-Davidson and Lehr, '[a]rguably, boredom is one of the more commonly experienced issues for translators in the context of their work' (2021: 59). We may feel bored at having to translate texts that we find repetitive or not very stimulating. This is something we should take seriously, as boredom has been found to lead to 'reduced motivation, decreased job satisfaction, poor performance, and counterproductive behaviours' (ibid.). Similarly, we may experience negative emotions (e.g. frustration) at having to translate poorly written source texts, especially if we are unable to clarify parts of the text with their author(s). At other times, a translation task may turn out to be linguistically or conceptually far more challenging than we had anticipated, which can make us feel anxious or overwhelmed. As professional translators, we should therefore recognise that our interactions with the source texts we translate can generate negative emotions that have the potential to affect our well-being. Further, '[h]uman-computer interactions, information sources, and language technology are also all factors related to the cognitive ergonomics of a translator's workplace' (Ehrensberger-Dow, 2019: 39). Research into translators' use of CAT tools, for instance, tends

188 *Continuing to grow as a professional translator*

to indicate that many translators 'are not entirely satisfied with the CAT tools they choose to use or are obliged to use' (O'Brien et al., 2017: 145). In fact, interacting with translation tools and technologies that we feel are not really tailored to our own needs, or that we don't always feel comfortable using, can be the source of a form of '**technostress**' that 'reduces performance and harms individual wellbeing' (Koskinen, 2020: 146). Cognitive stressors, we might conclude, are therefore a potential source of negative emotions that can lead to diminished well-being and decreased job satisfaction and, over time, make translation as a profession seem less sustainable (Hubscher-Davidson, 2020).

In 2020, Kaisa Koskinen published a whole book on the topic: *Translation and Affect*. To her, professional translating is 'affective labour' because it requires 'the creation and manipulation of emotions, the production and distribution of feelings, and the management of affinity or distance' (2020: 30). Koskinen thus focuses not only on the relation between the translator and the text to translate, but also on the wider context:

> The contemporary networked translation industry provides constellations of mutual dependence where translators, project managers, revisers, terminologists and IT people and other parties are in constant, albeit often virtual and indirect, contact. [...] These networks of relations provide a **second layer of affective labour**, tangential but not directly derived from the contents of the translatorial task at hand. [...] Managing, modulating and manipulating affects is indeed hard work, and the multiprofessional playgrounds, network economy, technological advances and tightening financial constraints are a constant source of negative affects in the current landscape. (Koskinen, 2020: 39, my emphasis)

This 'second layer of affective labour' described by Koskinen contributes to the **organisational stressors** that can affect us professional translators. Depending on our circumstances, we may find having to liaise with all the relevant stakeholders of a given project a source of stress. This is because contacts with other stakeholders are often indirect – as in virtual and mediated (e.g. communication with the end client via a project manager)–and, consequently, more challenging at times. As we saw in Chapter 3, in current translation production networks (see Figure 3.2), 'freelance translators commonly work in isolation with little collective power' (Moorkens, 2017: 467). Concretely, this means that often they lack direct access to supportive colleagues, which can lead to 'lower rates of job satisfaction, life satisfaction, and subjective well-being' (ibid.).

Not having direct access to supportive colleagues can be especially challenging when you work for a sector where 'recent rapid developments in CAT tools and increasingly usable MT output have led to higher organizational expectations with regard to productivity and consequently additional time pressure' (Ehrensberger-Dow, 2019: 44). Professional translators often have

Keeping it sustainable 189

to contend with ever-tighter deadlines. In order to meet them, they may feel that they have no other choice but to integrate CAT tools and MT into their workflows. This, in turn, can leave some of them feeling like they are **losing their agency** as translators:

> Dehumanization is related to translators' emotions and self-perception. It is one of the consequences of automation and fragmentation. Like Little Tramp, the character created by Charlie Chaplin who feels alienated by having to perform a repetitive task and is eventually swallowed by the machinic assembly line in *Modern Times* (1936), technology might negatively affect translators' emotions and self-perception [...]. (Alonso and Nunes Vieira, 2020: 398)

There are reasons for professional translators to fear being eaten alive by the metaphorical machinic assembly line of Translation 4.0. In a recent analysis of the contemporary translation industry, academics Joss Moorkens and Marta Rocchi identified key areas of ethical concern. Each can be seen as another potential organisational stressor for us translators:

- **Imbalance of power:** As we saw in Chapter 5, trust can be seen as the cornerstone of the industry's contemporary production networks (see Abdallah and Koskinen, 2007). As individuals, freelancer translators tend to be geographically isolated 'nodes' in these networks (see Figure 3.2). As a result, they have very limited collective power and must trust in the good faith of their – often, much more powerful – employers, especially when their employer is a translation agency. However, poor or unethical employment practices persist across the industry, with some employers putting profits before translators' well-being (Moorkens and Rocchi, 2021: 325);
- **Ownership of resources:** According to the 1886 Berne Convention for the Protection of Literary and Artistic Works, translators legally have rights to copyright ownership, subject to the rights of the original authors and depending on jurisdiction. Yet, 'it is common practice in the translation industry for translators to return translation memories via the project manager to their employers, retaining no ownership over the TM or the final translation' (Moorkens and Rocchi, 2021: 326). Very often in the industry, the end clients are seen as the rightful owners of the copyright and the TMs are retained by translation agencies to minimise costs (as they can be reused for future projects). Due to the growing demand for such data to train neural MT systems (machine learning), it is increasing in value, but some professional translators are missing out, in the absence of royalty payments (ibid.: 326);
- **Sustainability of the translation industry:** Despite the global language services industry being forecast to grow to a value of $84.9 billion by 2026 (Nimdzi, 2022), there are growing concerns about the long-term

190   *Continuing to grow as a professional translator*

sustainability of the freelance translation profession. Work stressors such as low rates, tight deadlines, imposed post-editing work with poor MTs and mandatory discounts are driving some translators out of the industry or encouraging them to produce lower-quality work. The increasing use of MT cannot compensate for this, as neural MT systems require a constant flow of large amounts of up-to-date bilingual data for training. Deteriorating conditions for translators could therefore make the whole industry unsustainable in the medium to long term (Moorkens and Rocchi, 2021: 327);

- **Trust:** We have just discussed how translators are required to trust in the good faith of their employers in the contemporary production networks. Trust is not just a matter for individuals, though, but also for organisations. Indeed, 'a company in the translation industry needs to establish relationships based on trust with all the stakeholders involved in its network' (Moorkens and Rocchi, 2021: 328). This is because mistrust has a cost; '[p]rocesses related to translation within a company become slower and more expensive due in particular to a lack of trust and information asymmetry'. Mistrust can also have a negative impact on translators' working conditions. In the case of the translation of pre-release materials, for instance, 'the need for secrecy impinges on the [translator's] ability to produce a high-quality text' (ibid.: 329).

TOPICS FOR DISCUSSION AND ASSIGNMENTS 9.3

Imagine that you work as a freelance translator or as a PM at a translation agency (feel free to use the same scenario as the one you used for the Topics for discussion and assignments 8.2–8.4 in Chapter 8). For each of the three categories, use what we have just discussed, what you know about the job and – just as importantly – what you know about yourself to identify one or two stressors that you feel are the most likely to affect your well-being in your chosen context:

- Physical stressors:
- Cognitive stressors:
- Organisational stressors:

9.2.2 Self-care as an ethical responsibility for professional translators

When they are organisational, work stressors can be the cause of **ethical stress**. Ethical stress is occupational stress 'resulting from disparities in the ethical values and expected behaviour of employees' (DeTienne et al., 2012: 377; see also Hubscher-Davidson, 2021b: 417). For example, depending on our own ethical values, for some of us, being asked to compromise the quality of a translation job to keep costs down will be a source of ethical stress. We may feel very uncomfortable with the request because we believe that the target text we will produce will not serve the end user's best interest. Yet, we may also feel we have no choice in the matter as we desperately need the work as freelance translators ... or we don't feel senior enough to challenge our line manager's request as in-house translators. Despite our serious reservations, we reluctantly decide to comply, thus compromising some of our ethical values. Our ethical values are the core personal or professional values we started exploring in Chapter 2 (see 'Topics for discussion and assignments Activity 2.4'). They are unique to us.

There are times where ethical stress emerges not from a clash between our **ethical values** and what others expect of us as translators ... but between our personal values and our internalised professional values or, to put it simply, what *we expect of ourselves* as professional translators.

In his book on *Translation Ethics*, UK academic Joseph Lambert gives a very helpful overview of some of the main drivers behind our desire to act ethically as translators ... as well as the many potential considerations that stem from these **overarching drivers**. As illustrated by Figure 9.1 below, some of these considerations are based on personal values (e.g. being a 'good' person, standing up against injustice etc.) while others are based on professional values we may have adopted and internalised (e.g. providing a service to your client, being accountable etc.). As we balance our responsibilities as translators, our professional values can sometimes clash with our personal values. There may be times, for instance, where our personal value of 'standing up against injustice' will seem irreconcilable with our internalised

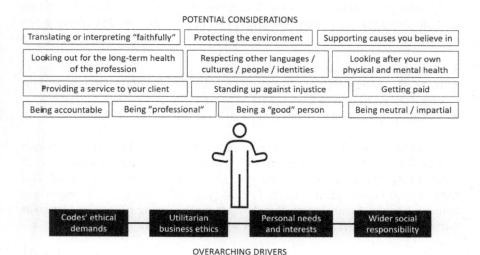

Figure 9.1 Potential reflections on responsibility in translation and interpreting (from Lambert, 2023: 171)

192 *Continuing to grow as a professional translator*

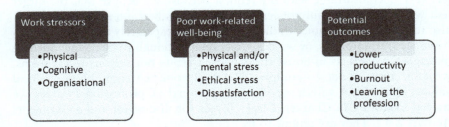

Figure 9.2 Potential impact of work stressors and poor work-related well-being on translators

professional value of 'remaining neutral/impartial'. Unless we manage to resolve them properly, the numerous potential **ethical dilemmas** between our personal and professional values can also become a powerful source of ethical stress for us as professional translators.

As can be seen from Figure 9.2, when endured over a period of time, physical, cognitive and organisational work stressors can lead to poor work-related well-being. If ignored, this can affect our productivity at work and even lead to **burnout** (see Hubscher-Davidson, 2021a: 425). Burnout, a term first coined by German-American psychologist Herbert Freudenberg, can be understood as a work-related process of 'wear[ing] out, or becom[ing] exhausted by making excessive demands on energy, strength, or resources' (1974: 159). As we start running low on physical and mental resources, work becomes increasingly unsustainable. These days, WHO recognises burnout as an 'occupational phenomenon' that results from 'chronic workplace stress that has not been successfully managed' (WHO, 2019). The three dimensions of burnout are:

- Feelings of energy depletion or exhaustion;
- Increased mental distance from one's job, or feelings of negativism or cynicism related to one's job;
- Reduced professional efficacy. (ibid.)

This risk of burnout is a very real one for professional translators, which is why there is broad agreement with Lambert that 'there is cause for all language professionals to consider the relationship between their work and their mental health' (2023: 142). To that end, **self-care** can be an important balancing tool for translators. Borrowed from the caring professions (such as nursing or social care), the concept of self-care refers to:

> activities or processes that are initiated and managed by the worker for the purpose of supporting one's health and well-being, attending to one's needs, or providing stress relief. (Bressi and Vaden, 2017: 34)

Keeping it sustainable 193

We know that, as professional translators, we operate in an industry that is complex and fast-changing and whose practices are not always ethical. We also know that, despite the toll work stressors can take on our well-being, we regularly have to resolve ethical dilemmas as we try to balance our many – and sometimes conflicting – responsibilities (see Figure 9.1). However, we are less likely to make the right ethical decisions for us if we suffer from poor work-related well-being. As Koskinen notes, 'when things become complicated, when the personal and the professional enter into conflict, and when there seems to be no right course of action, [...] one needs solid bearings' (2016: 176). This is why self-care can be seen as an **ethical responsibility** for professional translators. By supporting our well-being, self-care can help us keep 'fit and well-prepared to perform [our] assignments to the highest standards' (Costa et al., 2020: 40). It can also help us find the resources to make the right ethical decisions for us, avoid burnout and stay in the profession for longer. As stated by Gerard McAlester, ultimately as translators '[our] responsibility is not to the author, or the reader, or the commissioner, or to the translating profession but to [our]selves' (2003: 226).

TOPICS FOR DISCUSSION AND ASSIGNMENTS 9.4

The image in Figure 9.1 first appeared in *Translation Ethics*, where Joseph Lambert explained that it 'draws attention to the inescapably personal nature of ethics and the inescapably context dependent nature of our decisions. There is no one "right" answer in all situations' (2023: 171).

Activity 9.3 Have another look at Figure 9.1.

- Which potential considerations/values do you think will matter the most to you in a typical translation commission as a professional translator?
- Are there any other values – whether personal or professional – that do not feature in Figure 9.1 but that you feel are important to you (see 'Topics for discussion and assignments Activity 2.4' in Chapter 2)?

Activity 9.4 Imagine a situation where a translation job leads to a clash between some of the core values you have identified in Activity 9.3. This will be your ethical dilemma.

Activity 9.5 Now, get into pairs. Explain your ethical dilemma to your partner and discuss it using the following questions as a starting point:

194 *Continuing to grow as a professional translator*

- Why is this an ethical dilemma for you? How does it make you feel?
- Which 'overarching drivers' (in the black boxes at the bottom of Figure 9.1) do you feel could be the most helpful to help you solve this ethical dilemma?
- What (else)/who (else) could help you solve this ethical dilemma?
- How do you think you would feel if you couldn't find a way to solve this ethical dilemma satisfactorily?
- How do you think you would you feel if this ethical dilemma wasn't just a one-off, but something that arose on a regular basis in your work?

Activity 9.6 Group discussion. As a whole class, use what you have discussed in pairs (Activity 9.5) as a starting point to answer the following question:

- To what extent do you agree with professional translator Gerard McAlester that, ultimately as translators '[our] responsibility is not to the author, or the reader, or the commissioner, or to the translating profession but to [our]selves' (2003: 226)?

9.2.3 Self-care for professional translators

Just like with CPD, the guiding principle behind self-care is that it should support our own needs. We all experience work stressors in different ways, which means that we all have very specific well-being needs. This is why you should read what follows as mere pointers, meant to help you get started on your own self-care journey so you can continue to grow as a professional translator.

As you can see from the proposed self-care model in Figure 9.3, there are some concrete steps you can take to take care of yourself as a professional translator.

1. **Look after your physical well-being:** As well as making sure you take regular breaks and exercise, you should look out for potential sources of physical stress in your workspace. Too often, freelance translators pay little attention to their workstation set-up; they are happy to use 'laptop computers at desks and in seats that are not built for long-term use' (Moorkens, 2021: 331). However, following existing occupational health guidance on how to best set up your workstation could help prevent bad posture and, by extension, musculoskeletal injuries. Box 9.1 contains a few easy, and relatively inexpensive, tips taken from Queensland Government's Workplace and Safety Office in Australia.

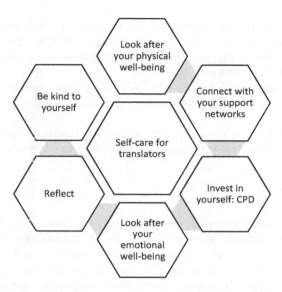

Figure 9.3 Proposed self-care model for professional translators

---

Box 9.1 Tips for setting up your workstation

- If you're working for long periods of time from a laptop or tablet, ideally you should use a separate monitor, keyboard and mouse. This will help your posture and visual comfort.
- Set the **monitor height** to your eye level or below, depending on what type of glasses you wear. If you don't have a monitor available, raise your laptop on a riser, stand, or another stable item such as reams of paper or large hardcover books.
- Ideally, set up your **monitor distance** at about an arm's length from where you're sitting. You can adjust the distance depending on the size of the monitor screen and what's comfortable for your eyes.
- If you use **two or more monitors** equally throughout the day, position yourself and your keyboard at equal distance to both screens so you don't have to twist your neck and spine. Also make sure the monitors are both at the same level.
- Put your **keyboard and mouse** on a flat surface, directly in front of you about 10 to 15 cm from the edge of the desk. This provides you with forearm shoulder and neck support. Keep your mouse next to and parallel to the keyboard as much as possible. This will reduce shoulder discomfort. Different keyboards and mouse designs can be more comfortable and useful for different workers.

196 *Continuing to grow as a professional translator*

> - After adjusting your chair, use a **footrest** if your feet can't comfortably sit flat on the floor. Check its height so your hips and knees are level. It should be stable and large enough to comfortably rest both feet and sloped for ankle comfort.
>   *This information was developed by the Queensland Government and is being used with permission.*
>
> Source: https://www.worksafe.qld.gov.au/safety-and-prevention/hazards/hazardous-manual-tasks/working-with-computers/setting-up-your-work station.

2. **Connect with your support networks:** As we saw in Chapter 3, in the current translation production model, where many translators are subcontracted as freelancers, translators are 'creative knowledge workers' (Groß, 2010: 98). As such, they 'rely heavily on their personal professional knowledge'. They must therefore 'ensure their competitive advantage on the labour market through the constant improvement of their unique selling propositions' (ibid.; see also Chapter 8). With that in mind, a translator's social and professional networks are therefore essential so that they can both exchange knowledge with and learn from other translators: 'When facing a cognitive deficit, having the possibility to ask someone for support or additional information can be of great help to a knowledge worker' (ibid.: 100). Developing these networks, however, does not just make business sense. We know that translators' relative isolation can be a work stressor, leading to 'lower rates of job satisfaction, life satisfaction, and subjective well-being' for some (Moorkens, 2017: 467). Connecting with your support networks can thus help you enhance your well-being by helping you become a 'networked lone fighter' (Groß, 2010: 98), as opposed to a 'lone fighter'. Please have another look at Chapter 3 for advice and guidance on how to set up your support networks as a translator.
3. **Invest in yourself:** CPD is not just about *what we know*, but also about *who we are*. When you engage with CPD, you invest in both your professional and personal development. As it is about your own growth and self-actualisation, CPD can therefore help you enhance your well-being and reduce the risk of burnout (Allen et al., 2019: 1096). Have another look at Section 9.1, 'Keeping on top of your game to keep on top of the game: CPD', in this chapter to find out more about CPD for professional translators.
4. **Look after your emotional well-being:** As we have already mentioned, recent studies have highlighted the importance of emotional and relational competencies for your well-being and performance as a translator (see

Keeping it sustainable 197

Georgiou and Perdikaki, 2020; Rojo López and Ramos-Caro, 2016). As translators, we should therefore:

- [Strive to] become self-aware and learn about adaptive responses and coping strategies when encountering ethically stressful situations;
- [Seek] guidance when it comes to attending to [our] own emotional, spiritual, psychological and physical needs;
- [Learn] preventive measures to manage [our] stress and solutions for processing challenging experiences.

(Hubscher-Davidson, 2021a: 426)

Attending CPD workshops on EI could be one way to develop your emotional efficacy and, therefore, enhance your resilience. However, this is not the only way. Other ways include strengthening your social connections by connecting with your support networks, identifying and practising activities that will help you reduce your stress levels (e.g. sporting activity, drawing, reading, walks, mindfulness etc.) and attending coaching or counselling sessions, among others.

5. **Reflect:** Caring professions such as nursing, social work and teaching have long seen reflective ability as a key skill to develop (see, for instance, Duffy 2007). This is because it allows practitioners to enhance their self-awareness and empathy. As such, reflective ability is 'strongly linked to ethics and professional judgement' (Hargreaves and Page, 2013: 2). Recently, a study into the reflective practice experiences of social workers employed in global development has shown that it can be an efficient form of self-care that improves the well-being of people working in challenging and complex conditions without formal supervision and support (Strumm, 2023). Supervision, here, should be understood as 'a process of professional learning and development that enables individuals to reflect on and develop their knowledge, skills, and competence, through agreed and regular support with another professional' (HCPC UK, 2021). Even though the working conditions of freelance translators are not directly comparable to those of social workers working in a global development capacity, both commonly share a lack of access to support (i.e. an absence of direct access to colleague support) and supervision. Reflective practice could therefore be another form of CPD that helps us as translators take care of our emotional well-being by increasing our self-awareness, boosting our confidence and reducing our work-related stress. As explained by UK-based HR professional and well-being expert Lauren Seward:

Acknowledging our wellbeing through reflective practice gives us permission to 'regroup' and identify a current picture for ourselves. Very simply it helps us recognise what we are doing well for ourselves, and what perhaps we are not doing so well with. In a positive and encouraging way, we can then coax ourselves to add some simple changes in the areas that will make a big difference. (Waite, 2023)

Figure 9.4 Driscoll's What? model of structured reflection

There are many – more or less complex – models of reflection we can use to revisit our professional experiences. When one is relatively new to reflective practice, however, adopting a relatively simple model such as Driscoll's 'What?' reflective model is often the best way to get started (see Figure 9.4 above). Originally developed for the supervision of healthcare professionals, this reflective model is based on three very simple questions: 'What?', 'So what?' and 'Now what?' When reflecting on a situation, you should seek to answer as many of the trigger questions in Table 9.3 as you can. You can use this model to reflect across a range of situations. It can, for instance, help you carry out a more detailed project post-mortem than the 'Start, Stop, Continue' exercise introduced in Chapter 6. In many instances, it will allow you to become more aware of your own emotions during complex situations and to identify your own development needs.

6. **Be kind to yourself:** As we reflect on our work as professional translators, we are reminded of all the responsibilities we need to balance during the course of our work (see Figure 9.1), as well as the many ethical dilemmas that emerge in the process. Sometimes, we do not manage to solve these completely satisfactorily. This can become a source of ethical stress. One of the features of ethical stress is the ontological guilt we feel; that is the guilt we experience at not being able to act in accordance with our own values (Hubscher-Davidson, 2021b: 417). However, carrying this guilt around can affect both our well-being and our ability to further develop our ethical maturity. Ethical maturity can be defined as

> the reflective, rational, emotional and intuitive capacity to decide [our] actions are right and wrong, or good and better; the resilience and courage to implement those decisions; the willingness to be accountable for ethical decisions made (publicly or privately); and the ability to learn from and live with the experience. (Carroll and Shaw, 2013: 138)

Keeping it sustainable 199

Table 9.3 Trigger questions for the 'what' model. Adapted from Driscoll (2007: 45)

1. What?	Start by briefly describing the situation you want to reflect on: • *What is the purpose of returning to this situation?* • *What happened?* • *What did I notice/do?* • *Who else was involved? What did they notice/do?*
2. So what?	Then, explain what makes this situation significant: • *How did I react? Why did I react this way?* • *Was I experiencing an ethical dilemma?* • *How did I feel at the time? And how do I feel about the situation now (if different)?* • *What were the – positive or negative – effects of what I did (or failed to do)?* • *How did the other person/people involved react? Why do I think they reacted that way? How do I think they felt?* • *Did past situations influence how I reacted during this situation, either positively or negatively? If so, how? If not, why not?*
3. Now what?	Finally, explain how you will use what you have learned to inform your practice moving forward: • *What are the implications for me? What could/would I do differently should a similar situation occur again?* • *What help and support might I need to act on the results of my reflection? How can I make sure I can access it?* • *What is the main learning experience that I can take from reflecting on my practice in this way?*

The implication is that, if we want to 'learn from and live with the experience', we must also learn to be kind to ourselves when we have to make difficult decisions that go against some of our core values. The same applies to any other mistakes we make as translators. Nobody is perfect. We must learn to forgive ourselves so we can learn from our mistakes and improve. When we reflect on our work, we would therefore do well to keep in mind the famous words of US lifestyle coach Lisa Hayes: 'Be careful how you talk to yourself because you are listening'!

TOPICS FOR DISCUSSION AND ASSIGNMENTS 9.5

Have another look at your answers to 'Topics for discussion and assignments 9.3'. With a course mate, use what we have just discussed to talk through some concrete self-care strategies you feel you could put in place to mitigate the negative effects of each of the potential physical, cognitive and organisational stressors on your well-being you identified in 'Topics for discussion and assignments 9.3'.

200 *Continuing to grow as a professional translator*

9.3 And finally ... Translation shouldn't cost the Earth!

Sustainability is about protecting existing resources, both ours and the planet's. The latter may just be one of the many responsibilities we have to juggle as professional translators (see Figure 9.1), but it is a crucial one. As explained by the United Nations' Environment Programme:

> The science is clear. The world is in a state of **climate emergency,** and we need to shift into emergency gear. Humanity's burning of fossil fuels has emitted enough greenhouse gases to significantly alter the composition of the atmosphere and average world temperature has risen between 1.1 and 1.2°C. And for every degree in rising temperatures, the cost of adaptation will rise exponentially. GHG emission must peak now yet the gap between ambition and action is growing. (UNEP, 2023)

Many of us are aware of the devastating effects of climate change and we therefore do our best to protect the environment in our personal lives. As professional translators, however, it may not be obvious to us how our work might contribute to the climate emergency. We may even feel we work for a rather green industry, as our work does not involve *visibly* polluting the planet by, for instance, requiring us to regularly jet off all over the world. Yet, in his seminal *Eco-Translation: Translation and Ecology in the Age of the Anthropocene*, Irish academic Michael Cronin argues that:

> there is nothing virtual about the consequences of the virtual. Creating the immaterial world of informations and communications technology (ICT) leads to very real, material effects for the environment, in everything from the extraction of precious metals to the constant drain on energy resources. (Cronin, 2017: 6)

How does this concern us professional translators? Well, first of all, through its work the translation industry can be seen to **facilitate** the world's energy dependency. Indeed:

> In part, the insatiable logic of ICT development is driven by and drives an economic model of endless, material growth. Translation as a practice through localisation that is indispensable in the development of foreign markets for goods and services is closely bound up with an ideology of infinite growth. (ibid.)

What's more, our industry also plays an active part in the exhaustion of the planet's resources, with its own reliance on ICT:

Keeping it sustainable   201

Technology as an indispensable component of contemporary translation practice is deeply implicated in forms of energy dependency that are increasingly unsustainable. Even when the emphasis is placed on energy efficiency, a paradoxical consequence is that the more energy that is saved, the more energy that is sought. (ibid.)

More concretely, recent research found that developing and training a neural network model for natural language processing (NLP) can emit as much as approximately 284 tonnes (626,155 lbs) of carbon dioxide (CO_2) (Strubell et al., 2019). This roughly corresponds to the total carbon output of five petrol cars during their lifetime (including production).

As individuals, we may rightly feel that we have little control over what Cronin calls 'the consequences of the virtual' (2017: 6). There are, however, some simple measures we can put in place to try and make sure that translation doesn't cost the Earth. According to the European project Fight Climate Change, every text-based email we send emits 4 g of CO_2 ... and this can increase to 50 g for emails with multiple attachments (Mawby, 2022). This may seem insignificant. However, in 2019, research conducted by a UK energy supplier showed that 'if every [British person] sent just one email less per day, 16,433 tonnes of carbon would be saved per year, or the equivalent to 81,152 flights from London to Madrid' (ibid.). Storing emails and files in the cloud also produces CO_2 emissions, as 'the cloud is actually huge servers storing data for us to access at any moment, and these big data centres consume massive amounts of fossil fuels each day' (ibid.). Considering the nature of our work, this is an area where we can all help protect the environment by, for instance:

- Deleting old emails and old client files as part of the 'closing administration' of a project (see Chapter 6);
- Deleting unwanted emails in our spam box on a regular basis and unsubscribing from the newsletters we never read;
- Asking ourselves 'Do I really need to send this email?' before sending an email;
- Sending links to documents wherever possible rather than attaching them to emails;
- Using a free online email carbon calculator to understand our own impact.

TOPICS FOR DISCUSSION AND ASSIGNMENTS 9.6

Group presentation: in groups of two to three, prepare a five-to-ten-minute presentation on one of the questions that follow (adapted from Lambert, 2023: 172–173):

202　*Continuing to grow as a professional translator*

- How can we reconcile our social responsibility to protect the planet with our personal need to survive financially as translators? What impact does this have on our professional role?
- How can we ensure the future sustainability of the translation profession in light of the various threats it faces?
- What is a successful professional translator?

Further reading

Courtney and Phelan (2019) offers fascinating insights into what professional translators perceive to be the main sources of stress in today's translation industry.

Ehrensberger-Dow (2020) shows how applying an ergonomics perspective to translation can help us identify potential sources of strain for professional translators, as well as some of the resources we can draw upon to avoid potential physical and/or mental health problems.

Published as part of the same Routledge Introductions to Translation and Interpreting series as this textbook, Lambert (2023) is an essential, thought-provoking read for any budding translator wanting to further develop their professional and ethical maturity. To that end, I suggest you start with chapter 7 ('Standards'), which shows some of the potential limitations of codes of ethics/conduct. For those of you wishing to explore this in greater depth, I recommend you also read chapters 4 ('Responsibility'), 6 ('Commitment'), 8 ('Ethical Professionals') and 9 ('Other Viewpoints').

Bibliography

Abdallah, K. (2010). 'Translators' agency in production networks.' In T. Kinnunen & K. Koskinen (eds.), *Translators' Agency*. Tampere: Tampere University Press, 11–46.

Abdallah, K. & Koskinen, K. (2007). 'Managing trust: Translating in the network economy.' *Meta*, 52:4, 673–687.

Adams, N. (2013). *The Little Book of Social Media Marketing for Translators: Network – Learn – Profit*. North Charleston, SC: CreateSpace Independent Publishing Platform.

Allee, V. (2000). 'Knowledge networks and communities of practice.' *OD Practitioner*, 32:4. Retrieved from: https://citeseerx.ist.psu.edu/viewdoc/download?doi= 10.1.1.465.3908&rep=rep1&type=pdf

Allen, K. R. (2012). *New venture creation*. 6th edition. Mason, OH: South-Western Cengage Learning.

Allen, L. M. et al. (2019). 'Categorising the broad impacts of continuing professional development: A scoping review.' *Medical Education*, 53:11, 1087–1099.

Alonso, E. (2016). 'Conflict, opacity and mistrust in the digital management of professional translation projects.' *Translation & Interpreting*, 8:1, 19–29.

Alonso, E. & Nunes Vieira, L. (2020). 'The impact of technology on the role of the translator in globalized production workflows.' In E. Bielsa & D. Kapsaskis (eds.), *The Routledge Handbook of Translation and Globalization*. London: Routledge, 391–405.

Anderson, A. R. & Warren, L. (2011). 'The entrepreneur as hero and jester: Enacting the entrepreneurial discourse.' *International Small Business Journal*, 29:6, 589–609.

Angelone, E. et al. (2020). *The Bloomsbury Companion to Language Industry Studies*. London: Bloomsbury.

Angelone, E. & Garcia, A. M. (2022). 'Reconceptualizing breaks in translation: Breaking down or breaking through?' *The International Journal of Translation and Interpreting Research*, 14:2, 68–83.

APTIS Association of Programmes in Translation and Interpreting Studies, UK & Ireland (2021). *APTIS 2021: Evolving Profiles. The Future of Translation and Interpreting Training*. A. Carnegie-Brown. 'The Evolving Role of Language Service Provision'. Dublin City University, 18–19 November 2021.

ATC UK (2021). *Language Services Industry Survey and Report 2021*. Association of Translation Companies UK. Retrieved from: https://atc.org.uk/wp-content/uplo ads/2018/06/ATC-UK-Survey-and-Report_2021.pdf

204 Bibliography

AUSIT (Australian Institute of Interpreters and Translators) (2012). *AUSIT Code of Ethics and Code of Conduct.* Retrieved from: https://ausit.org/wp-content/uploads/2020/02/Code_Of_Ethics_Full.pdf

Barabé, D. (2021). 'Translation status – A professional approach.' *Journal of Specialised Translation*, 36, 165–183.

Barnes, M. (1988). 'Construction project management.' *International Journal of Project Management*, 6:2, 69–79.

Barnes, R. & de Villiers Scheepers, M. (2018). 'Tackling uncertainty for journalism graduates.' *Journalism Practice*, 12:1, 94–114.

Bednárová-Gibová, K. (2021.) 'Organizational ergonomics of translation as a powerful predictor of translators' happiness at work?' *Perspectives*, 29:3, 391–406.

Biel, Ł. (2011). 'Training translators or translation service providers? EN 15038:2006 standard of translation services and its training implications.' *The Journal of Specialised Translation*, 16, 6–76.

Bond, E. (2018). 'The stunning variety of job title in the language industry'. *Slator News*. Retrieved from: https://slator.com/the-stunning-variety-of-job-titles-in-the-language-industry/

Bowker, L. (2004). 'What does it take to work in the translation profession in Canada in the 21st century? Exploring a database of job advertisements.' *Meta*, 49:9, 960–972.

Bowker, L. (2019). *Machine Translation and Global Research: Towards Improved Machine Translation Literacy in the Scholarly Community*. Bingley: Emerald Publishing.

Bowker, L. (2020). 'Fit-for-purpose translation.' In M. O'Hagan (ed.), *The Routledge Handbook of Translation and Technology*. London: Routledge, 453–468.

Bowker, L. (2023). *De-Mystifying Translation: Introducing Translation to Non-Translators*. London: Routledge.

Bressi, S. K. & Vaden, E. R. (2017). 'Reconsidering self care.' *Clinical Social Work Journal*, 45:1, 33–38.

Burns, P. (2018). *New Venture Creation: A Framework for Entrepreneurial Start-Ups.* 2nd edition. London: Palgrave.

Byrne, J. (2009). 'Localisation – When language, culture and technology join forces'. *Language at Work – Bridging Theory and Practice*, 3:5. Retrieved from: https://doi.org/10.7146/law.v3i5.6190

Calvo, E. (2018). 'From translation briefs to quality standards: Functionalist theories in today's translation processes.' *The International Journal of Translation and Interpreting Research*, 10:1, 18–32.

Candel-Mora, M. (2016). 'Translator training and the integration of technology in the translator's workflow.' In M. Carrio-Pastor (ed.), *Technology Implementation in Second Language Teaching and Translation Studies: New Tools, New Approaches*. Singapore: Springer, 49–70.

Carroll, M. & Shaw, E. (2013). *Ethical Maturity in the Helping Professions: Making Difficult Life and Work Decisions*. London: Jessica Kingsley Publishers.

Castells, M. (1996). *The Rise of the Network Society*. Malden: Blackwell Publishers.

Castells, M. (2004). *The Network Society: A Cross-Cultural Perspective*. Cheltenham & Northampton: Edward Elgar Publishing.

Castells, M. & Cardoso, G. (2006). *The Network Society: From Knowledge to Policy*. Washington, DC: Centre for Transatlantic Relations, Johns Hopkins University.

Bibliography 205

Catford, J. C. (1965). *A Linguistic Theory of Translation*. Oxford: Oxford University Press.

Chiesa, R. et al. (2018). 'Enhancing substainability: Psychological capital, perceived employability, and job insecurity in different work contract conditions.' *Sustainability*, 10:7, 2475.

Chodkiewicz, M. (2012). 'The EMT framework of reference for competences applied to translation: perceptions by professional and student translators.' *Journal of Specialised Translation*, 17, 37–54.

Chriss, R. (2006). *Translation as a Profession*. London: Lulu.

CIM (Chartered Institute of Marketing) (2015). *Marketing and the 7Ps: A Brief Summary of Marketing and How It Works*. CIM. Retrieved from: https://www.cim.cc.uk/media/4772/7ps.pdf

CIOL (Chartered Institute of Linguists). (2020). 'CIOL Insights: The Languages Professions 2019–2020'. CIOL. Retrieved from: https://www.ciol.org.uk/ciol-insights-languages-professions

Costa, B. et al. (2020). 'Self-care as an ethical responsibility: A pilot study on support provision for interpreters in human crises.' *Translation and Interpreting Studies*. 15:1, 36–56.

Courtney, J. & Phelan, M. (2019). Translators' experiences of occupational stress and job satisfaction. *Translation & Interpreting*, 11:1, 100–113.

Cronin, M. (2017). *Eco-Translation: Translation and Ecology in the Age of the Anthropocene. New Perspective in Translation and Interpreting Studies*. London: Routledge.

Daems, J. & Macken, L. (2021). 'Post-editing human translations and revising machine translation: Impact on efficiency and quality.' In M. Koponen et al. (eds.), *Translation Revision and Post-Editing: Industry Practices and Cognitive Processes*. London: Routledge, 50–70.

Dam, H. V., Brøgger, M. N. & Zethsen, K. K. (2019). 'Introduction.' In H. V. Dam et al. (eds.), *Moving Boundaries in Translation Studies*. London: Routledge, 1–11.

Dam, H. V. & Zethsen, K. K. (2008). 'Translator status – a study of Danish company translators.' *The Translator*, 14:1, 71–96.

Dam, H. V. & Zethsen, K. K (2011). 'The status of professional business translators on the Danish market: A comparative study of company, agency and freelance translators.' *Meta*, 56:4, 976–997.

Dam, H. V. & Zethsen, K. K. (2012). 'Translators in international organizations: A special breed of high-status professionals? Danish EU translators as a case in point.' *Translation and Interpreting Studies*, 7:2, 211–232.

Dam, H. V. & Zethsen, K. K. (2016). '"I think it is a wonderful job": On the solidity of the translation profession.' *Journal of Specialised Translation*, 25, 174–187.

Dastyar, V. (2019). *Dictionary of Education and Assessment in Translation and Interpreting Studies (TIS)*. Newcastle upon Tyne: Cambridge Scholars Publishing.

Dave, H. P. et al. (2021). 'Stability and change in trait emotional intelligence in emerging adulthood: A four-year population-based study.' *Journal of Personality Assessment*, 103:1, 57–66.

Depraetere, I. (2011). *Perspectives on Translation Quality*. Berlin: De Gruyter.

Desjardins, R. (2017). *Translation and Social Media: In Theory, in Training and in Professional Practice*. London: Palgrave.

206 Bibliography

DeTienne, K. et al. (2012). 'The impact of moral stress compared to other stressors on employee fatigue, job satisfaction, and turnover: An empirical investigation.' *Journal of Business Ethics*, 110:3, 377–378.

do Carmo, F. & Moorkens, J. (2021). 'Differentiating editing, post-editing and revision.' In M. Koponen et al. (eds.), *Translation Revision and Post-editing: Industry Practices and Cognitive Processes*. London: Routledge, 35–49.

Doherty, S. et al. (2018). 'On education and training in translation quality assessment.' In J. Moorkens et al. (eds.), *Translation Quality Assessment*. Cham: Springer International Publishing, 95–106.

Driscoll, J. (2007). *Supervision: A Reflective Approach for Healthcare Professionals*. 2nd edition. Edinburgh: Bailliere Tindall.

Drugan, J. (2013). *Quality in Professional Translation: Assessment and Improvement*. London: Bloomsbury.

Drugan, J. & Tipton, R. (2017). 'Translation, ethics and social responsibility.' *The Translator*, 23:2, 119–125.

Duffy, A. (2007). 'A concept analysis of reflective practice: Determining its value to nurses.' *British Journal of Nursing*, 16:22, 1400–1407.

Dunne, K. (2012). 'The industrialization of translation: Causes, consequences and challenges.' *Translation Spaces*, 1, 14–168.

Dunne, K. J. & Dunne, E. S. (2011). *Translation and Localization Project Management: The Art of the Possible*. Amsterdam: John Benjamins.

Durban, C. (2011). 'Translation: Getting it right. A guide to buying translation.' Institute of Translation and Interpreting. Retrieved from: https://www.iti.org.uk/resource/getting-it-right-english-uk.html

Ehrensberger-Dow, M. (2019). 'Ergonomics and the translation process.' *Slovo. ru: Baltic Accent*, 10:1, 37–51.

Ehrensberger-Dow, M. (2020). 'Translation, ergonomics and cognition.' In F. Alves & A. L. Jakobsen (eds.), *The Routledge Handbook of Translation and Cognition*. Milton Park: Taylor and Francis, 147–160.

Ehrensberger-Dow, M. & Jääskeläinen, R. (2019). 'Ergonomics of translation.' In H. V. Dam et al. (eds.), *Moving Boundaries in Translation Studies*. London: Routledge, 132–150.

ELIS Research (2022). *ELIS 2022 Language Industry Survey*. Retrieved from: https://elis-survey.org/repository/

EMT (2009). 'Competences for professional translators, experts in multilingual and multimedia communication.' Retrieved from: https://ec.europa.eu/info/ resources-partners/european-masters-translation-emt/european-masters-translation-emt-explained_en#documents

EMT (2017). *Competence Framework 2017*. European Commission. Retrieved from: https://commission.europa.eu/system/files/2018-02/emt_competence_fwk_2017_en_web.pdf

EMT (2020). *European Master's in Translation (EMT) Explained*. European Commission. Retrieved from: https://ec.europa.eu/info/resources-partners/european-masters-translation-emt/european-masters-translation-emt-explained_en#network-activities

EMT (2022). *Competence Framework 2022*. European Commission. Retrieved from: https://commission.europa.eu/system/files/2022-11/emt_compete nce_fwk_2022_en.pdf

Bibliography 207

EU-OSHA (European Agency for Safety and Health at Work). (2017). 'Ergonomics in office work.' Retrieved from https://oshwiki.osha.europa.eu/en/themes/ergonomics-office-work

European Parliament Talent Selection Unit (2021). 'Intercultural and language professional – PE/260/2021 (AD5) M/F.' European Parliament. Retrieved from: https://op.europa.eu/en/publication-detail/-/publication/edd25fc2-ae3c-11eb-9767-01aa75ed71a1/language-en

FIT (Fédération Internationale des Traducteurs/Federal Association of Translators) (n.d.). 'What is FIT?' FIT. Retrieved from: https://www.fit-ift.org/about/

FIT (Fédération Internationale des Traducteurs/Federal Association of Translators) (2022). 'Position Paper on Continuing Professional Development (CPD).' FIT. Retrieved from: https://library.fit-ift.org/public/Publications/positionpapers/PDP_202207_Continuing_Professional_Development_EN.pdf

Folaron, D. (2006). 'A discipline coming of age in the digital age.' In K. Dunne (ed.), *Perspectives on Localization*. Amsterdam: John Benjamins, 195–219.

Folaron, D. & Buzelin, H. (2007). 'Introduction: Connecting translation and network studies.' *Meta*, 52:4, 605–642.

Fraser, J. & Gold, M. (2001). 'Portfolio workers: Autonomy and control amongst freelance translators.' *Work, Employment and Society*, 15:4, 679–697.

Freudenberger, H. J. (1974). 'Staff burn-out.' *Journal of Social Issues*, 30:1, 159–165.

Froeliger, N. (2019). 'Are we getting it right for our translation programs? A tentative method to measure if we are.' In M. Koletnik and N. Froeliger (eds.). *Translation and Language Teaching: Continuing the Dialogue*. Newcastle upon Tyne: Cambridge Scholars Publishing, 215–238.

Fulford, H. (2012). 'The translator's bookshelf: The role of reading in a freelance translator's continuing professional development portfolio.' *The Journal of Specialised Translation*, 17, 271–283.

GALA (2022). 'What is localization?' Globalization and Localization Association. Retrieved from: https://www.gala-global.org/knowledge-center/about-the-industry/language-services

Georgiou, N. & Perdikaki, K. (2020). 'Do you second that emotion? An empirical study on the emotional impact of subtitling on the subtitler.' *Journal of Audiovisual Translation*, 3:2, 186–203.

Göpferich, S. (2008). *Translationsprozessforschung: Stand – Methoden – Perspektiven*. Tübingen: Gunter Narr Verlag.

Göpferich, S. (2009). 'Towards a model of translation competence and its acquisition: the longitudinal study "TransComp".' In S. Göpferich, A. L. Jakobsen and I. M. Mees (eds.), *Behind the Mind: Methods, Models and Results in Translation Process Research*. Copenhagen: Samfundslitteratur, 11–37.

Göpferich, S. (2019). 'Competence, translation'. In M. Baker and G. Saldanha (eds.), *Routledge Encyclopaedia of Translation Studies*. 3rd edition. London: Routledge, 89–95.

Gouadec, D. (2007). *Translation as a Profession*. Amsterdam: John Benjamins.

Gouadec, D. (2010). 'Quality in translation.' In Y. Gambier & L. van Doorslaer (eds.), *Handbook of Translation Studies Vol. 1*. Amsterdam: John Benjamins, 270–275.

Groß, M.-L. (2010). 'Personal knowledge management and collaborative actions: synergies in social networks of professional translators.' In U. Schroeder

208   Bibliography

(ed.), *Interaktive Kulturen: Workshop-Band: Proceedings der Workshops der Mensch & Computer 2010 - 10. Fachübergreifende Konferenz für Interaktive und Kooperative Medien, DeLFI 2010 - die 8. E-Learning Fachtagung Informatik der Gesellschaft für Informatik e.V. und der Entertainment Interfaces 2010.* Berlin: Logos Verlag, 98–101.

Groß, M.-L. (2012). 'Networked lone fighters? Knowledge flows and functional support in social networks of freelance translators.' In L. Zybatow et al. (eds.). *Translationswissenschaft: alte und neue Arten der Translation in Theorie und Praxis.* Frankfurt: Peter Lang, 391–396.

Groß, M.-L. (2014). *The impact of the social web on the support networks of freelance translators* (PhD thesis, University of Vienna).

Hale, S. (2007). *Community Interpreting.* New York: Palgrave Macmillan.

Hargreaves, J. & Page, L. (2013). *Reflective Practice.* Cambridge: Polity Press.

Harvey, L. and Green, D. (1993). 'Defining quality.' *Assessment & Evaluation in Higher Education*, 18:1, 9–34.

Havumetsä, N. (2012). *The client factor: A study of clients' expectations concerning non-literary translators and the quality of non-literary translations* (PhD thesis, University of Helsinki).

Hayton, J. C. et al. (2002). 'National culture and entrepreneurship: A review of behavioral research.' *Entrepreneurship Theory & Practice*, 26:4, 33–52.

HCPC UK (Health and Care Professions Council UK). (2021). 'What is supervision?' Health and Care Professions Council. Retrieved from: https://www.hcpc-uk.org/standards/meeting-our-standards/supervision-leadership-and-culture/supervision/what-is-supervision/

Heilbrunn, S. et al. (2017). 'Perceived feasibility and desirability of entrepreneurship in institutional contexts in transition.' *Entrepreneurship Research Journal*, 7:4, 785–796.

Herbert, J. (2009). 'Test translations – tips for success'. ProZ.com. Retrieved from: https://www.proz.com/translation-articles/articles/2312/1/Test-Translations---Tips-for-Success

Hlavac, J. (2013). 'A cross-national overview of translator and interpreter certification procedures.' *Translation and Interpreting*, 5:1, 32–65.

Holz-Mänttäri, J. (1984). *Translatorisches Handeln. Theorie und Methode.* Helsinki: Suomalainen Tiedeakatemia.

House, J. (1977). *A Model for Translation Quality Assessment.* Tübingen: G. Narr Verlag.

House, J. (2001). 'Translation quality assessment: Linguistic description versussocial evaluation.' *Meta*, 46:2, 243–257.

Hubscher-Davidson, S. (2018a). *Translation and Emotion: A Psychological Perspective.* London: Routledge.

Hubscher-Davidson, S. (2018b). 'Do translation professionals need to tolerate ambiguity to be successful? A study of the links between tolerance of ambiguity, emotional intelligence and job satisfaction.' In R. Jääskeläinen & I. Lacruz (eds), *Innovation and Expansion in Translation Process Research.* Amsterdam: John Benjamins, 77–103.

Hubscher-Davidson, S. (2020). 'The psychology of sustainability and psychological capital: New lenses to examine wellbeing in the translation profession.' *European Journal of Sustainable Development Research*, 4:4, em0127.

Bibliography 209

Hubscher-Davidson, S. (2021). 'ITI: Position Statement on translators' mental health and wellbeing.' Institute of Translation and Interpreting. Retrieved from: https://www.iti.org.uk/resource/position-statement-on-translators-mental-health-and-wellbeing.html

Hubscher-Davidson, S. (2021a). 'Ethical stress in translation and interpreting.' In K. Koskinen & N. Pokorn (eds.), *The Routledge Handbook of Translation and Ethics*. Abingdon: Routledge, 415–430.

Hubscher-Davidson, S. & Lehr, C. (2021). *Improving the Emotional Intelligence of Translators: A Roadmap for an Experimental Training Intervention*. London: Palgrave Macmillan.

Huifant, L. et al. (2018). 'China's language services as an emerging industry.' *Babel*, 63:4, 370–381.

Hurtado Albir, A. (2008). 'Compétences en traduction et formation par compétences.' *TTR - Traduction, terminologie, rédaction*, 21:1, 17–64.

Hurtado Albir, A. (2015). 'The acquisition of translation competence: Competences, tasks, and assessment in translator training.' *Meta*, 60:2, 256–280.

Hurtado Albir, A. (2017). *Researching Translation Competence by PACTE Group*. Amsterdam: John Benjamins.

IBM (2023). 'What is data security?' IBM. Retrieved from: https://www.ibm.com/uk-en/topics/data-security

IEA (2023). 'What is ergonomics (HFE)?' International Ergonomics Association. Retrieved from: https://iea.cc/about/what-is-ergonomics/

Ilari, M. (2021). 'How to successfully tackle translation tests.' *The ATA Chronicle*. Retrieved from: https://www.ata-chronicle.online/featured/how-to-successfully-tackle-translation-tests/

Ilja, M.-E. (2023). 'Translation-related CPD at the European Commission.' In T. Svoboda et al. (eds.). *Institutional Translator Training*. New York: Routledge, 216–225.

Inbox Translation (2021). *Freelance Translator Survey 2020*. Inbox Translation. Retrieved from: https://inboxtranslation.com/resources/research/freelance-translator-survey-2020/

International Organization for Standardization (1995). *Quality management and quality assurance (ISO 8402:1995)*. International Organization for Standardization.

International Organization for Standardization (2015). *Translation Services – Requirements for Translation Services (ISO 17100:2015)*. International Organization for Standardization.

International Organization for Standardization (2017). *Translation Services – Requirements for Translation Services (ISO 17100:2015+A1:2017)*. International Organization for Standardization.

International Organization for Standardization (2017b). *Translation Services – Post-Editing of Machine Translation Output. Requirements (ISO 18587:2017)*. International Organization for Standardization.

Iseli, F. (2021). *Social Media for Small Business: Marketing Strategies for Business Owners*. Melbourne: John Wiley & Sons.

ITI (Institute of Translation and Interpreting) (2013). *ITI Code of Professional Conduct*. Institute of Translation and Interpreting. Retrieved from: https://www.iti.org.uk/about-iti/professional-standards.html

210 Bibliography

ITI (2023). Benefits of CPD. Institute of Translation and Interpreting. Retrieved from: https://www.iti.org.uk/training/continuing-professional-development/benefits-of-cpd.html

Jakobsen, A. L. (2019). 'Moving translation, revision, and post-editing boundaries.' In H. V. Dam, M. N. Brøgger & K. K. Zethsen (eds.), *Moving Boundaries in Translation Studies*. London: Routledge, 64–80.

Kafi, M., Khoshsaligheh, M. & Hashemi, M. (2018). 'Translation profession in Iran: Current challenges and future prospects.' *The Translator*, 24:1, 89–103.

Kang, J. (2019). 'Institutional translation.' In M. Baker & G. Saldanha (eds.), *Routledge Encyclopedia of Translation Studies*. 3rd edition. London: Routledge.

Kappus, M. & Ehrensberger-Dow, M. (2020). 'The ergonomics of translation tools: understanding when less is actually more.' *The Interpreter and Translator Trainer*, 14:4, 386–404.

Karoubi, B. (2016). 'Translation quality assessment demystified.' *Babel*, 62:2, 253–277.

Katan, D. (2011). 'Occupation or profession: A survey of the translators' world.' In R. Sela-Sheffy & M. Shlesinger (eds.). *Identity and status in the translational professions*. Amsterdam: John Benjamins, 65–88.

Katan, D. & Taibi, M. (2021). *Translating Cultures: An Introduction for Translators, Interpreters and Mediators*. 3rd edition. London: Routledge.

Kelly, N. et al. (2012). *Voices from the Freelance Translator Community (Report)*. Boston: Common Sense Advisory.

Koskinen, K. (2016). 'Pym, Anthony. 2012. On Translator Ethics: Principles for Mediation between Cultures.' *Target: International Journal of Translation Studies*, 28:1, 170–177.

Koskinen, K. (2019). 'Tailoring translation services for clients and users.' In E. Angelone et al. (eds.),*The Bloomsbury Companion to Language Industry Studies*. London: Bloomsbury Academic, 139–152.

Koskinen, K. (2020). *Translation and Affect: Essays on Sticky Affects and Translational Affective Labour*. Amsterdam: Benjamins.

Kotler, P. (n.d.) 'Quotes by Philip Kotler.' pkotler.org. Retrieved from: https://www.pkotler.org/quotes-from-pk

Krajcso, Z. (2018). 'Translators' competence profiles versus market demand.' *Babel*. 64:5/6, 692—709.

Kujamäki, M. (2020). 'Applying service-dominant logic to translation service provision.' *HERMES – Journal of Language and Communication in Business*, 60, 191–207.

Kujamäki, M. (2021) 'Translation as a professional service: An overview of a fragmented field of practice.' *Perspectives*, 31:2, 331–346.

Kuznik, A. & Miquel Verd, J. (2010). 'Investigating real work situations in translation agencies: Work content and its components.' *Hermes – Journal of Language and Communication Studies*, 44, 25–43.

Lafeber, A. (2023). 'Skills and knowledge required of translators in institutional settings.' In T. Svoboda et al. (eds.). *Institutional Translator Training*. New York: Routledge, 30–49.

Lambert, J. (2023). *Translation Ethics*. London: Routledge.

Lambert, J. & Walker, C. (2022). 'Because we're worth it: Disentangling freelance translation, status, and rate-setting in the United Kingdom.' *Translation Spaces*, 11:2, 277–302.

Bibliography   211

Larsonneur, C. (2019). 'The disruptions of neural machine translation.' *Spheres – Journal for Digital Cultures*, 5. Retrieved from: https://mediarep.org/bitstream/han dle/doc/14415/spheres_5_0701_Larsonneur_Disruptions.pdf?sequence=1

Law, J. (2009). *A Dictionary of Business and Management*. 5th edition. Oxford: Oxford University Press.

Lee, J. 'Professional interpreter's job satisfaction and relevant factors. A case study of trained interpreters in South Korea.' *Translation and Interpreting Studies*, 12:3, 427–448.

Lepore, M. (2020). 'You have 7.4 seconds to make an impression: How recruiters see your resume'. *TheLadders.com*. Retrieved from: https://www.theladders.com/car eer-advice/you-only-get-6-seconds-of-fame-make-it-count

Loock, R. (2020). 'Social media and translators: A survey.' *European Master's in Translation Network Blog*. Retrieved from: https://european-masters-translation-blog.ec.europa.eu/articles-emt-blog/social-media-and-translators-survey-2020-07-01_en

Massey, G. & Ehrensberger-Dow, M. (2012). 'Investigating information literacy: A growing priority in translation studies.' *Across Languages and Cultures*, 12:3, 193–211.

Massey, G. et al. (2023). 'Meeting evolution with innovation: an introduction to (re-) profiling T&I education.' *The Interpreter and Translator Trainer*, 17:3, 325–331.

Matis. N. (2005). 'La gestion de projets de traduction et sa place dans la formation de traducteurs.' *Equivalences*, 32:1, 47–62.

Matis, N. (2011). 'Quality assurance in the translation workflow – A professional's testimony.' In I. Depraetere (ed.). *Perspectives on Translation Quality*. Berlin: De Gruyter, 147–160.

Matis, N. (2014). *How to Manage your Translation Projects*. Nancy Matis. Retrieved from: https://www.translation-project-management.com/en/book/how-manage-your-translation-projects

Matis, N. (2016). 'The main steps of a translation project.' *LinkedIn*. Retrieved from: https://www.linkedin.com/pulse/main-steps-translation-project-nancy-matis/

Matis, N. (2017). 'How to deal with questions during a translation project.' American Translator Association. Retrieved from: https://www.atanet.org/resources/how-to-deal-with-questions-during-a-translation-project/

Mawby, A. (2022). 'The environmental cost of email.' Fight Climate Change. Retrieved from: https://fightclimatechange.earth/2022/05/22/the-environmen tal-cost-of-email/

Mbotake, S. (2015). 'The standard profile of the 21st century translator and its impact on translator training.' *International Journal of English Language and Translation Studies*, 3:3, 86–104.

McAlester, G. (2003). 'A comment on translation ethics and education.' In G. Anderman & M. Rogers (eds.), *Translation Today: Trends and Perspectives*. Clevedon: Multilingual Matters, 225–227.

McDonough, J. (2007). 'How do language professionals organize themselves? An overview of translation networks.' *Meta*, 52:4, 793–815.

McDonough Dolmaya, J. (2010). 'A window into the profession: What translation blogs have to offer translation studies.' *The Translator*, 17:1, 77–104.

McDonough Dolmaya, J. (2011). 'Moral ambiguity: Some shortcomings of professional codes of ethics for translators.' *The Journal of Specialised Translation*, 15, 28–49.

212 Bibliography

McDonough Dolmaya, J. (2018). 'Translation and collaborative networks.' In S.-A. Harding & O. Carbonell Cortés (eds.), *The Routledge Handbook of Translation and Culture*. London: Routledge, 347–360.

McDonough Dolmaya, J. (2022). 'Translator associations and networks.' In K. Malmkjær (ed.). *The Cambridge Handbook of Translation*. Cambridge: Cambridge University Press, 198–213.

McKay, C. (2015). *How to Succeed as a Freelance Translator*. 3rd edition. Boulder, CO: Two Rat Press.

Megginson, D. & Whitaker, V. (2007). *Continuing Professional Development*. 2nd edition. London: Chartered Institute of Personnel and Development.

Mihalache, I. (2008). 'Community experience and expertise: Translators, technologies and electronic networks of practice.' *Translation Studies*, 1:1, 55-72.

Mitchell, K. et al. (1999). 'Planned happenstance: Constructing unexpected career opportunities.' *Journal of Counseling and Development*, 77, 115–124.

Mitchell-Schuitevoerder, R. (2020). *A Project-Based Approach to Translation Technology*. London: Routledge.

Moorkens, J. (2017). 'Under pressure: Translation in times of austerity.' *Perspectives*, 25:3, 464–477.

Moorkens, J. (2020) 'Comparative satisfaction among freelance and directly-employed Irish-language translators.' *The International Journal of Translation and Interpreting Research*, 12:1, 55–73.

Moorkens, J. (2021). 'Translation in the neoliberal era.' In E. Bielsa & D. Kapsaskis (eds.), *The Routledge Handbook of Translation and Globalization*. London: Routledge, 323–336.

Moorkens, J. (2022). 'Ethics and machine translation.' In D. Kenny (ed.), *Machine Translation for Everyone: Empowering Users in the Age of Artificial Intelligence*. Berlin: Language Science Press.

Moorkens, J. & Rocchi M. (2021). 'Ethics in the translation industry.' In K. Koskinen & N. Pokorn (eds.), *The Routledge Handbook of Translation and Ethics*. Abingdon: Routledge, 320–337.

Mossop, B. (2019). *Revising and Editing for Translators*. 4th edition. London: Routledge.

Müller-Prothmann, T. (2005). 'Knowledge communities, communities of practice and knowledge networks.' In E. Coakes & S. Clarke (eds.), *Encyclopedia of Communities of Practice in Information and Knowledge Management*. Hershey, PA: IGI Global, 264–271.

Munday, J., et al. (2022). *Introducing Translation Studies: Theories and Applications*. London: Routledge.

Nimdzi (2022). 'The 2022 Nimdzi 100–The Ranking of the Top 100 Largest Language Service Providers.' Nimdzi. Retrieved from https://www.nimdzi.com/nimdzi-100-top-lsp/#state-of-the-language-industry

Nitzke, J. & Gros, A-K. (2021). 'Preferential changes in revision and post-editing.' In M. Koponen et al. (eds.), *Translation Revision and Post-Editing: Industry Practices and Cognitive Processes*. London: Routledge, 21–34.

Nitzke, J. & Hansen-Schirra, S. (2021). *A short guide to post-editing*. Volume 16. Berlin: Language Science Press.

Nitzke, J. et al. (2019). 'Training the modern translator – the acquisition of digital competencies through blended learning.' *The Interpreter and Translator Trainer*, 13:3, 292–306.

Bibliography 213

Nord, C. (2018). *Translating as a purposeful activity: Functionalist approaches explained*. 2nd edition. London: Routledge.

O'Brien, S. (2012). 'Translation as human–computer interaction.' *Translation Spaces*, 1:1, 101–112.

O'Brien, S. et al. (2017). 'Irritating CAT tool features that matter to translators.' *Hermes*, 56, 145–162.

O'Hagan, M. (2020). 'Introduction.' In M. O'Hagan (ed.). *The Routledge Handbook of Translation and Technology*. London: Routledge, 1–18.

Olohan, M. & Davitti, E. (2017). 'Dynamics of trusting in translation project management: Leaps of faith and balancing acts.' *Journal of Contemporary Ethnography*, 46:4, 391–416.

Orozco, M. & Hurtado Albir, A. (2002). 'Measuring translation competence acquisition.' *Meta*, 47:3, 375–402.

Ottmar, A. (ed.). (2017). *Best Practices - Übersetzen und Dolmetschen: Ein Nachschlagewerk aus der Praxis für Sprachmittler und Auftraggeber*. BDÜ Weiterbildungs- und Fachverlagsgesellschaft mbH.

PACTE (2000). 'Acquiring translation competence: Hypotheses and methodological problems of a research project.' In A. Beeby et al. (eds.), *Investigating Translation*. Amsterdam: John Benjamins, 99–106.

PACTE (2003). 'Building a translation competence model.' In F. Alves (ed.), *Triangulating translation: Perspectives in process oriented research*. Amsterdam: John Benjamins, 43–66.

PACTE (2005). 'Investigating translation competence: Conceptual and methodological issues.' *Meta*, 50:2, 609–619.

Patels, W. (2008). 'Rules for dealing with translation clients'. *Translationdirectory.com*. Retrieved from: https://www.translationdirectory.com/article121.htm#:~:text= Here%20are%20a%20few%20tips%20for%20dealing%20with,what%20tran slation%20is%20all%20about.%20...%20More%20items

Pavey, N. (2020). 'Debunking the myths about freelance translators.' NP Translations. Retrieved from: https://www.traductionsnp.com/freelance-translators-versus-tran slation-agencies/

Payment Practices. (2022). 'About us'. Retrieved from: http://www.paymentpractices. net/About.aspx

Phelan, M. et al. (2020). *Ethics in Public Service Interpreting*. London: Routledge.

Pielmeier, H. & O'Mara, P. (2020). 'The state of the linguist supply chain.' CSA Research. Retrieved from: https://insights.csa-research.com/chapters/305013106/ MethodologyandInform

Pierrzak, P. (2022). *Metacognitive Translator Training: Focus on Personal Resources*. London: Palgrave Macmillan.

Plassard, F. (2007). 'La traduction face aux nouvelles pratiques en réseaux.' *Meta*, 52:4, 643–665.

Plassard, F. (2010). 'Les 'communautés de traducteurs' communautés réelles, communautés virtuelles en traduction.' In J. Peeters (ed.), *Traduction et communautés*. Arras: Artois Presses Université, 197–209.

Pym, A. (2003). 'Redefining translation competence in an electronic age: In defence of a minimalist approach.' *Meta*, 48:4, 481–497.

Pym, A. (2013). 'Translation skill-sets in a machine translation age.' *Meta*, 58:3, 487–503.

Pym, A. (2014a). *Exploring Translation Theories*. 2nd edition. London: Routledge.

214 *Bibliography*

Pym, A. (2014b). 'Translator associations: From gatekeepers to communities.' *Target*, 26:3, 466–491.

Pym, A. (2020). 'Quality.' In M. O'Hagan (ed.), *The Routledge Handbook of Translation and Technology*. London: Routledge, 437–452.

Pym, A. (2021). 'Translator ethics.' In K. Koskinen and N. Pokorn (eds.), *The Routledge Handbook of Translation and Ethics*. Abingdon: Routledge, 147–164.

Pym, A. et al. (2012). *The Status of the Translation Profession in the European Union*. Studies on translation and multilingualism 7/2012. Luxembourg: Publications Office of the European Union.

Reiss, K. & Vermeer, H. J. (1991). *Grundlegung einer allgemeinen Translationstheorie*. 2nd edition. Tübingen: Niemeyer.

Reiss, K. & Vermeer, H. J. (2014). *Towards a General Theory of Translational Action:Skopos Theory Explained*. Translated by Christiane Nord. London: Routledge.

Reza Esfandiari, M. et al. (2019). 'An evaluation of the EMT: Compatibility with the professional translator's needs.' *Cogent Arts & Humanities*, 6:1. https://doi.org/10.1080/23311983.2019.1601055

Risku, H. (2016) *Translationsmanagement: Interkulturelle Fachkommunikation im Informationszeitalter*. Tübingen: Narr.

Risku, H. & Dickinson, A. (2009). 'Translators as networkers: The role of virtual communities.' *Hermes: - Journal of Language and Communication Studies*, 42, 49–70.

Risku, H., Pein-Weber, C. et al. (2016). '"The task of the translator": Comparing the views of the client and the translator.' *International Journal of Communication*, 10, 989–1008.

Risku, H., Rogl, R. et al. (2016). 'Mutual dependencies: Centrality in translation networks.' *Journal of Specialised Translation*, 25: 232–253.

Risku, H. & Schlager, D. (2021). 'Epistemologies of translation expertise.' In S. L. Halverson & Á. Marín García (eds.), *Contesting Epistemologies in Cognitive Translation and Interpreting Studies*. New York: Routledge.

Roberts, D. (2021, 13 December). 'Personal branding with Kelsey Frick.' *Meet the Translator*. Podcast. Retrieved from: https://www.dotrobertstranslation.com/meet-the-translator/episode/4ddba8d2/personal-branding-with-kelsey-frick

Roberts, D. (2022, 27 July). 'CPD with Lloyd Bingham.' *Meet the Translator*. Podcast. Retrieved from https://www.dotrobertstranslation.com/meet-the-transla tor/episode/7ebce45a/cpd-with-lloyd-bingham

Robinson, D. (2020). *Becoming a Translator: An Introduction to the Theory and Practice of Translation*. 4th edition. London: Routledge.

Rodríguez-Castro, M. (2016). 'Intrinsic and extrinsic sources of translator satisfaction: An empirical study.' *Entreculturas*, 7:8, 195–229.

Rodríguez de Céspedes, B. (2019). 'Translator education at a crossroads: The impact of automation.' *Lebende Sprachen*, 64:1, 103–121.

Rojo López, A. & Ramos Caro, M. (2016). 'Can emotion stir translation skill? Defining the impact of positive and negative emotions on translation performance.' In R. M. Martín (ed.), *Reembedding Translation Process Research*. Amsterdam: John Benjamins, 107–129.

Rothwell, A. et al. (2023). *Translation Tools and Technologies*. London: Routledge.

Bibliography 215

Ruokonen, M. (2013). 'Studying translator status: Three points of view.' In M. Eronen & M. Rodi-Risberg (eds.), *Point of view as challenge*. Vaasa: Vakki Publications, 327–338.

Ruokonen, M. & Mäkisalo, J. (2018). 'Middling-status profession, high-status work: Finnish translators' status perceptions in the light of their backgrounds, working conditions and job satisfaction.' *Translation & Interpreting*, 10:1, 1–17.

RWS Translation Services (2022). 'Translation spectrum: Transcreation.' RWS. Retrieved from: https://players.brightcove.net/6202477137001/default_default/index.html?videoId=1704610753620665352

Samuelsson-Brown, G. (1996). 'Working procedures, quality and quality assurance.' In R. Owens (ed.), *The Translator's Handbook*. London: Aslib, 103–136.

Samuelsson-Brown, G. (2010). *A Practical Guide for Translators*. 5th edition. Bristol: Multilingual Matters.

Schäffner, C. (2012). 'Translation competence: Training for the real world.' In S. Hubscher-Davidson and M. Borodo (eds.). *Global Trends in Translator and Interpreter Training: Mediation and Culture*. London: Continuum, 30–44.

Schäffner, C. (2020). 'Translators' roles and responsibilities.' In E. Angelone et al. (eds.), *The Bloomsbury Companion to Language Industry Studies*. London: Bloomsbury Academic, 63–89.

Schmitt, P. (2019). 'Translation 4.0–Evolution, revolution, innovation or disruption?' *Lebende Sprachen*, 64:2, 193–229.

Schnierer, M. (2021). 'Revision and quality standards: Do translation service providers follow recommendations in practice?' In M. Koponen et al. (eds.), *Translation Revision and Post-Editing: Industry Practices and Cognitive Processes*. London: Routledge, 109–130.

Sela-Sheffy, R. (2022). 'The translation professions.' In K. Malmkjær (ed.), *The Cambridge Handbook of Translation*. Cambridge: Cambridge University Press, 160–180.

Setton, R. & Guo Liangliang, A. (2011). 'Attitudes to role, status and professional identity in interpreters and translators with Chinese in Shanghai and Taipei.' In R. Sela-Sheffy & M. Shlesinger (eds.), *Identity and status in the translational professions*. Amsterdam: John Benjamins, 89–117.

Slator (2021). *Slator 2021 Language Industry Market Report*. Slator. Retrieved from: https://slator.com/slator-2021-language-industry-market-report/

Slator (2022). *Slator Machine Translation Expert-in-the-Loop Report*. Slator. Retrieved from: https://slator.com/machine-translation-expert-in-the-loop-report/

Sofer, M. (2013). *The Global Translator's Handbook*. Taylor Trade Publishing.

Stalder, F. (2006). *Manuel Castells: The Theory of the Network Society*. Cambridge: Polity Press.

Starr, J. (2021). *The Coaching Manual*. 5th edition. Harlow: Pearson Education

Stasimioti, M. (2023). 'Here are 30 new jobs language industry CEOs expect to hire for in the AI age.' *Slator*. Retrieved from: https://slator.com/30-new-jobs-language-industry-ceos-expect-to-hire-ai-age/

Statista (2023). 'Number of social media users worldwide from 2017 to 2027.' Statista. Retrieved from: https://www.statista.com/statistics/278414/number-of-worldwide-social-network-users/

Stevenson, H. & Jarillo, J. C. (1990). 'A paradigm of entrepreneurship: Entrepreneurial management.' *Strategic Management Journal*, Summer Special Issue 11, 17–27.

216 *Bibliography*

Strubell, E. et al. (2019). 'Energy and policy considerations for deep learning in NLP.' Proceedings of the 57th Annual Meeting of the Association for Computational Linguistics (ACL). Stroudsburg, PA.

Strumm, B. (2023). 'Reflection for well-being: The reflective practice experiences of social workers employed in global development.' *Reflective Practice*, 24:2, 238–250.

Suttie, C. (2022, 11 November). 'What's the saddest job you've ever had?' *LinkedIn*. Retrieved from: http://bit.ly/3GRxQlQ

TAC (2019). *China Language Service Industry Development Report*. Translator Association of China.

Taebi, E. & Mousavi Razavi, M. S. (2020). 'Towards a CPD framework of reference for the translation profession.' *Lebende Sprachen*, 65:2, 303–326.

Tang, J. & Gentzler, E. (2009) 'Globalisation, networks and translation: A Chinese perspective.' *Perspectives: Studies in Translation Theory and Practice*, 16:3–4, 169–182.

Templer, A. & Cawsey, T. (1999). 'Rethinking career development in an era of portfolio careers.' *Career Development International*, 4:2, 70–76.

Terra Translations (2019). 'What is Desktop Publishing (DTP)?' Terra Translations. Retrieved from: https://terratranslations.com/web/2019/08/02/what-is-desktop-publishing-dtp/

Thelen, M. (2016). 'Professionalisation in the translator training curriculum'. In Ł. Bogucki et al. (eds.), *Translation and Meaning*. New Series, 2:2. Bern: Peter Lang, 117–142.

Tomozeiu, D. et al. (2016). 'Teaching intercultural competence in translator training.' *The Interpreter and Translator Trainer*, 10:3, 251–267.

Tomozeiu, D. & Kumpulainen, M. (2016). 'Operationalising intercultural competence for translation pedagogy.' *The Interpreter and Translator Trainer*, 10:3, 268–284.

Torresi, I. (2021). *Translating Promotional Texts*. 2nd edition. London: Routledge.

Tyulenev, S. (2014). *Translation and Society*. London: Routledge.

UNEP (United Nations Environment Programme) (2023). 'The Climate Emergency'. United Nations. Retrieved from: https://www.unep.org/climate-emergency

UNWCED (United Nations World Commission on Environment and Development) (1987). *Report of the World Commission on Environment and Development: Our Common Future*. United Nations. Retrieved from: http://www.un-documents.net/our-common-future.pdf

Valliere, D. (2019). 'Refining national culture and entrepreneurship: The role of subcultural variation.' *Journal of Global Entrepreneurship Research*, 9:47, 1–22.

Vandepitte, S. (2017). 'Translation product quality: A conceptual analysis.' In T. Svoboda et al. (eds.), *Quality Aspects in Institutional Translation*. Language Science Press, 15–29.

Van Egdom, G.-W. et al. (2020). 'A turn to ergonomics in translator and interpreter training.' *The Interpreter and Translator Trainer*, 14:4, 363–368.

Waite, K. (2023). 'The role of reflection in workplace wellbeing.' Workplace Wellbeing Professional. Retrieved from: https://workplacewellbeing.pro/analysis/karen-waite-the-role-of-reflection-in-workplace-wellbeing/

Walker, C. (2023). *Translation Project Management*. London: Routledge.

Way, A. (2013). 'Traditional and emerging use-cases for machine translation.' *Proceedings of Translating and the Computer*, 35. London: Aslib, 1–12.

WHO (World Health Organization). (2019). 'Burn-out an "occupational phenomenon": International Classification of Diseases'. WHO. Retrieved from: https://www.who.int/news/item/28-05-2019-burn-out-an-occupational-phenomenon-international-classification-of-diseases

WHO (World Health Organization). (2021). *Health Promotion Glossary of Terms 2021*. Retrieved from: https://www.who.int/publications/i/item/9789240038349

WIPO (World Intellectual Property Organization) (2023). 'What is copyright?' WIPO. Retrieved from: https://www.wipo.int/copyright/en/

Index

Note: Entries in **bold** denote tables; entries in *italics* denote figures.

Abdallah, Kristiina 83
abstracting 136–7
added-value 175
administration, for freelancers 28–9
administrative documentation 125
advertising, codes of conduct on 48
affective labour 188
African Development Bank 34
agencies *see* translation agencies
agency: losing 189; renewed sense of 171
agency-mediated procurement model 45
alignment function 120
American Translators Association 47, 71, 86
angst 72
artificial intelligence 12, 155, 175
audiovisual translation xii, 36, 47, 51, 109, 180
AUSIT (Australian Institute of Interpreters and Translators) 19, 177
automation 16, 22, 149, 154–5, 189
autonomy 35, 158
availability 45, 79, 111

B2B (business-to-business) 159, **160**
B2B (business-to-consumer) 159, **160**
Barabé, Donald 85
Barnes, Martin 115, 130, 163
BDÜ (Bundesverband der Dolmetscher und Übersetzer) 177
bespoke MT systems 147
bilingual sub-competence 7–9
boredom 187
Bowker, Lynne 63–5, 146
breaks 29
burnout 112, 175, 177, 192–3, 196

business and marketing skills 12
buyers' expectations 81

Cameroon 24
Canada: Translation Bureau 34; translation industry in 63–4, 73
career coaching xi–xii
career guidance 58
career progression 32–5
Carnegie-Brown, Anu 65
Castells, Manuel 44, 46
CAT (computer-assisted translation) 9, 112–13, *142*; and cognitive stress 187–9; documents used by 110; for freelancers 30; further reading on 127, 150; MT integrated into 147, 149; and QA 141–6; and quoting 114, 116; skill set in 182; and social networks 52; translation memories and termbases for 119–20
certification 20, 67
chance events 38–9
China 20; data confidentiality in 94; language industry of 60; professional translating in 24; social media in 54–5
CIOL (Chartered Institute of Linguists) 20, 30, 48, 184
client confidentiality 94
client expectations 35, 97, 103, 110–11, 115, 128–9
client management 101, 103
client relationships 77
client retention 122
client-orientation 5, 16, 42
clients: access to 51, 54; rules for dealing with 95–6; seeking new

Index 219

78–80; understanding 80–3; *see also* direct clients
climate emergency 200–1
closing projects 123–5, 201
cloud computing 201
codes of conduct and codes of ethics 21; CPD in 177–8; and ethical issues 14, 19; of professional associations 48–9, 51, 96; and professional standards 93–4
cognitive demands 29, 146
cognitive friction 148
cognitive load 11
cognitive stress 186–8
collective power 188–9
commercial companies 32–6, 44, 71, 104
commissioner 42
commissions: information asymmetry around 84; negotiating 85; unclear or unrealistic 86
commitment, professional 176–7
communication engineering, multilingual multimedia 4, 6, 14
communication strategy 80, 82; and project monitoring 121–2; and quotes 117; and trust 83–9
communication style 86–7, 124, 163
communicative competences 9, 13
communicative function, main 68
communities of practice 50–2, 177; virtual 51–3, 114
competence, in codes of ethics 93–4
competence-based training 15
competition, fair 14, 48
competitive factors 163–5, **163**
complementary services 122
confidentiality 14; accusations of breaching 30, 49, 98; in codes of ethics 93–4; and co-working spaces 55–6; guidance on 48; and MT 148; in project agreement 119
conflict of interest 48
content marketing 169–70, 172
contracting phase 107, 118–19, 121, 129
contracts 49, 84, 96
copyright 95
copywriting 61, 66
core values 37–8, *38*, 193, 199
cost: as client criterion 81; and marketing strategy 85; of professional association membership 50; and project management 103, 114–15

covering letters 67, 70, 73
co-working spaces 55–6
CPD (Continuing Professional Development) 13, 28–9, 35, 175–83; in CVs 69; as self-care 194–7
creative services 61, 66
creativity 17, 158, 164, 184
CSA Research 59–61, 147, 168
cultural awareness 5, 89
cultural backgrounds 89, 91
cultural conventions 54, 68
cultural differences 77, 86, 89–92
cultural sub-competence 179–81
curiosity 16–17, 39, 89–90
currencies 117–18
customer profiles 160–2, **161**
customer service 78
CVs (curriculum vitae) ix, 58, 67–71, 73, 79, 84

daily throughput 28, 111
Dam, Helle V. 23–4, 36, 40
data, trusting and mistrusting 16
data confidentiality 94–5, 124
data management and archiving 124
Data Protection Officer 94
data security 22n1, 94
Davitti, Elena 79–80, 87, 100
deadlines 13–14; ability to meet 13, 35, 81; in feasibility study 110–12; for freelancers 27–8; imposed by translation agencies 27; negotiating 14; premium for 28, 115; and project management 103; as stressors 189; for test translations 72; and translation quality 84, 88
DeepL 147, 175
dehumanization 189
delivering projects 123
Denmark 23, 36
dependency, mutual 46, 83, 188
Depraetere, Ilse 128–9
Desjardins, Renée 171
DG TRAD (Directorate-General for Translation) 12, 66, 146–7, 177
digital genres 24
digital literacy 4, 13, 22n1
Digital Taylorism 148
direct clients 27–9; information asymmetry with 86; reaching out to 79–80; and social media 55; test translations from 71–2
directories 47–8, 166

220 Index

disrupters 154, 175
document review 109
documentation department 33
domain competences 9
domain specialists 119, 133
Drugan, Joanna 63, 130
DTP (Desktop Publishing) 61, 109, 113, 116
Durban, Chris 85

economic exploitation 47–8
Ehrensberger-Dow, Maureen 184–6, 202
EI (emotional intelligence) 87, 183, 197
ELIA (European Language Industry Association) 60
ELIS (European Language Industry Survey) 60, 79, 147
emails: and carbon emissions 201; to clients 86–7; and cultural differences 89, 91–2; and data security 94
emotion management 180
emotional competency 196
emotional efficacy 183, 197
emotions: negative 187–8; processing 73
empathy 87, 89–90, 93, 197
employer's needs 70
employment status xii, 25, 36
EMT (European Master's in Translation) xii; Competence Framework 11–15, 17, 42, 171, 179; University Network 60; Wheel of Competences 12, 14, 78
entrepreneurial mindset 155–8
entrepreneurial sub-competence 180
entrepreneurship 153–7, 156
environmental factors 185–6
equivalence paradigm 42
ergonomics 13, 185–7, 202
ergonomics sub-competence 180
ethical decision-making, informing 48
ethical dilemmas 48–9, 108, 192–4, 198
ethical maturity xii, xv, 198, 202
ethical responsibility 193
ethical stress 190–2, 198
ethical support 48
ethics: in client relationship 93; see also codes of conduct and codes of ethics
EUATC (European Federation of National Associations of Translation Companies) 60
European Agency for Safety and Health at Work 186
European Commission, Language Industry Platform 60

European Union: data confidentiality in 94; small claims courts 98; as translation employer 11–12, 34, 144
expert knowledge 8
expert-in-the-loop production model 59, 147, 149
expertise 8–9; in pre-production phase 108, 111
extra mile, going the 122
extra-linguistic sub-competence 7–9

Facebook 55, 154, 168, 170, 172
feasibility studies 106–9, 113, 118–19
feedback: for freelancers 27, 123–4; for in-house translators 31–2; negative 97, 141; from test translations 72
final verification and release 123, 137, 144
first translation job 58–9, 65
FIT (Fédération Internationale des Traducteurs) 47, 96, 176
FIT Europe 60
fitness for purpose 130, 134–6, 147
5 Ps model 166, **167**
flexibility 16–17; and professional translating 35, 39; as soft skill 182–3
formal CPD 183–4
forums: of professional associations 47, 49; of virtual communities 52–3
freelance translators 16, 25–31, 35–6; client feedback for 97; communication methods 91; CPD for 176; criteria for choosing 81; and customer service 78; hiring for revision 138, 141; information on payment practices 99; marketing for 153, 159; and outsourcing 44–5, 103–4; and portfolio careers 40; potential clients 101–3, 102; project management by 106–7, 141; rates charged by 113–14; researching potential clients 81; seeking clients 78–80; support networks of 55–6, 112; sustainability of industry 189–90; and trust 83; use of MT 147
frontier technologies 59
functionalist approach 42, 68, 136
future-proofing 181

GALA (Globalization and Localization Association) 60
game localisation 47

Index 221

gaming industry 33
GDPR (General Data Protection Regulation) 94–5, 168
General Enterprise Tendency test 157–8
geographical location xii
GIGO effect 146
globalisation 44, 63, 89
glossaries: client-provided 119; retaining 125; in test translations 72
Google Translate 146–7
Göpferich, Susanne 9–11; Translation Competence Model 9–12, *10*
governmental organisations 34–5
Groß, Marie-Luise 46
guilt, ontological 198

happenstance theory 39–40
hard skills 18, 65, 163, 180–2
harmonisation phase 112
Havumetsä, Nina 78, 81, 85, 115
health insurance, private 31
Hofstede, Geert 92
holistic translation competence models 6
Holz-Mänttäri, Justa 42–5
honesty 38, 84, 164
House, Juliane 130
human resources 27, 111–12, 119
human skills 17
human-in-the-loop model 147

ICT *see* information technology
IEA (International Ergonomics Association) 185–6
Ilari, Marina 71
Ilja, Merit-Ene 177
imponderables 112
industry intelligence 59–60
industry standards 20, 132, 134–5
influence at work 36
informants 119–20
information asymmetry 83–4, 86, 93, 190
information technology 182; environmental impact of 200–1; as translation subject 50, 60
in-house translators 25, 31–6; CPD for 176, 182; as entrepreneurs 155; personal branding 171; and portfolio careers 40; and Start, Stop, Continue exercise 126; translation tests for 71
Initiator 42
in-person marketing 169

Instagram 168, 170, 172
instinct 108
instrumental sub-competence 8–9
integrity 49, 164
intellectual property 54, 95
intended purpose 42, 68–9, 110–11, 135–6
intercultural competence 89–91
intergovernmental organisations 34–5
internal documentation 33–4
Internet access, reliable 30, 112
interpersonal activity 42
interpersonal skills 33, 77
interpersonal sub-competence 180
intrepreneurs 155
invoicing 27–8, 106–7, 117, 123–5
Iran 20
Iseli, Franziska 168–9, 172
ISO 17100:2015 xii, 20, 108, 123; role of reviser in 139; translation process 132–5, *133*
isolation 46, 52, 55, 77, 188, 196
ITI (Institute of Translation and Interpreting) 47–50, 85, 183; Code of Professional Conduct 48–9; on CPD 176–7; on health and well-being 183–4

job advertisements 4–6, 41; job titles in 63–4, 66–7
job satisfaction 24, 36; and CPD 177; and isolation 46, 188, 196; and MT 147
job search: research before 58–9; *see also* first translation job
job security 26
job titles 24, 64–6

Karoubi, Behrouz 129–30
Katan, David 39
kindness to self 198–9
know-how 8
knowing yourself 164
knowledge: exchanging 46, 196; underlying system of 6
knowledge workers 46, 52, 196
knowledge-about-translation sub-competence 8–9, 11, 13
Koskinen, Kaisa 83, 188
Kotler, Philip 153–4
Krajcso, Zita 15
Krumboltz, John D. 39

222 Index

Lambert, Joseph 48, 191, 193, 202
language and culture competences, in EMT framework xii, 13
language competence 4, 11
language industry: entrepreneurship in 156–7; global value of 23, 189; job titles in 65–6; market positioning in 157–65; role of MT in 147; trends in 59–61, 63
Language Industry Market Report 59
language industry sub-competence 179–80
language pair xii; cultures and subcultures of 7; in CV 69; in feasibility study 108–9; and market rate 114
Language Services Market report 59
language subcompetence, and CPD 179–81
language technology 16–17, 59–60, 187
late payments 98
learning to learn 16–17
legacy translation 143
legal advice 50
legal constraints 168–9, 172
legal dilemmas 48
legal obligations 94, 118
legal statuses 29–30
legal support 48, 50
legal texts 137–9
life satisfaction 188, 196
lifelong learning 176
limited company status 29
linguistic resources 119–20, 125, 143
LinkedIn 54–5, 172; job titles on 65; marketing on 168, 170–1
literary translation xii, 36, 47, 51–2, 130
LLMs (large language models) 175–6, 179
localisation xii, 33, 65–6, 200
loyalty 38, 48, 99, 164, 166
LSPs (language service providers) 14, 25, 103–4; growth of sector 60–1; QA checks 144; reports aimed at 59–60; and transcreators 65

McAlester, Gerard 193–4
McDonough Dolmaya, Julie 93
machine learning 146, 189
McKay, Corinne 79, 153
market rates 114–15, 118
market research 59, 82, 158, 160–2

market segments 159–60, 162, 164
marketing 16, 28–9, 153, 165–72; further reading on 172–3; transcreation in 66
marketing channels 166–8, 171
marketing department 89; translators in 33
marketing mix xv, 166–7, **167**, 180; personal branding in 170; social media in 169
marketing strategy 154, 162, 164–6; and client research 80, 82; and quotes 117; virtual communities discussing 52
marketplaces 48, 52–3, 166, 169, 176
master copy 69–71
matches 110, 116
Matis, Nancy 86, 109, 123
Mbotake, Sakwe 24
medical, translation 51–2
MemoQ 5–6, 141
mental health and well-being 99, 183–4, 202
mentors 156–7
Microsoft Word 112, 141
monitoring of translation projects 106–7, 118, 121, 129
MOOC (massive open online course) 179–80, 182
Moorkens, Joss 189
moral hazard 47–8, 56, 56n1
Mossop, Brian 138, 140
Mousavi Razavi, Mir Saeed 179
MT (machine translation) 9, 61; and CAT tools 112, 141; competition from 21; and confidentiality 94; in EMT Framework 13; human advantages over 175–6, 181, 184; online discussion of 52; and QA 146–9; revising 16; risks of 85; as stressor 189–90
multilingual projects 27, 45, 92, 102
multilingualism 11; political commitment to 34

national cultures 92, 154
National Network for Translation 17
NATO 34
negative feelings 187
negotiation 84, 107, 116–18, 167
network economy 46, 83, 188
network society 44, 46
networked lone fighters 46, 196

Index 223

new media 66
new translation projects 27; assessing and quoting 107–18; final tasks before launching 118–20; and purchase orders 96
Nimdzi 59–61, 189
NLP (natural language processing) 201
NMT (neural machine translation) 16, 146–7, 175, 189–90
non-compete clauses 28
non-disclosure agreement 27
non-literary translators 36
non-payment 97–8
non-solicitation clauses 28
nonstandard components 116

occupational status 23, 36
official documents 34
Olohan, Maeve 79, 87, 99
online reputation 170
online translator communities 51–3
open-mindedness 39–40
operational issues 16
opportunities, pursuing 155
organisational skills 33
organisational stress 188–9
outsourcing 44–6, 52, 83, 104, 112
overarching drivers 191, 194
overheads 114
over-revising 139–40

PACTE (Procés d'Adquisició de la Competència Traductora i Avaluació): and professionalisation turn 15; Translation Competence Model 6–9, 7, 179
parallel texts 120, 176
Patels, Werner 81, 95
Pavey, Natalie 112
payment terms 97, 117, 119
PDFs 109–10
pedagogical dimension 85, 122
pedagogical models, new 15
pedagogical translation 3–4
PEMT (post-editing of machine translation) 148–9
pensions 30–1
perfectionism 132
perishable texts 137
personal and interpersonal competence xii, 13–14, 42
personal branding 153, 168, 170–3
physical stress 186, 194

PIPL (Personal Information Protection Law) 94
PMI (Project Management Institute) 103, 121
PO (Purchase Order) 96, 119, 125
podcasts 60, 168, 172–3, 181–4
politeness 86, 91, 96, 141
portfolio careers 39–40
post-editing (PE) 16, 24, 61, 147–9; automated 176
post-mortem 123, 125, 198
post-production phase 104, 125, 129, 132; checklist for 106
power imbalance 189
prejudicial texts 85, 110, 136–8
pre-production phase 104, 107–8, 129; checklist for 105
pressure, working under 5, 16, 64, 186
proactiveness 90
problem-solving 11, 19
production models, new 52, 83, 103
production networks 44–6, 45, 89, 90; different stakeholders in 77; and isolation 46, 55; and organizational stress 188–90; trust in 83, 190
production phase 104; checklist for 106; QA in 129, 132–3
professional associations 19–20; directories of 166; membership requirements of 50; as support networks 46–51, 98–9
professional autonomy 19
professional competences 11, 20, 132
professional development 46, 124; see also CPD
professional experience 20–1, 67
professional growth 175
professional identity 21, 24, 36, 52, 177
professional indemnity insurance 30, 51, 99
professional knowledge, personal 46, 196
professional maturity xii, xv, 202
professional obligation 48
professional profile 55, 177
professional profiles 66
professional responsibilities xv, 77
professional service 100, 148
professional standards 93, 96; harmonisation of 47; meeting 12, 20
professional support networks xiii, 41, 124
professional translating xi–xiii, xv; in Canada 63–4, 73; communities

224 *Index*

of practice 52; cost and added value of 85; CPD for 178–83, **180**; entrepreneurship in 154–6; fragmentation of 25; in-house and freelance 26–38; job satisfaction 23–4; myths about 3; and pedagogical translation 4; project management in 106–7; qualifications needed 19–21; as situated activity 185; skills needed 15–19; things going wrong in 96–9; visibility of 171

professional values 38, 70, 93, 191–2
professionalisation 22n2, 48
professionalisation turn 15
professionalism 16, 47, 93, 95
profession-oriented networks 46–7, 52
project agreement 118
project domain: in feasibility study 109; and market rate 114–15
project management xiv, 16; checklist for **105–6**, 129; further reading on 127; real-time 175; as sub-competence 180; use of term 103
project management triangle 114–15, *115*, 122, 130, 163
project managers (PMs): communicating with clients 87; and feasibility studies 108; quoting 106; at translation agencies 27, 33, 79–80, 103–4; translators as 101
project negotiation phase 86
project schedule 109–12, 114, 119
project type 109
proofreading, and test translations 71–2
provisional schedule 111
ProZ.com 52–4, 73, 114, 169
psychological skills 183
psychomotor competences 10–11
public-facing documents 34
purpose of text 139
Pym, Anthony 16, 42, 68, 149

QA (quality assurance) 128–9; CAT functions 144; extra checks 122; models of 130; resources 141
QA steps: and CAT 144; for ISO 17100:2015 132–5, *133*; and post-editing 149; right 136–8
qualifications 19–22; in ISO 17100:2015 132; for professional associations 50; sought by employers 64, 67, 69; as USP 162–3
quality xiii–xiv; compromising on 85, 93, 190; conceptualisations of **131**;

defining 128–32; further reading on 150; industry standards for 132–4; right level of 135–8, 141, 148
quality control 13, 27, 32, 34, 175
quality gaps 136
quality level, expected 84–5, 93, 110–11, 114–15, 122, 134, 148–9
quality management xiv, 16, 121
questions, during translation projects 86–7
quoting 27, 87, 107–11, 113–17

referral marketing 169–70, 172
reflective approach xii–xiii
reflective practice 126, 180, 197, *198*
relational competency 196
relationship management 80, 167
reliability 80, 157
renegotiation 122
repetitions 110, 116
resilience 29, 35, 197–8
resources: human and technological 111, 141; organising 119; ownership of 189
résumés *see* CVs
return on investment 113
revision 16, 70–1; of CVs 70; as QA step 133–4, 138–41, 149; quoting for 116; and TMs 143
revision kit 139
risk management 16, 22n1
risk-taking 39
Robinson, Douglas 174
Rocchi, Marta 189
RWS 66

Samuelsson-Brown, Geoffrey 28, 134, 136–7
Schmitt, Peter 175
Schnierer, Madeleine 134
scope management 121–2, 127
Sela-Sheffy, Rakefet 155
self-awareness 197
self-care xiii, 184; as ethical responsibility 190–4; for professional translators 194–9, *195*
self-directed CPD 183–4
self-discipline 29
self-evaluation 13
self-motivation 77
self-promotion 68
senior translator status 32, 34, 180
service provision competence xii, 12, 14, 42

Seward, Lauren 197
6 Model of national culture 92
skill sets 16–17, 41, 182
Slator 59–61, 65, 175
small claims courts 98
Smartcat 141, *142*
SME (small or medium enterprise) 159–61
social aspect of networks 46
social capital 57, 99
social constraints 168–9, 172
social justice 44
social media 12–13, 22n11; building support networks on 54–5; marketing on 28, 153, 168–72
social media networking 169
social positioning 89–91
social responsibility 135, 202
socio-economic status 25, 35
soft skills 13–14, 16–18, 42, 65, 164, 180–3
software 27
sole trader status 29
source text (ST): authors 77; emotional reactions to 187; finalising 85; producer 42–3
specialisation 28, 32–3
specialist domain xii, 10, 36–7, 48, 71, 117; CPD in 179, 181–2; as market segment 159; as USP 163; *see also* project domain
stakeholders, liaising with 89, 121
Start, Stop, Continue exercise 125–6, 198
Stevenson, Howard 155
strategic sub-competence 6, 8
streaming content 63
stressors 184–90, 199; potential impact of *192*
stronger ties 56
style 70; and translation quality 137, 139
style guides 5–6, 72, 120; retaining 125
stylistic expectations 97, 137
sub-competences 7–9, 179–81
sub-specialisations 181–2
subtitling 36, 52, 61
superdiversity 89, 91
support networks 58; building 54–6; global 51–4; and self-care 196–7; traditional 46–51
sustainability: ecological 200–2; and entrepreneurship 156; MT and 148; psychology of 174–5; of the translation industry 189–90
Suttie, Clare 187

TAC (Translator's Association of China) 47, 60
Taebi, Ehsan 179
tags, placeable and localisable 144
target language, variety of 109, 120
target market 65; identifying 158
target text (TT) producer 42–3
target text (TT) receiver 43
target text (TT) user 43
target-language writing skills 181–2
task documentation 125
TAUS (Translation Automation User Society) 149
technological change 12–13, 63
technological competence 14
technological field 15–16
technological resources 108, 111–12, 141
technology competence xii, 13, 179–80
technostress 188
termbases 113, 119–20, 122, 125, 143–5
terminology 4; client's preferred 86, 144; in-house policy on 34
terminology management 34, 52, 127, 144
test revisions 72
test translations 29, 67, 71–3, 79
TikTok 168, 170
time management 16, 19, 124
TMs (translation memories): and CAT 143–5; client-provided 110, 112, 116, 119; lack of ownership over 189
tools and research competences 9
Torresi, Ira 68
Trados 5–6, 141
trainee translators 6, 14–16, 40
TransComp 9
transcreation xii, 61, 65–6
transferable skills 14, 18–19, 39–40
translating sub-competence 179–80
translation: concept of xii; as emerging profession 19; as interpersonal activity 41–2; responsibility in *191*; as a service 77–8
Translation 4.0 175, 181, 183, 189
translation agencies 25, 27–8, 32–3; client relationship management 80; communication strategies 87; contracts with 96; and customer service 78; engaging freelancers 79; and feasibility studies 108; and outsourcing 44–5; research about 81; test translations for 71; use of TMs 189; *see also* LSPs

226 Index

translation apps 3
translation buyers: criteria for purchase 81; trust in providers 84–5
translation checkers 32, 65
translation companies 25, 32
translation competence xii; and CPD 179–80; in EMT framework 13; real 4
translation competence models 6–15
translation ecosystem 181; changing 176
translation errors 34, 135, 137; objective 97, 140
translation graduates, roles open to 65–6
translation industry xiii; current trends in 58–63, **62**; energy dependency of 200–1
translation memories 6, 110, 113; retaining 125
translation networks: informal 70; practice-oriented 52, 54; traditional 46; and writing CVs 69
translation profession *see* professional translating
translation programmes ix, xi, 9, 11, 19, 69; skills and competences taught in 15–17
translation routine activation competence 10–11
translation scholars 6, 16, 42, 130
translation service industry 11
translation service providers *see* TSPs
translation service provision 14, 78, 103, 126, 135
translation technologies 10, 13; and CPD 28; in CVs 69; job ads requiring knowledge of 64, 67
translation tests *see* test translations
translation workflow 104; MT in 13; and project management 107, 119
translation-related jobs 64
translatorial action 42–4; key players in *43*
TranslatorsCafé 52–4, 114
transparency 84
trust: in client relationships 77–8, 92–6; further reading on 99–100; managing 83–9; and quotes 115, 117; and stress 189–90
trusted network 111–12
trustworthiness 48, 50–1, 54, 57

TSPs (translation service providers) 20, 77–8; and B2C 159; competitive factors for 162–4, **163**; criteria for choosing 81, 85; feasibility studies 108; new roles for 176; trust in 84–5
Twitter 55, 168, 170

unique blend 164
unit price 114–16
United Nations 34, 144, 174, 200
units, number of 109, 111, 113
unsolicited work 80–1
urgency 115
USP (unique selling point) 162–6, *162*, 168, 180

value proposition 154, 164–6, 169
vertical network 45
visibility 20, 36

Walker, Callum 103, 111, 124–5, 127
weaker ties 56
Web 2.0 52
websites 30
weekends, working 31, 79
well-being 175; emotional 196–7; importance of 184–5; mental 183; and networks 41, 46, 188; physical 185, 194; and things going wrong 99
What? model of structured reflection *198*; trigger questions **199**
WhatsApp 170
WHO (World Health Organization) 184–5, 192
willingness to learn 182
WIPO (World Intellectual Property Organization) 95
Women in Localization 60
Word documents 109–10
word of mouth 166–7, 169
working conditions 24–5; for freelance translators 26; for in-house translators 31; and trust 190
working from home 30
working languages 34
work-life balance 31
workstation 186, 194–6

YouTube 172

Zethsen, Karen Korning 23–4, 36, 40